THE
PHILOSOPHY
OF
GABRIEL MARCEL

THE
PHILOSOPHY
OF
GABRIEL MARCEL

KENNETH T. GALLAGHER

With a Foreword by GABRIEL MARCEL

CLUNY

Providence, Rhode Island

Cluny Media edition, 2020

This Cluny edition is a republication of the 1962 Fordham University Press
edition of *The Philosophy of Gabriel Marcel*.

For more information regarding this title
or any other Cluny Media publication,
please write to info@clunymedia.com, or to
Cluny Media, P.O. Box 1664, Providence, RI 02901

VISIT US ONLINE AT WWW.CLUNYMEDIA.COM

ISBN: 978-1952826368

Cover design by Clarke & Clarke
Cover image: Paul Cézanne,
Bend in the Road Through the Forest,
detail, 1873, oil on canvas
Courtesy of Wikimedia Commons

CONTENTS

❖   ❖   ❖

TO MY WIFE, RAY
Pignus amoris

KEY TO ABBREVIATIONS

BH   =   *Being and Having*
HP   =   *L'homme problématique*
HV   =   *Homo Viator: Introduction to a Metaphysic of Hope*
MMS   =   *Man Against Mass Society*
MJ   =   *Metaphysical Journal*
MB (I) =   *The Mystery of Being*, Vol. I: *Reflection and Mystery*
MB (II) =   *The Mystery of Being*, Vol. II: *Faith and Reality*
PE   =   *The Philosophy of Existence*
PAC   =   *Positions et approches concrètes du mystère ontologique*
PI   =   *Presence et immortalité*
RI   =   *Du refus à l'invocation*

PREFACE

THE PRINCIPAL aim of a book on the philosophy of Gabriel Marcel
ought to be to send the reader back to the original works in all their
non-expoundable concreteness. Actually, in the case of this relentlessly unsystematic thinker, even to speak of "his philosophy" has
a hollow ring, for it suggests just the kind of carefully constructed
edifice of doctrine which Marcel deliberately renounces. An attempt to
"expound" such a thought inevitably runs the risk of distorting it. And
yet the risk seems worth running. For Marcel's thought, while original
and fascinating, is so extremely elusive that it is a rare reader for whom
it does not seem to cry out for interpretation. The paradox is that this
elusiveness is an essential constituent of his thought, and any exposition which sought to eliminate it would be self-defeating. In the pages
that follow, I have sought to find the source of this elusiveness, not
in order to banish it, but rather in order to discover its philosophical
significance. My hope has been that, through a progressive penetration of Marcellian themes, the animating principle behind his thought
will gradually emerge. What follows, then, is an exposition—in the
sense that an attempt has been made to bring the contours of Marcel's
thought into clear focus—but one which preserves the freshness of his
approach. The success of such an attempt is bound to be uneven, but it

is hoped that it will be of service in providing much-needed direction to many a reader drawn to Marcel's style of thought, yet adrift in its uncharted expanse.

It is certainly time that such an attempt was made. Marcel has been for over thirty-five years one of the world's most influential thinkers, but he is still too superficially categorized as an "existentialist," a title which has a limited validity but is about as misleading as any other. He does not derive from the line of descent to which so many of the "existentialist" thinkers owe their origin, the line that is vaguely drawn from Kierkegaard and Nietzsche; the influence of these thinkers on his formation was next to nil. If we were deliberately seeking to reconstruct formative influences, we might do better to cite philosophers who engaged his attention at an early age: Schelling, who was the subject of Marcel's undergraduate thesis, which compared his metaphysical ideas with Coleridge's; or Josiah Royce, about whom Marcel wrote in 1917 a study which remains standard today. But the truth seems to be that he is a largely underivative thinker, stubbornly resistant to classification. Calling him a "Catholic philosopher" would not do, for that suggests a sectarianism altogether alien to his work; furthermore, his thought after his relatively late conversion in 1929 is perfectly continuous with that prior to it, and his appeal transcends religious barriers.

Marcel's thought seems to stem much more from his life than from philosophical influences. Born in Paris in 1889, of a father who had been French minister to Stockholm, he benefited from his early youth from a vast, multi-lingual culture and from extensive foreign travel. At twenty he obtained the agrégation in philosophy from the Sorbonne, and by twenty-four had completed the first part of the brilliant speculations which form the *Metaphysical Journal*. But he has been only intermittently a teacher of philosophy, at various lycées; his philosophy does not have an academic origin but rather represents the reflective expression of a life endowed with remarkable intellectual vitality: Marcel is a prolific and award-winning playwright, has been for decades a regular music and drama critic for leading French journals, and is not only an

accomplished pianist who improvises for hours daily but also a some-
time composer. All of these activities he regards as perfectly integral to
his highly concrete philosophical reflection, and he further stresses the
role of several crucial personal experiences in giving direction to his
thought. His mother died before his fourth birthday, but remained as a
strongly felt presence throughout his childhood, providing a prototype
of the polarity between the visible and the invisible which looms so large
in his thought. Raised by his father and his aunt in an essentially irreli-
gious atmosphere, he tells us that his early religious life was nurtured by
the music of Bach. During the first World War, his work with the Red
Cross in responding to the despairing inquiries of families about loved
ones missing in action brought painfully home to him the drama of
human existence and the inability of abstract thought to make contact
with that drama. His own thought may be looked upon as an effort to
discover the light by which that drama is ultimately illuminated.

The notion which has been taken in the present book as the leitmo-
tif of Marcel's thought is that of "participation." To be, says Marcel, is
to participate in being. There is no such thing as an isolated experience
of existence, and therefore no problem of breaking through to realism.
The purely private self is an abstraction: the ego given in experience is
a being-by-participation. This participation might be said to have more
than one level, but at every level a similar statement may be made: we
cannot effectively divorce the self from that in which it participates,
because it is only the participation which allows there to be a self.
Participation, in other words, is the foundation—the only foundation—
for my experience of existence. If this is so, then a philosophy whose
aim is to construct an overall, systematic view of reality has already
forsaken existence for abstraction. A system is only there for a detached
observer, a spectator; but the existing self (and the existing thinker) is
not a spectator but a participant. If the task of philosophy is to think
the existent and actual, it must apply itself not to the construction of a
system, but to tracing out the richness and depth of the experience of
participation.

It is here suggested, perhaps over-neatly, that there are three levels of participation discerned by Marcel: the level of incarnation, which is actualized through sensation and the experience of the body as "mine"; the level of communion, which is actualized through love, hope, and fidelity; the level of transcendence, which is actualized through the ontological exigence, primitive assurance, and "blinded intuition" of being. This scheme can serve as a handy guide for the interpretation to be set forth in this book, but its divisions are admittedly fluid. The third level is the realm of what Marcel calls "being" or "plenitude," and it is undoubtedly with the mystery of being in this sense that his philosophical reflection is ultimately concerned. A major aim, indeed, of the present interpretation is to stress the metaphysical, rather than merely phenomenological, character of Marcel's thought. In this area, the central interpretive insight is the notion of "creation." The contention is that being is only revealed to creative experience (in a signification of that phrase to be made clear), that in fact being's role in thought is not so much that of a concept as it is a creative intuition analogous to that of the artist. The presentiment of transcendence haunts human experience, as the artist's intuition haunts his consciousness. Just as the artist's intuition only comes to be recognized in the artistic process which it alone makes possible, so the presence of being is only recognized by being read back out of the human experiences which it alone makes possible. Which experiences are these? Marcel concentrates on love, hope, and fidelity; it is his conviction that the ontological exigence cannot be recognized by a solitary ego, but only by a subject-in-communion. Therefore, the acts which found me as subject-in-communion, as I in the face of a thou, are also those which give me access to being. The recognition of the ontological value of these experiences and therefore of the transcendent dimension of man's existence is free—it is the response by which thought freely sustains itself in its own source. Thus, the fundamental philosophical affirmation, "being is," is a truth spoken by and to my liberty. My participation in being is ultimately, then, a creative participation. Such in brief is the theme of this book.

I cannot close without expressing my deepest thanks to M. Gabriel Marcel for the kindness and encouragement he has extended to me in conversations and correspondence relative to this study. I shall not try to put into words the poignant impression which my meetings with him, after so many years of acquaintance with his thought, made upon me. Suffice it to say that this was one occasion where none of the hazards of expectation were borne out; just the opposite, for Gabriel Marcel is a living testimony, a man who far outruns his works.

I would also like to pay my tribute of gratitude to an extraordinary philosopher, Dr. Robert C. Pollock of Fordham University, under whose guidance my researches into Marcel were initially carried on.

Finally, I wish to thank the following journals for their gracious permission to republish material which originally appeared there: Chapter II, "Being in a Situation," appeared in *The Review of Metaphysics*, Vol. 13 (December 1959), pp. 320–339; Chapter III, "Problem and Mystery," appeared in *The Modern Schoolman*, Vol. 39 (January 1962), pp. 101–121.

FOREWORD

How could I not accept the invitation to write a few lines by way of preface to this fine study, the very first in the United States to be devoted to my thought in its entirety? I am especially glad to do this because Kenneth Gallagher has had the merit of emphasizing an idea which is absolutely central to my work, an idea, in fact, that in a way even provides the key to my thought, although this has rarely been perceived by others as clearly as I would like. I think that the author is mistaken when he writes that I myself do not seem to him to have fully recognized its decisive role. It would be more accurate to say that this role has only progressively become clear to me, and this all the more distinctly as I have concentrated more and more on the relations between my philosophical thought, my dramatic work, and even the attempt I have made at musical composition, embodied in a certain number of unpublished melodies and in countless improvisations. Only a few of the latter—and not the most important ones—have been put down on tape. I am in complete agreement with Mr. Gallagher when he stresses the importance of the following phrase: as soon as there is creation, in whatever degree, we are in the realm of being (p. 93). But the converse is equally true: that is to say, there is doubtless no sense in using the word "being" except where creation, in some form or other, is in view.

Certainly in my own case, if I have had any experience of being, it is to the extent that it has been my privilege either to create in the precise sense of the word or to participate in an order which is in reality that of love and admiration, within which the creative act can be described. This last particular is essential: for there could be no question of denying the experience of being to innumerable human beings who have never written a line nor attempted to express themselves in music or painting. This experience exists from the moment that a person reaches a certain plenitude, provided that this does not degenerate into an illusory self-sufficiency.

We do not belong to ourselves: this is certainly the sum and substance, if not of wisdom, at least of any spirituality worthy of the name. I prefer not to speak here of wisdom, because this word is sometimes applied to an ethics that is basically egocentric and shut off from all transcendence.

I have been re-immersing myself lately in the very last works of Beethoven, which in my opinion mark a level of perfection that no other composer ever attained, except perhaps for a few fleeting moments. Surely this music could only have welled up in the most profound solitude, and yet it is there for us, for each one of us: it *is* not before *giving itself*, it itself *is this gift*, the inexhaustible gift of a soul which in the same degree as Shakespeare or Rembrandt—these are certainly the only names that can be mentioned in the same context—was able to concentrate in itself the totality of being and human destiny. Moreover I employ the term totality with regret, for since Hegel and especially in our own day it has, in my opinion, been used rashly.

If I have felt the need to refer here to this ultimate creation of Beethoven, it is because it represents for me the extreme limit of what I myself have sought to achieve by ways that have often been exceedingly narrow and winding, and actually without always having been distinctly conscious of my goal. The German word *Verklärung* expresses perhaps better than the French or English term *transfiguration* the sort of transmutation of human experience which is antipodal to a purely abstract or conceptual thought. In the final analysis it seems that being reveals or entrusts itself to me only in the measure, always woefully incomplete, in which this transmutation is accomplished in me and for me.

I do not doubt that what I am trying to say here will be much more accessible to those who have been initiated into the deepest secret of the art of music than to those for whom this is a closed book. And it is for this reason, I think, that whoever approaches my work will have to conceive the drama in function of music, and the philosophy in function of drama—which implies a complete reversal of traditional perspectives. But I insist very firmly that all this must not be interpreted in an irrational sense: or rather, that such an interpretation would postulate a degraded conception of reason which would amount to identifying it with understanding. The latter fills, in our spiritual economy, an indispensable but subordinate office, that of the calculable. Certainly this calculating understanding finds plenty of work to do, but it is by definition impossible for it to explain anything, to plumb the depths of anything. I cannot refrain from inserting here some lines of Claudel from *La Ville*. The engineer Besme speaks to the poet Coeuvre[1]:

> Make clear to me whence came this breath by your mouth trans-
>   formed into words.
> For when you speak, like a tree that with all its leaves
> Stirs in the silence of Noon, within our hearts peace impercepti-
>   bly succeeds to thought.
> By means of this song without music and this word that has no
>   voice, we are put in accord with the melody of the world.
> Naught you explain, O poet, but all things grow comprehensible
>   through you.

Of course these lines refer to a lyric poet, but I think that in spite of that they retain their meaning for someone like me, of whom it could be said that the union of philosophy and music has not ceased to wave like a kind of bright banner before his thought.

When I conjure up the very sinuous and almost unforeseeable development that has been mine, I observe that the rather vast ambitions which I no doubt initially entertained had to give way little by little under the pressure of experience, as I gradually became aware of the immense area it was proper to cede to the control of positive science. It is upon man himself and very precisely upon the hidden springs of his life that my attention came to be centered, and this above all in the light of the dramas that I composed and about which I felt so utterly convinced that they were not invented but on the contrary in essence given to me, and even imposed upon me. Under these conditions, the limited but quite delicate task which fell to my lot was to penetrate, by a fraternal impulse, sufficiently deep into the interior life of others to become for them, so to speak, *helpful from within*, and not from without. But this sort of help could only be rendered at the level of thought, and thus it may be clear why even, and perhaps especially, after my conversion it was to the most spiritually destitute persons or to those most disturbed that I turned by preference: for those who had achieved fulfillment had no need of me and it is rather in the other direction that the current could have run between us.

I will add only one more reflection, but one that seems to me indispensable: the more that technical development quickens and spreads, extending to realms which recently seemed necessarily excluded from it, the more there yawns that central void which I have striven to fill, proceeding by what I believe I once called a kind of magical fomentation, That there are found everywhere in the world a few readers to welcome what I would not like to call a message—for this word is misused—but rather a sympathetic stimulation, emanating often enough from suffering and frustration, I find a grace, which has been dispensed to me by powers it appears presumptuous to wish to name. Just so it would be absurd and arrogant to commit oneself to some conjecture or other about the future of such an endeavor. May it not be that we are entirely ignorant of what the man will be like who very shortly will have to take his bearings and find his way in the world which is taking shape before

our eyes? On this point, it seems to me, we have to confess our ignorance, which is the same as saying that we must not take our desires
for reality. We do not even know if certain of the works which move
us most deeply will not be in a quarter of a century a dead letter for
our descendants. But this ignorance, I feel, is at the origin of an obliga-
tion which we cannot shirk with impunity: that of remaining faithful to
what is essential in ourselves, rather than striving to anticipate a future
about which we know nothing.

Gabriel Marcel
De l'Institut
March 26, 1962

CHAPTER I

The Winding Path

Nothing could be more uncustomary than the thought of Gabriel Marcel: there seems to be no direct precedent for it in the entire history of philosophy. Presenting elements of phenomenology, existentialism, idealism, and empiricism all consorting together in symbiotic bliss, it completely defies classification. A provoking and fascinating situation, and all the more fascinating because the net effect of the *mélange* is a strange feeling of authenticity such as is aroused by relatively few writers. This impression might be conveyed by the inevitably cryptic statement that from him we may now and then fear to hear error, but never untruth. This does not simply mean that he shows himself to be "sincere," but that his thought itself does not seem capable of serving as an instrument for the advancement of falsehood. And we are soon driven to wonder about the nature of that thought. What is the method which Gabriel Marcel follows in philosophy? What is it in that method which accounts for the haunting note of conviction which his thought carries?

This does not mean that we are anxious to pin a label on him, but that there is a pressure on us to understand what he conceives philosophy to be or, better still, what he conceives philosophizing to be. Certainly there are not wanting many indications that he repudiates that kind of cumulatively erected structure so dear to the heart of the more "orderly" thinker. Philosophy does not build step by step on results that have been achieved once and for all, like a continually extended and ramified sorites. For he makes it quite clear that philosophical thinking is not a matter of drawing conclusions from established premises, and it is to be doubted even if the phrase "established premise" has much meaning for him. Does he not explicitly say that "the thinker…lives in a state of continual creativity, and the whole of his thought is always being called in question from one minute to the next"?[1] The very notion of a result is a philosophically suspect category, we hear him assert.[2] Under such conditions, why does not his whole philosophy dissolve into the mists of skepticism? What can be the meaning of truth when a man declares that his thought is fundamentally anti-dogmatic,[3] and apparently means by dogma any formulation that can be regarded as final, as achieved, as public property? The most minimal definition of truth would seem to imply this minimal dogmatism.

To gloss over this aspect of his thought would be a mistake, since Marcel has made it part of the basis for naming, or renaming, his philosophy. Having long since declined the ambivalent title of "existentialist," he now prefers the appellation "neo-Socratic," and it does seem an oddly apt term.[4] However, there is another side to his thought which is, if anything, even more fundamental. That is, the pervading impression of *assurance* which is everywhere. It is not too much to say that it is this other aspect which is most strongly felt even at those times when the questioning tendency of Marcel has full rein. The attitude of interrogation is at the same time an attitude of listening. And the manner of listening is strangely tranquil, unafraid, patient, expectant.

Here is where Marcel begins—not with the calling into question, but with the assurance, the primitive assurance which underlines all questions and which makes all questions possible: "The soul which despairs shuts itself up against the central and mysterious assurance in which we believe we have found the principle of all positivity."[5] This assurance is not a formulated proposition, but a presence. It is not an affirmation that we make, but an affirmation by which we are made: "the whole reflexive process remains within a certain assertion which I *am*— rather than *which I pronounce*—an assertion of which I am the place, and not the subject."[6] Being affirms itself in us. In our being there is the presence of the Being by which we are. This presence is not something about which we can make an assertion, any more than we can make an adequate assertion about ourselves. We know ourselves as inexpressible presence: and the self arises in the interior of a presence which founds it. To be is to be in the presence of being.

All this we know obscurely simply because we are: to be, and to know oneself as being, is to know being as indubitably present to us. We do not grasp this as communicable information, but as a forefeeling,[7] which is, as it were, the first intelligible emanation from the act of being itself. If being is present to us, to the whole self, and if our knowledge arises out of that self, then there is a point at which being is present to our knowledge. At a certain level the intellect is face to face with being,[8] not with the idea of being but with that being which is the "inexhaustible concrete" at the very source of the self.[9] In that source we live and move and are. From that source we draw the assurance of fulfillment for the exigences of mind and heart which originate the questioning process.

It will not do to interpose impatient queries as to what precisely the being *is* which overflows our boundaries, and, failing to get it properly delineated, to excoriate the whole doctrine as vague. What can be characterized is already an object enclosed within its own limits; as such it is not present within mine. We cannot apply the norms of characterization to the presence which makes all characterization possible. Someone is sure to say: "In that case all propositions in regard to it become equally valid because equally meaningless. If I do not know *what* I am talking about, no assertion I make can even rise to the dignity of being disputable. Thus, to say that being is present to me is to say that there is present to me—what? No one can argue with Marcel's statement, for no one really has much of an idea what it means. For the same reason, he could not give a very stout rebuttal to its negation."

Now, however incisive this objection may sound within the confines of logic, it has a glaring existential irrelevance. For exactly what is said here of being can equally well be said of the self: we are totally unable to characterize it, to say *what* it is. Yet who but the most unredeemed of logicians would be dutiful enough, on that account, to deny the unbounded meaningfulness of the assertion of his own existence? The presence of being is exactly as mysterious as the presence of the self; both can only be alluded to, not communicated.[10] We are in the realm not of found objects, but of founding presences. Being is not given: it is the giver of givens. The self is the space in which being makes its entry. Thus, self and being are but two sides of one mystery. To ignore the second would be to let slip the first.

The objector persists that either we know the being which is present under definite attributes (as a person, as good, as infinite), or we do not. In the first alternative, we are contending for a direct intuition of God; in the second, we are in touch either with nothing at all, or with a pure indeterminate the means to the discernment of which we lack by definition. If being is uncharacterizable, then little good it does us to be assured of its presence. There is no denying that this is a recurrently bothersome objection, and we must wait and see how Marcel is able to answer it. For the present we will content ourselves with foreseeing that, since there is really only one mystery, in some way the elucidation of the self will simultaneously be an elucidation of the nature of being. The ontological exigences of the spirit are the hither side of the magnetic presence of being. Try as we will, we will only awake to being within being.

If it be urged against him that this way of proceeding in some way predetermines the conclusion, the only reply is that this is not really an objection at all, but simply an indication of the inevitable nature of metaphysics. We may lay it down as a fundamental axiom that in the domain of metaphysics the end is in the beginning. The idea of a completely novel bit of knowledge—a "totally unlooked-for"—can only apply to the realm of factuality, not to the realm of philosophical truth. Here, whatever we shall know is already in some way known. We cannot come to it from an experience which in no way contains it. Since metaphysics is not the search for a particular object within experience, but for the ultimate implications of experience itself, then by definition the end is implicit in the experience with which we begin. If an ultimate knowledge is possible, then it is already in some way actual. If we can reach the transcendent, then the transcendent is already immanent in our own experience. Given its complete absence, there would always be its complete absence. We may make use of a sentence of Marcel's to summarize this: "Either there is not and cannot be experience of being, or else this experience is in fact vouchsafed us."[11]

We may transfer this to the psychological order, where our initial attitude announces the way in which we awake to being. What is the last thing I may say about reality? It is a unilinear descendant of the first thing I have to say about it. Leaving out the details of my answers (for they will only develop in the piecemeal hammering-out of my conclusions) the *kind* of answer I will give is predicted by the initial attitude I take up at the portals of thought. The manner in which I describe the real depends upon the posture in which I approach it—it could hardly be otherwise. A scrupulous distrust of every experience which cannot be reduced to an exact formulation; a dull predilection for the sensibly verifiable; an imperturbable reliance on common sense in all its forms—these are not so much conclusions of a thinking process as pre-philosophical attitudes which, by turning the philosophical quest unalterably in a certain direction, delimit and even create its discoveries. Whether a man turns out to be a Cartesian, a Positivist, or an Aristotelian, is therefore not simply dependent upon the aptitude with which he sifts "objective evidence" which is there for everybody. It would not be too much to say, as we shall see, that he makes his own objective evidence; for there is no evidence until we encounter being, and our attitude determines the level at which we encounter it.[12]

Now Marcel declares that at the origin of philosophy there must be an attitude of humility, of "ontological humility."[13] This is axial:

without it, our thought would lose all properly philosophical character and would slip back into the "problematic." Given this humility as the source out of which we philosophize, is it not easily seen that his whole philosophy is in some sense already there? For this humility is not the virtue of modesty, which is a perfection in the moral order. It is not an assessment of our inferiority in some circumscribed field, which is either commendable candor or social bashfulness. It cannot be assimilated to prudent scholarly hesitancy in assertion; it is not a mere refraining from aggressiveness in thought, nor a submissive waiting upon the evidence, like the humble patience of the scientific researcher. That sort of humility is a predominantly intellectual quality. What Marcel refers to is ontological humility, which is an existential attitude: it is a recognition of a depth in being which surpasses and includes us. In a word, it is the profound acknowledgment of finitude. To assent to finitude is not simply to acquiesce in the theoretical limits of the essence of man, for this can be done by an unruffled and self-confident rationalism. To experience finitude in the existential order is to experience the continued duration of a being which is not the master of its own being, and which therefore must appear to itself as a gift renewed through time.[14] For that reason the experience of our limits is simultaneously an experience of the invasion of our limits by a source which we cannot shut out from the self, since it is only its presence which permits there to be a self.[15] Humility is at the farthest possible remove from a theoretical attitude, and a philosophy that arises out of humility must of its very nature be anti-theoretical.

"Arising out of" humility is the salient phrase. We do not merely pass through humility as a preliminary phase and then put it aside, returning to it occasionally as a corrective for over-confidence. Even more strictly, we do not first experience humility *and then think*—as if the two processes were external to each other. Our thought is not juxtaposed to our being: our thinking arises out of our ontological humility. Humility and finitude are the fountainheads of human thought, and not simply safeguards against temerity.

What repercussions such a realization will have both in epistemology and metaphysics can only be suggested in these preliminary
sentences. Surely it ought to be clear, however, that any form of humility is an analogously intentional response and must tell us much about
the being before which we are humble. It must adumbrate, for instance,
the doctrine of the non-objectifiability of being, for the reality which
is encountered in humility simply cannot be an "object" in Marcel's
sense of the word. Likewise humility cannot bring forth a system,
for systematic thought only flourishes on the soil of "objectivity."
Even more—there is pre-contained in the experience of humility an
inherent incompatibility with all rationalist thought as such, for the
very notion of a clear and distinct idea is suspect except in the order
of "having" and the reality which humility reveals is pre-eminently
non-possessible. Finally, it follows that in authentic philosophy any
autonomous functioning of a purely impersonal reason is impossible:
since thought, as the instrument of our adhesion to being, only unfolds
within a continuing act of humility, there is always a fundamental,
concrete, free commitment interior to the most abstract of speculations. It goes without saying that the full meaning of every one of these
statements must be developed at length, but it is astonishing to observe
how simply they flow from the initial attitude, how completely the end
is in the beginning.

Does someone object that this is not fair, that the verdict on reality
ought to be delivered after a genuinely impartial evaluation? But what
does this mean? Does it not really suppose the very thing which we
must begin by denying, that the mind can stand outside of being like
a disinterested spectator and pass a totally external judgment? Yet the
very standards by which such a presuppositionless *tabula rasa* decided
would have to be drawn from within being itself. Any mind detached
from being could only deliver a verdict that was a pure construction:
but knowledge which is a pure construction can only issue from a self
which is a pure construction. Such a self would be absolutely transparent to itself, and this is clearly not the case with men. To recognize the

non-transparency of the self is the supremely philosophical act: it is the intellectual counterpart of ontological humility.[16]

Suppose a man refuses this recognition and entrenches himself behind the barriers of an objectivity which stands as a coequal in the face of being and demands with rigid protocol that reality certify its credentials. Shall he thereby escape the charge of pre-determining his end? Hardly, for he has effectively blocked any passage to the transcendent. The attitude of strict propriety which seals off the self and secures it against any existential porousness at the same time empties reality of transcendent significance. To neutralize the self in the face of being is to neutralize being itself; not to feel one's finitude is, reciprocally, not to recognize the transcendence of being. Are we not inextricably caught in a dilemma here? The man who begins in humility prejudges things in one way; the man who abstracts from humility prejudges them in another. Does not this mean that philosophy is an arbitrary construction of the subject which cannot be justified in one way or the other?

Here we have touched the paramount epistemological question to which the philosophy of Gabriel Marcel gives rise. If we acknowledge that all philosophical thought is tributary to an option which stands at its source, and if that option is a function of freedom, then how can philosophy deal with objective truth?[17] Is not the truth that which does not leave us free to reject it? If philosophy is a mode of thought which does not impose its results with necessity, then it is in no way scientific knowledge and we wonder how the category of truth can apply to it at all. Before we have reached the conclusion of our study, we shall have followed Marcel a long way in the pursuit of his "methodology of the unverifiable." Suffice it to point out now that this is the novel and crucial epistemological aspect of a philosophy which in its metaphysical orientation can unhesitatingly be called Augustinian. The Augustinian experience is of a self whelmed in being and truth. Nothing could better express the central Marcellian insight than St. Augustine's "To know the truth, we must be in the truth." We might even attempt to sum up his essentially un-abbreviable method with this shorthand expression:

to philosophize is to utter the being which is present unuttered. The cardinal point which Marcel does not cease to emphasize is that this utterance is an effluence of our liberty: being can only be attested freely.

The indubitable presence of being, its free attestation—upon these two points hinges our understanding of almost everything in Marcel's thought. And yet this is not enough. There is a further precision which has to be made in regard to the manner in which being is present to the self. It would be erroneous to think that Marcel sees man's existential situation as some kind of solitary encounter with the real. We do not withdraw from others in order to ensconce ourselves within being. The self to which being is present is not an insular ego which abuts upon a transcendent. The experience of being arises in communion; even more strictly, it is an experience *of* communion: *esse est co-esse.* Whatever genuine value a conception like the Plotinean "alone to the Alone" may have, it is not the register in which Marcel's metaphysical symphony is played. Although we may rightly say that the transcendent is present to the self, we must immediately make clear that there is no self except insofar as there is communion. My self apart from other selves quite simply *is not.* It comes to be in communion.[18] In coming to be, it emerges to a mode of existence which is at once limited and opened beyond its limits. In terms we have already used, my experience of finitude, my experience of the invasion of my limits, includes my permeability to other finite selves. To be in a limited way is to be related: it is to be-in-relation to others. Conversely, it is *not to be* apart from the co-presence of others. Not only is the continuing existence of the self a gift from a transcendent generosity, but the most intimate treasures of the self are minted by the communal generosity of other finite selves. I am literally given to myself by others. Unless I am a self, being will not be present to me; unless I am with others, I will not be a self.

It is the windows of interpersonal experience which open on to transcendence. Marcel fully shares the conviction of E. M. Forster that "it is personal life and it alone which holds up the mirror to infinity."[19] This conviction is the basis for his absorption with such non-traditional

themes as love, hope, and fidelity. Habitually, the metaphysician has
conducted his research into the ultimate nature of reality by a concentration upon being as it is apprehended in the structures of language:
as we shall see, even though this is not fruitless, it is at best unduly
restricted and at worst dangerous, for language is the instrument of the
objectification of communion and is itself susceptible to an objectifying
treatment that would wither away its transcendent roots. Even though
ideas and words may be grounded in the immediacy of existence, they
are *par excellence* detachable, and inclined to tip over into a totally
neutral universe of discourse where abstraction has proceeded to its
devitalized limit.

What a debilitated and derivative metaphysics too often does is to
begin within this de-existentialized conceptual universe and then to try
to work its way out, allowing room for spiritual experiences only insofar
as they are willing to adapt themselves to what is an essentially irrespira-
ble environment. Men then begin to wonder whether such profoundly
primary experiences as fidelity and love can pass muster in the face of
careful critical scrutiny. Do they tell us anything ultimate about how
things are or are they only (possibly illusory) subjective states which
have to be checked and validated by businesslike and unsentimental
minds? For Marcel, there is no hesitation: these experiences manifest
the true face of being, and the objective structures which presume to
judge them are in fact only partial products of the indubitably actual
spiritual world which they reveal.[20] They are the focusings to a fine point
of that light which is present to us even through its source is obscured.
They are the projections onto the plane of particularized experience of
the being which hovers below experience, eruptions into consciousness
out of the abyss that consciousness cannot plumb, eminences of that
"metaphysical Atlantis"[21] which is the archetypal object of what we
might call the ontological memory of man.

Many of the key ideas which will enable us to move freely in the
chambers of Marcel's thought now lie in our hands, but let us pause
for a moment over the word "light" which has been used above. It may

be that the individual strands of interpretation all converge in this one center. More than once Marcel has suggested that there must lie at the beginning of philosophy what he calls a "blinded intuition."[22] We may take this as an alternative expression for the primitive assurance, a transposition of that phrase into the visual realm. Both expressions point up the same truth: our thought sets out from a source which may be inaccessible to us but which illuminates and comforts us on the whole road's journey. It is in this sense that the end is in the beginning: the assurance which derives from fulfillment is not wholly missing even in need. The holy city may not be possessed from the start but the vision of its reality initiates the pilgrimage.[23] This does not mean that our philosophical conclusions are there to begin with, but that that which makes them philosophical is there to begin with. What actually specifies philosophical knowledge proper is the vision of its object as transfigured in the aboriginal light.

> In this sphere everything seems to go as if I found myself acting on an intuition which I possess without immediately knowing myself to possess it—an intuition which cannot be, strictly speaking, self-conscious and which can grasp itself only through the modes of experience in which its image is reflected, and which it lights up by being thus reflected in them.[24]

We see and we do not see: here is almost the literal translation of Marcel's "blinded intuition." There is a world entirely there, and yet it escapes our possession. The light is not that which is seen, but that in which all else is seen. We may not ever capture the light; we are the aperture through which the light breaks.[25]

It is assuredly at this point that attention ought to be called to a remarkable fact: it is entirely possible, and even likely, that we may grasp the philosophical method of Gabriel Marcel in the order of metaphor before we grasp it in rational terms. Read with absorption in the pages of this philosopher and you find a primordial image spontaneously arising in the mind: the image of a winding path. This man's thought is a winding path: here is the original certitude. Nor does it signify a mere extrinsic embellishment of a comprehension already conceptually clear. We do not first know what his method is and then apply to it a conscious figure of speech. Rather, here it seems that the understanding in the dimension of metaphor precedes the intellectual knowledge; the metaphor is a principle of comprehension. We know that the metaphor applies, and applies profoundly, before we know why it applies.

Certainly the application is not simply to the form of Marcel's work, where the circuitous and hesitant nature of the journals, their false starts and divagations, clearly confer a superficial validity on it. It is the inner meaning of this thought which the metaphor communicates, not the quasi-spatial meanderings of its formal expression. Emphasizing the readily apparent union of form and content also falls short, for the real referent of the image is neither what he says nor the way he says it, but the very act of thinking which creates both form and content. To think—to think philosophically—is to walk a winding path. Or to put it more exactly: to think is to engage in an interior movement which imposes itself on the mind of the observer under this dominant and non-contingent metaphor. Once again, this is evident before we know why it should be so.

Without treating the image as a convenient sampler, along whose patterns we industriously stitch our rational insights—thus affectedly trivializing the whole approach—it would still be helpful to examine it in the light of our later intellectual understanding with a view to uncovering its genuine cognitive value. For if the metaphor is really non-arbitrary, then it must possess such value. Although the metaphor taken alone is not yet knowledge and must be rationally explicated if it is to become such, there is no title to despise the heuristic power that it may possess. Marcel himself, following Bergson, stresses the irreplaceable contribution of certain basic structural metaphors.[26] What we are soon struck by in reading his commentators is the apparently unconscious manner in which so many of them seize his thought via the mediating

image of a "*chemin sinueux*,"[27] and we are confirmed in the belief that
in this we have found the basic structural metaphor which corresponds
to his philosophical method. To accentuate the sinuosity of a man's
thought is not, as it might seem at first sight, merely to say that he goes
off on tangents or that he cannot carry an argument in a straight line;
for a sinuous movement is not a random deviation—it contains the
notion of a direction. When eventually we discover in Marcel himself
the realization that he is engaged in a work of reclamation that is both
"*sinueux et deroutant*"[28]; when he talks of the "winding journey"[29] of his
reflections, and says that "I will only reach my goal through roundabout
ways"[30]; when in the very context of his remarks on fundamental metaphors he chooses to apply to his own thought the image of a road[31]—
then the conviction of the non-contingent character of this image no
longer appears fanciful.

Our problem simply is to find in the thinking of Marcel those
elements which, insinuated into the "spatiality of inner experience"
which is "coextensive with the whole spiritual life,"[32] inevitably recom-
pose themselves into this involuntary metaphor. And we have not far to
look. For a little consideration will show us that the image of a winding
path embodies exactly those paradoxical elements of assurance and
tentativeness to which we have already alluded. The act of walking a path
is indissolubly linked to the assurance of a goal; the winding nature of
the journey signalizes the uncertainty of the traveler. If we subsume the
image under the dominant symbol of light, the complete interpretation
emerges. Every act of thinking is a movement towards the light. None of
these thoughts ever captures or possesses the light; it is continually lost
and refound in the individual experiences which radiate it. When our
spiritual imagination surveys these successive impulses, it must translate the renewed surges into a single movement which veers and swerves
without losing its constant forward vector, thus giving the impression of
sinuosity. As Marcel says, a thought which does not lay hold of a manipulable object must exhibit a vacillating character[33]; it is this temporal
vacillation which the spontaneous spatiality of our spiritual eye unifies

into the metaphorical *gestalt* of a winding path. It is only upon reflection that the intellect can disengage the rational implication of a symbol
which has imposed itself without reflection.

The full exegesis of that symbol will also lay bare the reason for the
perpetual "beginning over" which Marcel attributes to authentic philosophical thinking. Since this vision can never become a possession, it
can never be retained, and therefore philosophy is a constantly renewed
vision rather than a persevering deduction from a premise achieved
once and for all.[34] This is what it means to begin from zero, to call one's
thought continually into question: a "result" in philosophy is only an
incantation to put us in the presence of the light. All philosophical
reflection is a thinking for the first time, because it is a passage into that
region which is first absolutely—where the category of the "customary"
has no meaning. That is why Marcel's thought, which so perfectly fulfills
this ideal, has the appearance of absolute freshness and authenticity: a
thought steeped in the inexhaustible can never be stale.

CHAPTER II

Being in a Situation

THE POINT of departure in philosophy is strictly correlative to the goal we set ourselves.[1] One who aims only at a security in thought, a harmonious system of consistent propositions, needs only to embark from a purely logical indubitable, a proposition which it would be self-contradictory to deny. Such a system of transmittable theorems, over which the mind feels a comfortable mastery, Marcel himself at first had aimed at, and his *Metaphysical Journal* represents a series of notes recorded for that kind of construction. It did not take him long to become conscious, however, that the undertaking was a futile one.[2] What it would entail is the installation of the mind in the vantage point of the absolute observer, one who had the best possible seat from which to view the totality of the real.[3] In effect, this means a depersonalized observer, a nobody-in-particular, for every personal point of view is the opposite of absolute: it is *mine*. Personal experience—my experience inasmuch as it is mine—could therefore never be integrated into such a system.[4] Singular experience is forever recalcitrant to inclusion in a totality which is available for anybody; indeed, Marcel later shows that the very concept of a totality is erected by a withdrawal from the un-summable immediacy of being.[5] This means that the pronouncement on ultimate reality cannot be made by a detached and universalized subject, by pure thought.

Not only that, but the very attempt to do so is impossible of attainment, for the human mind cannot, even in pure thought,[6] reach the central observatory of the absolute onlooker, for the startlingly simple reason that it is only by participating in reality that it exists at all. A system is a spectacle which is there for a disengaged mind, a mind which is not itself enclosed within the panorama it beholds. For the human subject such a disengagement is unthinkable. Where its possibility seems plausible—for pure reason—it is only because the systematizer neglects the one element which can never be included within his structure: his own act of thinking.[7] Our thought does not lie open to our gaze—we cannot stand outside it and treat it as an object, and it is only the objectified (that which I can observe without being involved in) which is systematizable. Because I am altogether engaged in being, no merely objective judgment upon it is possible.[8]

Now if truth cannot be found by detaching ourselves from our situation, it follows that it can only be found within the situation. To philosophize is not to flee from the situation into the arid certainties of pure thought, but to "*approfondir mon expérience*,"[9] elevating and immanentizing its singular secrets through the power of a properly philosophical reflection. It is true that we can discover universally valid structures within the situation, but this is the work of science, not philosophy. The world of universal validity which abstraction creates is there only for a universalized mind.[10] At the level of pure thought, every man is a universalized mind, but the philosophical undertaking is the *élan* of an ontological exigence which is not a drive for formal correctness but a demand for singular fulfillment. This fulfillment, therefore, can be derived not by setting up a system of ultimate propositions which are valid for everyone, but by lighting up the promise latent in my situation. Philosophy is not a construction which is built upon a situation but an excavation into a situation, which aims at finding the underground springs that feed it from the beyond.[11]

Still, philosophy must start somewhere, and it ought to start with an indubitable. Otherwise its later positions will be vitiated. The point is, what kind of indubitable are we offered? There is the famous proffer of the Cartesian *cogito*—will not that do? Not as far as Marcel can see. There is more than one objection to it. First, there is the use to which Descartes put it—using it as an absolutely punctiliar given, by focusing on which he could filter out all else needful. But if the *cogito* is transparent, it is not an existential indubitable, for the self given existentially is the acme of non-transparency. Actually, as far as Marcel can judge, the *cogito* of Descartes is transparent, which is as much as to say that it is non-existential.[12] Descartes discovered not the existential subject, but himself as a thinking being, a universal subject: the *cogito*, then, is a purely formal *a priori* which guards the threshold of the valid.[13] The *cogito-self* is the self which stands ready to put its seal of clear and distinct approval on a world which meets its standards—on a world of objects, then, for the existential world shares the opacity of the existing self.

Some might quarrel with this as a proper interpretation of Descartes, on the solid grounds that what Descartes intuited really was an existing singular self and not a universal ego. There are undoubtedly the strongest reasons for believing this to be his own understanding, but we must remember that the certainty revealed in the *cogito* bore upon a consciousness in which only the subjective pole had an unchallengeable status in existence: his certainty was of a self for whom the existence of the non-self had still to be demonstrated. Now Marcel looks upon consciousness as an undifferentiated unity in which even the polarity of subject-object is rather discovered than given.[14] If we isolate one term of this polarity, the thinking self, in total unrelatedness to the other, what do we have left, even if we insist on the singularity of this thinking self? The attribute of existence which we would like to confer on it has been derived from the immediate situation from which we have now withdrawn and whose existence we now pose as problematical. Then what non-problematical idea of existence are we bestowing upon the *cogitans*? To call the *cogito-self* existent while leaving the "external world" still in doubt, we would have to appeal to a privileged idea of existence drawn from a source other than the polar situation of immediate reality, for in that situation existence is a *totum simul*. Where would we get such a privileged idea of existence?

Can the *cogito* draw it from within itself? Not in Marcel's view, for even if it grasps in self-consciousness the uniqueness of its own subjectivity, it soon withdraws to that portion of the subject in which a mind intent upon guaranteed certitude feels most at home—the area of pure thought, the area where the individual appears to himself as a mere representative of the universal. It is from this area that the sortie to existence must then be made. "Inasmuch as I think, I am a universal, and if knowledge is dependent on the *cogito*, that is precisely in virtue of the universality inherent in the thinking ego."[15] This view comes very near to placing the *cogito* as the first step on the road which led to the transcendental self of Kant, where the thesis maintained by Marcel becomes more obviously applicable. But the general burden is acceptable enough: the rationalist, the man who emphasizes transmittable certainty in thought, is functioning primarily as a universal reasoner. It does seem that at a certain story of the mind, the Averroist opinion begins to recommend itself: the intellect appears as a hyper-individual principle which utilizes empirical selves for its operation.

Descartes' self-as-thinker is a subject which has cut the umbilical cord which binds it to things; even after establishing this validating matrix of pure thought, he still has the task of making the passage back to existence. How can the existential world be resuscitated starting from a self which does not take part in it? According to Marcel, it cannot be. There can be no passage to existence from a vantage point outside it. Existence is not a *demonstrandum*: it is there from the beginning or it is not there at all.[16] Now, as a matter of fact, existence *is* given in the beginning, and we may call it into question only by means of a pseudo-idea of it conjured out of nowhere and supposedly more evident than existence itself, an obviously vicious procedure. The moment of doubt is not the initial phase of our meeting with reality; it represents a withdrawal from a more primary experience and actually lives off the primary experience.

Up to a point the movement of the mind in which it poses the world as in front of itself, as an object over against a subject, is a legitimate operation of abstraction which sets up the public universe of the sciences. But to extend this process of abstraction to a global scale is absurd[17]: how can I detach myself *in toto* from reality? Purified of every intruding connection with the empirical, what is the self? It is a mere intersection of the abstract forms of thought, not anyone's self at all—just a self-in-general. The world as constituted for a self-in-general is a formally valid and universally verifiable system of propositions—but it does not exist. What exists is what is present for an incarnate consciousness.

The existential indubitable is the self as incarnate in the body and as manifest in the world[18] Existence is said in reference to a body; it is presence to a body. The first moment of my experience is an exclamatory awareness of myself not as curled up tight, but as *ex-sisting*, as standing out, as manifest to a world which is also indubitably existent. It is my body which sets me down in a world of real beings. It is this self in which my philosophical concern flares up. And the great datum for this self is the non-contingency of the empirically given.[19] The past, my family, my surroundings—these are not something over and above me, not something in any way outside my self. I am constituted by my situation. What is real is the altogether. The *cogitans* is erected by a retreat from the altogether; to that extent it is unreal, and if we want to restore its existential density we must re-cross to the *cogitatum*. But if we do we find that we recover not our isolated existence, but a global reality which is given *en masse* and which alone can give the *cogitans* real roots.

It is the body through which we are inserted into the world of real existence; it is conjunction with the body which is the criterion for the existence of what is not the body.[20] (Marcel has never completely disentangled the possible difficulties raised by this *identification* of existence and the spatially related.) That is why an idea cannot be said to exist; it may somehow be real, but it is not an existent.[21]

Now, to speak of the body is to use a word which is not unambiguous.[22] The body as object is merely one among others in a world

that can be described by an observer. But the body as *mine* is object for
nobody, including, of course, myself.[23] The inevitable manner in which
we construe the relationship between self and body is to consider the
body as an *instrument*, something which we use, and therefore something which we have. Just as every tool we use is an extension of the
power of the body, so the body itself seems to be a utensil of the self,
or of the soul. However, this way of looking at things leads to insoluble
problems. The instrument which is a prolongation of the body always
has a community of nature with the body, both being extended entities.
If we project this instrumental relationship, will we not be forced to say
that the self which uses the body as its extension is itself bodily? But if
it is, then it is an instrument of something further, and this regress will
go on to infinity. This shows us that our approach has misled us—my
body cannot be equated with something that I have. All having is said
in relation to the body; if the body itself is in turn a form of having, then
by what is it possessed? Furthermore, any such view clearly makes the
body to be something outside me, external to the true self; but the only
self which is not related to the body is a universal subject which is a pure
construction, which does not exist but is only thought of. The body is
the mode of presence of the self to the actual world.

Remember that we are talking about *my* body, under the precise
character which makes it mine, which allows me to say mine. If I choose
to regard my body as a mere something, as a spatial structure governed
by various physiological laws of functioning, as a *quid* which belongs
to a *qui*, then I have bypassed the ambiguity. Unfortunately, I have also
vanished from the actual world. Once I begin to concentrate on the
"my" aspect of my body, I see the impossibility of treating the duality between body and soul as an instrumental one. This conviction is
enforced on me by my feelings, which are least of all to be apprehended
in anonymous terms. My body is the absolute mediator between me and
the actual world, the vehicle in which the self deploys itself in existence.
To refuse the duality between body and soul is to say that no merely
objective judgment on their relationship is expressible.[24] Marcel sums

up with the proposition: "I am my body."[25] The body *is* myself insofar as
I am manifest. This is, naturally, not a version of the materialist formula,
which actually suppresses the self in favor of an objectified structure
hypostasized as real. It is the limit-statement of the refusal to objectify
the body-soul relationship.

I cannot, without contradiction, think of my body as non-existent,
for my body is the existential indubitable which is the touchstone of
all existence. Incarnation is the central given of metaphysics[26]; it is the
rock-bottom of my being-in-a-situation. The assurance of the incarnate nature of the self is simultaneously an assurance of the existence
of the world. First of all it must be emphasized that this issue cannot be
discussed in terms of a prior dichotomy of existence and the existent[27];
we cannot detach existence as a predicate and then look around for a
subject to which it might just possibly belong. It is only in virtue of a
rupture which thought makes in reality that we are obliged to ask if
there is *something which* possesses existence. For we do not really have
an idea of existence which we must conscientiously match up with an
essence. All thought is a mediation within existence; existence itself is
therefore unthinkable. The existential judgment is just the transposition
of the experience-limit into the intellectual order.[28] Existence is not a
predicate in search of a subject. Existence must be assured from the
start, as we have seen it to be. What is there for us from the beginning is
the "indissoluble *unity of existence and the existent.*"[29] This assurance is
of a global character; it is not confined to my incarnate self but extends
to the reality within which my self is incarnate. "What is given to me
beyond all possible doubt is the confused and global experience of the
world inasmuch as it is existent."[30] The "I" of the "I exist" is not an ego
isolated from the world, but a self in the world, a self whose incarnation
is not completed within its own limits but by the being-together with
the whole world; thus the affirmation "I exist," Marcel declares, "tends
to merge with an affirmation such as 'the universe exists.'"[31] All this
is not demonstrated—the very attempt would be absurd—but simply
there in the immediacy of exclamatory awareness. Marcel goes so far as

to say that the union between soul and universe is of the same nature
as that between soul and body,[32] meaning by this that I am no more
detachable from the world than I am from my own body.

This comes out very strongly in his critique of the familiar view of
sensation, which is really based on a naïve objectification.[33] His remarks
here form the second half of what he himself calls his "sensualist metaphysics,"[34] and although they are doubtless occasioned by the crude
form of sensory epistemology indulged in by Locke and the empiricist
school, it is difficult to see how his impugnments do not as well fall
on the Scholastic doctrine as it is usually expressed. The kernel of his
indictment is that by a mind operating at a certain stage of reflection,
sensation is invariably regarded as the translation of a message received
from a physical object, and that this is a falsification of its true nature.
The uncritically critical thinker proposes the situation in these terms;
There is a body A, situated in space, which sends out a stimulus that
impinges on my body-organ B, this entire process being physical and
pre-sensorial. I then translate this purely physical event into psychical
terms and produce a sensation. The process is conceived along the lines
of transmitter and receiving-station. What is wrong with it? Only that
it assumes conditions which cannot be realized. Literally, a translation
is the rendering of one set of data in terms of another; naturally it is
impossible to a subject which does not possess the data in the first form.
Now the physical events, taken purely as physical, are not known to the
subject which is supposed to do the translating—if they were known
they would already *be* sensations (and our whole problem would repeat
itself: how did they get to be sensations?). There is no way in which the
data can be given to the senses for it is of the very nature of a physical
event that it be infra-sensorial and not given to me as datum. Sensation
is the basis for all communication and all interpretation: how can we
look upon it too as an interpretation? This would be to apply to sensation a category which only arises within sensation.

Sensation is not the translation of something other than itself. The
opinion that it is unfailingly leads to uncertainty as to whether or not it

is a correct translation, and our critic finds himself trying to escape the trammels of solipsism. Sensation is a way of being; it is a pure immediate and inexpressible in objective terms. Whenever I do try to give an account of it, I instinctively begin by separating object and subject as discrete entities and then try to close the circuit between them. This view of sensation is unalterably bound up with the instrumentalist notion of the body. I see my body as an instrument for the reception of a message. I try to grasp according to the categories of having what is in reality a way of being. Sensation is not a reception, but an immediate participation in being. It is the operation which actualizes my incarnation in the world.

The word participation must give us pause, for it is the notion on which Marcel's metaphysics turns. Participation is at once his manner of piercing through to realism and his avenue of escape from individualism. To be is to participate in being. Do not fail to note the twofold affirmation of this formula: in existing, we trans-exist. In virtue of our being we are swept beyond our being. Sensation represents but one side of this participation. And what can be said of it can also be said of all ontological participation: it is non-objectifiable. We cannot effectively isolate that in which we participate from ourselves as participants, since at every level it is the participation which founds the being of the participants.

True enough, there is a participation in the order of having, such as occurs when I claim my share of a cake that is being cut up.[35] Here I literally take a part of an object external to my being. We may slide down the scale of objectification, however, if we imagine our participation in a ceremony, let us say a thanksgiving for the deliverance of a nation from war; even if I cannot take part in the objective event due to sickness, I recognize that in the truly significant order I can share in the national prayer. And the objective element can be eliminated completely if we allow ourselves to realize that this one ceremony is only a particular expression of an act of adoration which is continuous and in which I participate through every movement of prayer. This melting into a larger act of love helps to convey the meaning of non-objective participation; in it there is an internalization of the reality in which I participate. In the flowing river of love, separate spirits are ineffably *with* one another.

To be sure, on the level of cognitive activity this *emergent* participation is always under the aegis of some informing idea (here, e.g., the idea of God), but we are now in a position to turn towards the possible meaning of a *submerged* participation, below the level of thought. It is to this kind of participation that both sensation and feeling bear witness. Feeling is comprehensible only in non-instrumentalist terms. To externalize it, to regard it as something which I have, is equivalent to nullifying it: it is only feeling insofar as it is *my* feeling. Only because I can say that I *am* my feeling must I say that I *am* my body. And it is probably, by analogy, as a fundamental feeling that we ought to conceive that non-objectifiable thrust into existence which can never be reduced to a thought-content and which therefore plays the role of the "*non-mediatizable immediate*"[36] at the root of all participation. Through feeling my body is mine; through sensation my body is immediately present to the world; through sensation and feeling I participate, at one level, in a reality from which it would be strictly nonsensical to try to divorce myself.

Feeling is a mode of participation, but there is more to participation than feeling alone. The situation affects me at all levels of my being. There is a temptation to use the term "incarnation" for the purely spatial plane of the situation and to reserve "participation" for the more spiritual levels, but Marcel himself has not really consistently followed such a terminology. However, we ought to suggest in some way that there is more than one level to our participation. We might be prompted to call the body-level the plane of existence and the intersubjective level the plane of being; yet this too—even though it comes close to our eventual decision—would leave us with certain difficulties if followed too rigidly. The point is that my situation affects every facet of my self. Essentially what is always connoted is that I am not autonomous, not self-contained, that I am permeable to others.[37] To be living is to be open to a reality with which I enter into some sort of commerce. My presence to the world is *by* spatiality, but it is *for* communion. Just as my body is a co-immediate of the incarnate world in which it emerges, a focal point within that enfolding world, so my self in its personal aspects is a co-immediate of the "intersubjective element from which the *ego* seems to emerge like an island arising from the waves."[38] My body is given to me as presence-in-the-world; my person is given to me as presence-in-communion. "*Esse est co-esse*" is true not only on the plane of sensible existence but above all on the plane of personal being. The proper beginning of metaphysics is not "I think" but "we are."[39] The tie which binds me to others gives me to myself.

Marcel is not indulging in pious sentimentality here; he means this quite literally. I have no right to treat myself as prior to or more indisputably real than others: I only exist within a certain fullness of experience which is not private but trans-subjective.[40] If anything, it is the other who takes priority, for "it is of the essence of the other that he exist"[41] and I only give definition to my own existence by separating myself from him. This being so, a little thought will make it obvious that communion will be a function of the particular way in which I relate myself to the other. Characteristically, Marcel never troubles to sort out the connections between the possible varieties of communal existence. What really interests him is authentic ontological communion, in which the other is given to me as a thou, as a non-objectifiable presence. This ontological communion is sanctioned by a creative response of our freedom, and is the direct route to transcendence. Yet, after all, our relations with others precede the flowering of our liberty; in childhood we are one among others long before we either freely acknowledge or freely reject them. Following, with some modifications, Troisfontaines' terminology,[42] we might classify this original togetherness as the stage of *community*; here the presence of others (our family, in particular) is as pervading as the air we breathe, and there is no question of taking up a position in regard to it. At some time along the way, however, the realization of the measure of our autonomy leads us to disengage the self as one element, a privileged element, over against others; this phase of analysis we may call the stage of *communication*. It is this which makes possible the crucial experience upon which Marcel concentrates. For until we have arisen out of the slumber of community, a human response in the fullest sense is not forthcoming. Not that the love and devotion of the child within the family can be reduced to the level of mere biology, not that the familial cocoon does not represent a shielding and truly spiritual presence, but because the capacity for a refusal in the real sense is missing, the intersubjectivity here has more the character of a lovely fact than an invitation. When, beyond the egocentric enticements of communication, I freely open myself to a thou in a truly personal encounter, I reach the stage of ontological *communion*.

The passage back to togetherness which is accomplished in communion is a work of my freedom. I may, if I wish, immure myself in the privileged specialness which the stage of communication uncovers, and refuse to surrender to communion. Yet, strangely, even this kind of convoluting egotism is achieved only with a view to the other: egotism is a claim to recognition by the other. He becomes for me a kind of reflector in whose eyes I must read the image of my own worth. At the same time he is a threat against which I must be carefully on guard: the consciousness of my vulnerability forces me to speed the calcifying process which encases me in the warm and protecting shell. When I have finished, I dwell in a Sartrean universe where the other is purely and simply other—and the self I have fashioned by means of this alienating process, this self of mine is also a boring and joyless stranger. When the "thou" is ejected from the front door, the "I" leaves by the back.

But it is not only rampant egotism which loses consciousness of presence. The distinction of egotism is its hostility to communion: a more prosaic neglect of communion is less an exception than a normal condition of the human predicament. By and large, my fellow man is a mere "he" for me—not a "thou," but a third in an ideal dialogue I conduct with myself, an absent party who serves various useful and even interesting purposes but who is hardly *present* to me in the true sense.[43] The faces that hurry by me on the street, the dismal fellow-travelers in the subway, the stereotyped co-workers with whom I engage in perfunctory and tedious conversation—their very "being-there" is hardly to be distinguished from an absence. A "thou" is one who is present to me in a living dialogue, a respondent in an authentic *con-versatio*. Any exchange, it is true, presupposes a minimal second person who is there to listen to my questions, but is there a danger that even this minimum can vanish from my view? The man whom I stop in the street to ask directions to the park—is he much more to me than an animated signpost? The fact which he recounts for me is a pure third, an "it," and the man himself as a mere filing cabinet for facts is a "he." Between two filing cabinets communication is possible, but not communion. We need not think, of course, that one's relation to the great body of men actually reaches this condition; it is enough that it approach the condition asymptotically for Marcel's point to be made.

Communion arises only in a personal response, in an encounter. Suppose I meet a stranger by chance on a railroad train and we engage absently in desultory conversation about the weather, traveling conditions, and the like: even while we respond to each other in a kind of dialogue, he remains for all that a "someone" to me, "that fellow over there." Gradually, perhaps, I learn many things about him, as if he were filling in a biographical questionnaire. Then let there be the sudden discovery of a hidden but profound tie between us, and quickly we pass out of the zone of exterior communication into the "elsewhere" in which our spirits are vivified in communion. How often do I hear the tale of the misfortunes and ills of others with whom I know I ought to sympathize, and yet inwardly feel nothing? I cannot respond; they are just not there for me. But let me open a letter from a friend a thousand miles away telling me that he has been struck down by a terrible disease, and at once I am with him, I suffer with him, we are *together* without qualification. In examples like this the peculiar perfection of communion calls

attention to itself because of the sudden passage into the dyadic relationship, but this instantaneity is not a necessary factor. The co-presence which unites husband and wife represents one instance in which
the triadic element has been more or less permanently replaced by a
habitual intimacy which both broadens and extends the victory over
exteriority won in the instantaneous encounter.

The thou which is given to me in an encounter is not a mere reper-
tory for facts; furthermore, he himself is not the subject of a factual
description. The reality of the thou cannot be grasped by a series of
predicates. Our awareness of the thou is not the awareness of a something, but of that which superabounds above every attempt to grasp him
as a something. We do not know *what* he is, but only *that* he is. Only
an absent third person can be the term of reference of a questionnaire.
"What is his background?"; "What are his talents?"; even "What pleas-
ant traits does he possess?"—all these questions bear on a "he" about
whom our curiosity is aroused. "Who are you?" is the only question
which can be asked of the thou, and it is not a request for information.
Although interrogative in appearance, it is really a form of invocation:
"Be with me." The thou who is present to me eludes all characterization
precisely in respect to his being present. It is only an absent other who
can be characterized; in fact, characterization, reduction to content, is a
form of objectification and is at the opposite pole to presence.

Nothing could be clearer than this if we confined it to self-presence:
the self in its ultimate reality simply transcends all description, all judgment, I can tell you all kinds of things about myself, but to speak *about*
something is to convert it into a third in a dialogue. To treat the self in
this manner is to deprive it of the precise character which makes it to be
a self—its non-absence, its first-personness, its presence. The self as self
cannot be converted into an "it." In the same way, the thou as thou, in
that exact respect which makes him to be a thou, cannot be transformed
into a "he," into a sum of contents, a locus of characteristics upon which
we might bring a judgment. The thou as thou is felt as co-presence and
only as co-presence. Can we not at least ask who is present? Only in the

way in which one can say to himself "Who am I?" What is the answer
to such a question? Certainly it is not to be had by toting up individual
traits, or even by arranging them into "patterns." What is the essence of
the self? To be more than an essence.[44] What is the essence of the thou?
To be more than an essence.

But this doctrine can be made more telling still. Not only are the
self and the thou both mysterious, they are one and the same mystery.
The uniqueness and ineffability of the self is founded by the co-presence
of the thou.[45] Apart from the presence of an other, I am not a unified
center at all; I am either a universal content of thought or a succession
of empirical states. What makes me to be a singular "I"? The presence
of the thou. If I shut myself off from the influx of others' presence, I
cannot be present to myself—present, that is, as a unique being. There
will remain, perhaps, a self-consciousness of a bundle of thoughts
and desires, but this falls short of real personal consciousness.[46] If, *per
impossible*, I had *never* been present to others (had even skipped the
stage of community), my "self" would be an amorphous possibility, not
an actuality at all. He who, having been shaped as an actual person by
the presence of others, withdraws from the living tissue of communion,
to that extent ceases to be an actual person. To live and think habitually without reference to the dimension of being which communion
reveals would be to approach asymptotically the condition of a merely
epistemological subject. Knowledge bears on universal; love reveals the
singular; loving knowledge is the definition of philosophy.

Marcel refers to that endowment of the person in virtue of which he
is open to others by the untranslatable term "*disponibilité*."[47] To render
this as "disposability" or "availability," as his translators are forced to
do, is really to replace a suggestive word with a rather unhelpful and
misleading one. The English words manage to convey the idea of "being
at the service" of the other, which would not be bad if correctly understood, but which is not self-explanatory. It would undoubtedly be better
to anglicize the French form, while realizing what it connotes: openness,
release, abandonment, welcoming, surrender, readiness to respond. The

attitude which it combats is admirably conveyed by the French word "*crispation*."[48] The disponible person is hospitable to others; the doors of his soul are ajar. The concept is one of the several most important in Marcel's whole philosophy and we will have to recur to it more than once. For the time being it is enough to see it as the dispostion that permits communion. Disponibility will be proclaimed in acts like love, sympathy, admiration. And if metaphysics is only possible through communion, then it is easy to see why Marcel will declare[49] that the inability to admire is a metaphysical fault: it is the mark of the indisponible man, and the indisponible man cannot be a metaphysician.

A meditation on the underlying implications of the preposition "with" insofar as it applies to personal experience will reveal the irreducible nature of communion.[50] For, two persons are not with one another as two things are with one another. The table may be with the chair in the sense of being in the same room, but its relation is an external one which leaves it unaffected within itself; its being with the other piece of furniture literally makes no difference to it. As long as another is merely with me in this sense, he is not with me at all, as a person. Only when he is present as "thou" does the new dimension of being arise which is irreducible to non-personal categories. At that point he is with me in an absolute sense—he is not juxtaposed to me at all. When one debouches upon the spiritual plane, the correlative categories of the "same" and the "other" are at once transcended. Beyond the closed systems in which the logical judgment encloses us, there is a sort of fecund indistinctness where persons commune. The preposition "with," at this level, corresponds neither to a relation of inherence, nor to a relation of exteriority: the being with whom I am is not only "before" me and not only "in" me. Between the I and the thou a bond exists which exceeds any means I have to take cognizance of it.

The intimacy which exists in communion cannot be expressed in categories which leave communion aside. Thus, if I begin by treating the persons involved in it as objects external to one another, I will inevitably conceive their "being-together" as something added to their being:

first they are, and then they are related. The best I could do, with such a scheme, would be to see co-presence as the idea of co-presence, an attitude which alters the bearing of the subject towards a thing outside him without introducing him to a plane of being on which he had not existed before. The distinction between thou and he would then be a purely psychological one, devoid of ontological import. It is not only possible to take this view but even a persistent temptation: the tendency of both my thought and my life is to disengage myself from the immediacy of participation and thus to degrade the thou to a he. Once we look upon him as a he, it is unimaginable how he can be anything else, or even what it can mean to be anything else. The thou then becomes an "x" which is assumed to be beyond a sensible facade and which is known by assimilating it to my own self—my own self being presumably first known to me. The "thou" then is one who is like unto me, whose presence I deduce from various objective data.

Now, actually, if the thou is a mode of existence, it cannot be deduced; existence is not a *demonstrandum*. It is only when we realize that communion is a primary mode of being that we understand its ineffability without doubting its ontological significance. What is primary cannot be conveyed in terms more ultimate than itself. Thus, Marcel would probably say that its ineffability is the sign of its ontological significance. If the person is a reality which only emerges in communion, then we cannot try to see communion in terms of the juxtaposition of already constituted personalities. Every relation of person with person must be interiorized in the most extreme manner possible. How are we to express this limit of the interiority of relationships? How but to say that *I am* my relationships? I am constituted by my relations with others.[51] It is the "we" which creates the "I." Intersubjective acts found the subject.[52]

Personal communion, then, like every form of authentic ontological participation, is strictly non-objectifiable. I cannot dissect it into components one of which confronts the other. It is a "participation without frontiers,"[53] and Marcel emphasizes this by the seemingly quaint statement that we cannot tell how far a personality extends[54]: We are part of all that creates us. ("Ask not for whom the bell tolls…" would on this basis, be not a mystical flight, but a sober assertion of metaphysics.) There is an easily perceived parallel between participation on the level of personal communion and participation on the level of corporeality. Just as the enclosing spatial universe founds me as corporeal existent, so the enclosing universe of intersubjectivity founds me as spiritual existent. If I were to consider myself *apart* from these participations, what would I be? Either nothing at all, or a pure potentiality for such participation. But as an actual subject, as an existent, I am a co-existent, a debtor to all that is.

Because of the ineradicable objectifying bent of language, we must even be on our guard against setting up intersubjectivity as a kind of something which can be designated. It is neither a this nor a that. "It is an implied understanding which remains an implied understanding even when I try to focus my thought on it."[55] How can I think that out of which my being and my thought arise? Marcel suggests a recourse to metaphors, especially to the non-optical metaphors drawn from music. In the realm of music everything is bound together in a living communication. It is a world of interpenetration, inseparability, where the harmony of the whole is present to every part. "All is in all"—this is at once a description of musical reality, of communion, and of Marcel's philosophy. Yet the metaphors can take us only so far, and at the ultimate point we must confine ourselves to saying that intersubjectivity shares with all truly ontological reality the fact that it cannot be designated but only alluded to.[56]

CHAPTER III

Problem and Mystery

OUR UNDERSTANDING of Marcel's classical distinction between a problem and a mystery hinges on our understanding of what he means by an object. The sources of this notion are twofold. The first is an inheritance from the views of Royce; the second is original with himself. According to Royce, an object is a third in a dialogue. What is primary is the communion of subjects. In relation to the dialogue between I and Thou, the object is an absent third which serves as a term of reference. This view of Royce comes out very clearly in the latter's conception of the way in which "nature" is set up by man as an independent entity. Nature is constituted as an object by human society, for by nature we mean the collection of processes which can be shared by all and verified. Thus, nature is "a realm which we conceive *as known or as knowable to various men*, in precisely the same general sense in which we regard it as known or knowable to our private selves."[1] Not everything need be so generalized—we can believe in a religious revelation, or in the reality of the interior life of another, without feeling that their secrets are open to public verification. But, "nature" considered as a complexus of verifiable processes is precisely the public property which exists between me and my fellow man; it is a social reality, and as civilization advances, it is distinguished more and more from privately experienced reality, until it becomes an alien and mechanical other. This treasure-trove of universal validities is the world which science investigates—and it is the only world which science as such can conceive. Eventually the latter concludes that the true world is a domain of unvarying necessity and presumes that everything must at last be subsumed under this category. Royce protests that science has no right thus to cast all reality in its own image; the public world has no absolute status, it is only the triadic common element between man and man.[2]

Enough has already been said to see how many of these elements Marcel has retained. We have seen that he conceives pure thought to operate in the realm of the public or universally verifiable. As a natural correlative of this, the world of public property exists for "anyone." What is universally valid is there for anyone at all; the knower of the universally valid functions as anyone at all, not as an individual self. This consideration merges with his own view of an object. Etymologically, an object is something which is thrown in front of me; it is something which I encounter as outside me and over against me. Here is the feature of objectivity on which Marcel's distinction between problem and mystery is grounded. In order to bring together the fairly widely scattered explanations of this distinction, let us resort to the method of systematically noting down the points of difference between the two modes of knowledge. These will be found to be four in number.[3]

1. The basis for all points of difference is in this view of an object as something external to me, something which is set over against myself. In an objective situation, I am here and the object is there, complete and open for inspection. For the reason that I meet the object as juxtaposed to myself and as not involving myself, I can envelop it in a clear and distinct idea which delineates its limits. With this clarity comes perfect transmissibility, and with the transmissibility the object begins to lead that public and independent life which is the privilege of the world of the problematic. Marcel does not fail to notice[4] the peculiar coincidence that the Greek roots of the word "problem" are perfectly correspondent to the Latin roots of "object"; a *pro-blema* is something which is thrown in my path, something which is met along the way.

A problem, then, is an inquiry which is set on foot in respect to an object which the self apprehends in an exterior way. Such would be a problem in algebra, or the problem a mechanic faces in fixing an automobile. The engine and the man are two quite isolable entities; the engine is something complete and entire outside of him, which he may literally inspect from all sides. Not every object, naturally, presents a spatial externality of this sort (an objectivity stemming from perception, from "*voir*") but the problematic datum is always *regarded* as juxtaposed (an objectivity which arises from converting it into a possessed thing, from "*avoir*"). Thus the attempt to solve the equation $2x^2 - 3x = 2$ would be a problematic inquiry even though the elements are essentially mental rather than spatial. The point is that the data as presented do not include myself; in conceiving the numbers I do not conceive myself, I retreat from them and regard them intently as posed in front of me. The area of the problematic covers a wide range of human knowledge. The mechanic and the mathematician may stand, perhaps, as types of the domination of nature which the problematic knowledge of science makes possible. Science, of course, embodies the ultimate achievement of problematic knowledge: from the theorists of cybernetics to the researcher pursuing the links between cigarette smoke and cancer, science is uniformly the application of the mind to an *object* in the strict sense of this word. But it is not only science which fulfills the notion of a problem. A bored student doing a crossword puzzle, a reader frowning over a whodunit, a clerk consulting an orderly office file, all are engaged in solving problems. In each case, the data of the questions are such that I can effectively divorce myself from them and concentrate upon them as upon manipulable external objects.

A mystery, on the other hand, is a question in which what is given cannot be regarded as detached from the self. There are data which in their very nature cannot be set over against myself, for the reason that as data they involve myself. If I ask "what is being?" can I regard being as an object which is thrown across my path? No—for being, as a datum, includes me; in order to conceive being as a datum, I must conceive it as including me. I cannot get outside of being in order to ask questions about it in a purely external way. The attempt to isolate what is before me from what is in me breaks down completely here. Being, then, is not a problem at all, but a mystery. If I decide to treat it as a problem, to stand on all fours with it and approach it as just one more manipulable object, I no longer have hold of my original question. A mystery is a question in which I am caught up. In the area of the problematic, the status of the questioner is completely prescinded from, and only the object is called into question. But if I ask "what is being?" the question recoils upon my own status as a questioner: who am I who question being? Am I? At this point the "problem" of being impinges upon the intrinsic conditions of its own possibility, and becomes the mystery of being. For the condition of a problematic research is that the subject wear the regalia of unquestionability, and it is only this privilege which qualifies him to render the object totally intelligible. But to question being is to question myself as questioner. That is, this "being" at which I would like to aim questions, is not an object given to a non-obscure subject which may direct all its uncertainty outward: for here in questioning the object I call myself into question.[5]

Being is not an object which I can inspect from all sides: if I were to have a clear and distinct notion of being, I would be completely an object for myself (since being envelops me, and in order to objectify being I would have to objectify myself). But I cannot objectify myself; I can not observe myself from the outside. The question "what am I?" is another example of a mystery. I do not even know for sure what the question means—and here we can say that as a problem it encroaches upon its own supposed data. In the case of a true problem, the elements are clearly given, so that I may use them to proceed to the unknown: in a problematic situation there are always traceable analogies of the splendidly lucid conditions of geometry, "given" and "to find." For instance, in a crossword puzzle: given, the dictionary meaning of "valley"; to find, a four-letter word which equivalently conveys it. Or, in the mechanical problem: given, the known functions of the various parts of the engine; to find, which has broken down. But in a mystery the given itself is not clear and distinct. Thus, the "I" which causes me to tremble when I call it into question contains no element exempt from the mystery which wraps the whole; there is in it no small segment framed within defined limits and exhaustively known, to serve as an opening wedge from which to launch an encircling ratiocination.

Therefore not every reality can be the target of a merely problematic inquiry. Wherever I deal with something which encompasses the self, I may never hope to keep contact with its authentic nature if I treat it as if it does not involve the self. The supreme example of this is, of course, the mystery of being. Perhaps we might even say that *every* example of a mystery is only a particular case of the mystery of being. I am a mystery to myself insofar as I *am*: all things are mysterious insofar as they *are*. We have seen that in any question bearing on being the ontological status of the questioner is of the highest significance. But does this not involve us in an infinite regress? To question myself is to question myself as questioner, and so on ad infinitum. No, says Marcel[6]; the very power to conceive such a regress already enables us to transcend it. For in our predicament is revealed the transcendence of being in relation to our thought. We grasp that all assertions that we make live off a profound assertion by which we are made. Reflection at length loses itself in the depth of an intuition which is blinded (in respect to objectifiable content) but which is at the root of all positivity. The recognition of mystery is the recognition of the self as besieged by being. We only *are* insofar as there is that in us which thought cannot lay bare: we only know we are by recognizing that there is a positing prior to our thought. But this means that wherever there is an encounter with *being* there is mystery; and it means that every other example of a mystery is a particular manifestation of the mystery of being. Only what is not being—or what is not encountered as being—is not mysterious. The only thought which does not run full tilt into mystery is de-ontologized thought, thought which, by immunizing itself against the opacity at its own center, succeeds in conferring the same kind of immunity upon its object. This operation is quite possible, and even desirable, in vast areas of human knowledge. But there are certain realities which in the nature of things are not amenable to this sealing-off process: because what they are involves the self in all its singularity, I cannot prescind from that singularity when I conceive them.

We have already seen examples of this. My body insofar as it is *mine* cannot be adequately rendered in problematic categories. I can say neither that I am the master of it nor its slave, since such relations break down in this, region. In fact my *situation* as a whole is non-objectifiable and refuses to be reduced to a problem. I cannot pass judgment on the world as if I am a spectator: every judgment on the world as a whole is passed on *my* world since I qualify it through my participation.[7] Again, suffering and evil only *are* what they are inasmuch as they involve me; looked at from the outside, evil seems the mere malfunctioning of a mechanism— that is to say, it is not seen as evil at all. Only one who participates with me in my suffering has the right to interpret it for me; that suffering only has a meaning in the respect that I confer a meaning on it through the way I experience it as mine.[8] As with my body, the world, evil, so with love and knowledge[9]: these are realities about which an observer can pass no verdict whatsoever, for they are only real for the participant. We will see this at some length in regard to love, but it may be helpful to empha- size the mysterious character of knowledge, which traditional philosophy has grasped without naming. If I say "what is knowledge?" it is all too obvious that I immediately plunge into the realm of mystery. For I can in no way get outside my own act of knowing in order to treat it as a possible object of description. This is what the famous refutation of skepticism stresses for its own reasons. The question "what is knowledge?" impinges upon its own intrinsic conditions of possibility: the act through which I would like to objectify knowledge in order to study it is already an act of knowledge. Certainly I can reflect on my own act of thought, but only as a *that*, not as a characterizable *what*, not as an object.

So it is, apparently, with all truly philosophical questions. They bear on non-objectifiable data, realities which it is forever impossible to externalize. Freedom, time, space, sensation—all seem to fall under this classification. The consequences of this assertion only slowly begin to dawn on us, but there is every reason to suspect, *a priori*, that it will make all the difference in the world between philosophy and other kinds of knowledge. It opens up a new territory in epistemology, of which others have had passing glimpses but which Marcel must get the credit for discovering and mapping out. Bergson, for instance, saw with unparalleled clarity that every attempt to define freedom conceptually must end by denying it.[10] Marcel allows us to see why that should be true. Freedom is least of all susceptible of being transformed into an object for our study. Freedom involves the self—it is the self; the more an act is free, the more it is *mine* in the absolute sense. Only an object is definable. Only what is definable is demonstrable. Therefore the attempt to demonstrate freedom is an attempt to deal with a mystery as if it were a problem. The most that discursive thought can hope for is to show that any attempt to refute the reality of freedom by problematic argumentation is likewise impossible. Do we not begin to have a premonition that this distinction is introducing us directly into a special realm of being?

2. The second characteristic of a problem derives immediately from the first. A problem admits of a *solution*. By the use of the proper techniques, a "period" can be put to our inquiries. With diligence (expended at the proper hourly compensation) the mechanic will eventually put his finger on the defective part of the engine and declare confidently, "There is your trouble." In the algebraic problem above, the inquirer may by suitable manipulations reach the ready conclusion that x = 2. At that point the problem is finished, over and done with. Final results have been attained and further thought is unnecessary. The possibility of a solution is directly linked to the objectified nature of the datum: because the datum is isolable, it is subject to being circumscribed and dissected by one who has the necessary skill. Its solvability is not what makes it to be a problem, but because it is a problem it is solvable. And

because it is solvable, the notion of a "result" applies to it in the strictest sense. Marcel remarks that in some cases the result seems able to lead a life of its own.[11] If a biochemist by dint of years of patient research has developed a serum for a specific disease, it is not necessary that those who come after duplicate his long investigation; they may simply detach and utilize the result. In the same way, formulas in physics, classifications in biology, logarithmic tables in mathematics can be known in complete isolation from the thought processes which first laboriously found them out. This is not the case in philosophy. I cannot be said to "know" a philosophical conclusion unless I retrace in thought the paths over which its discoverer traveled. The philosophical conclusion has no life independent of the philosophical quest. This is the significance, it would seem, of the Platonic dialogue form, and it is likewise the justification for Marcel's adoption of the metaphysical journal.

But even aside from this, the notion of a "result" cannot be applied in the region of mystery in the way it applies in the region of the problematic.[12] Here it is not possible to reach the point where I can say: "That is done with," the point at which further thought is unnecessary. There is no Q.E.D. in a mystery. What is being? What is freedom? What is the self? Those questions ceaselessly renew themselves. They are not susceptible of a solution in any proper sense. On the contrary, there is a prevailing impression of an inexhaustible profundity, of depths which no amount of thought can ever fathom. The best that we can do is to locate ourselves within the mystery, but this can hardly be said to be a solution.

It must be carefully noted, however, that it is not the characteristic of being insoluble which defines a mystery. This is an error into which hasty reading might betray us or the pseudo-reverence of a jejune apologetics which delights in the limitations of present knowledge because they afford it the chance to exclaim: "See how many things are mysterious. What is magnetism? What is electricity? We don't know! Small wonder that our tiny minds cannot traverse the inner nature of God." One accustomed to this edifying manner of speaking will seize knowingly on Marcel's words as the familiar fodder for his intellectual nourishment—and miss the whole point. For, the things he mentions are merely unsolved problems, not mysteries in Marcel's sense. The fact that an answer to a question is unknown does not make it a philosophical mystery. Suppose that man never does discover the cure for cancer. Does that make cancer a mystery? Not at all. It is an unsolved problem. The fact that it may be perpetually unsolved does not transform it into a mystery, for it is the kind of reality to which the concept of a solution could be properly applied. To repeat, it is not its insoluble character which defines a mystery, but the fact that it is not objectifiable, the fact that it is a reality which takes in the reality of the subject. Because it is non-objectifiable, we can never dispose of it; no technique will give us a hold over it, and all "results" are obtained by technique.

3. We have seen that an object is indifferent to me; it is simply there "for anyone" (and ultimately, Marcel says,[13] this means that it is there for "no one"). Because this is so, it follows that the self as conscious of an object is just anyone, an anonymous, impersonal mind for which any other mind might just as well be substituted. The object is what is thrown in front of a purely epistemological subject. As an epistemological subject, I am perfectly "interchangeable" with anyone else; I share the neutrality of the object itself. Marcel came across this aspect of objectivity quite early in his thought, in reflecting on the nature of faith.[14] The rationalist would like to say to the believer: "You think your belief bears on a real being, but if you were in my position you would see clearly that you are the victim of an illusion." His remark implies that he can put himself in the place of the believer and correct the latter's vision. This assumes that their places are interchangeable, and this is just what Marcel is moved to deny, holding that the subject of the act of faith is a singular self whose place absolutely no one else could take: his "place" is his being, his unique self. To take my place, the other would have to become me. This, of course, means that my faith is absolutely unverifiable by anyone else, for only what is available for all can be verified. So much the worse for the other: if he cannot be what I am, he cannot believe what

I believe. Most assuredly he cannot presume to judge my faith from *his* position, for my faith is not accessible from his position. As his grasp on his own thought tightened, Marcel substituted for the "unverifiable" of the *Journal* the term "mystery." This is not only a shift of terminology but represents a new level of understanding, since the latter term brings out the positive side of this kind of knowledge. Mystery is the more ultimate term since it is the ground of unverifiability. And yet the shift of terminology does not signalize a break, but is a perfectly continuous development. For at each stage of reflection he recognizes that it is a purely epistemological ego which is the correlative of the world of verifiability: what is objectively common is revealed to what is subjectively common.

Not so in the case of a mystery. It is the singular person who must ask these questions, with all his singularity. He becomes a person by asking them. For the reason that they cannot be juxtaposed to the self they evoke the self in their asking.

> It surely behooves us to renounce, once for all, the naïvely rationalist idea that you can have a system of affirmation valid for a thought *in general*, or for *any consciousness whatsoever*. Such thought as this is the subject of scientific knowledge, a subject which is an idea, but nothing else. Whereas the ontological order can only be recognized personally by the whole of a being, involved in a drama which is his own, though it overflows him infinitely in all directions—a being to whom the strange power has been imparted of asserting or denying himself. He asserts himself insofar as he asserts Being and opens himself to it: or he denies himself by denying Being and thereby closing himself to it. In this dilemma lies the very essence of his freedom.[15]

A definitively important conclusion is wrested from us on the basis of these reflections. The conclusion is that no "objectively valid" judgment bearing on being is possible.[16] A system of ontology which pretends to impose itself with the impersonal objectivity of scientific knowledge is ruled out. My verdict on reality will always be *my* verdict; and it will be at the same time my verdict on my self. The organ of affirmation in philosophy is the whole self. Inevitably this means that liberty is involved in the philosophical affirmation, since my self is a free self. An objectively valid judgment is imposed on me necessarily; but the verdict on being is had through an appeal to my freedom.

4. Finally, the mood in which these questions are asked differs widely. The moving force in a problematic inquiry is curiosity of some more or less intensity. At the bottom of it seems to be a kind of thirst or desire for acquisition—either for the acquisition of a stockpile of information, or for the subtler yet more real acquisition of an answer which eludes capture. The mind at the very moment it may feel itself restless and searching (whether for a twelve-letter word for thickening, or for a specific vaccine for polio) also feels that it will win out if only it persists and exercises its ingenuity. The mind is master of the problematic situation, and its temporary discomfiture only serves as a piquant appetizer for the triumph which it savors in advance. No matter what its initial bafflement, there is the confident realization that its ability is perfectly commensurate with the puzzle which so far refuses to be broken. It is a puzzle, and therefore it is at the mercy of techniques. The problematic is the arena of cleverness, where the expert is properly at home, the man who "knows how."

But a mystery is something else again.[17] What a degree of vacuity it would require to ask the mysterious questions in a mood of mere curiosity! What is being? What is time? Who am I? Is the man who asks such questions engaged in a search for information? Could we say about him that his curiosity is aroused? The inappropriateness of such a way of speaking is too evident to need emphasizing. Let us instead designate by the all-embracing word *wonder* the organ notes of emotion which sound in the soul in the asking of these questions. Humility, we have seen, is thematic, but this does not mean that ontological awareness is a pompously serious attitude ready-made for constitutional sobersides. If Marcel speaks with approval of Peter Wust's belief that philosophy lives off a fundamental piety or trust in being; if this is, in fact, only the reverse side of his own doctrine on ontological humility; if he further declares that a sentiment of reverence is interior to all authentic philosophy—none of this is in any way incompatible with a whole range of varied emotions. The holy, after all, is a dimension of experience, and may be present in states which are quite different psychologically. When philosophical reflection becomes conscious of its source, then the aspect of the reverential overpowers all else—yet one did not necessarily begin with this hushed seriousness, nor is seriousness the only legitimate expression of the sense of mystery. Astonishment, for example, as it rises in the eyes of a child plunged into the immediacy of an infinitely fresh reality, is an ontological attitude. No thought which loses the gift of astonishment can hope to maintain its vitality. Philosophy is nurtured by a sentiment of the holy; philosophy springs out of a delight in existence. Are these two statements in conflict? How so? Unless we take a conscientiously earnest view of the holy—that is, the secular man's view. Whatever the emotional concomitants, what is constant in all experiences of mystery is the implicit awareness of my own finitude. The knowledge of mystery is sacral knowledge because it reveals this finitude. But it is not gloomy knowledge, for who says that it is not the greatest joy to acknowledge one's creaturehood? Perhaps we might even say that creaturehood can only be truly acknowledged with joy, for gloom itself represents a kind of refusal or rebellion.

So much for the exposition of Marcel's doctrine. Certain misgivings obtrude with respect to it. Of these, one is a particularly grievous irritant. If a mystery really is irreducible to a problem, then how is it thinkable at all? Does not all thought tend to objectify its material in the manner which Marcel describes? This being so, the attempt to *discuss* or even indicate a mystery defeats itself; as one of his critics says, to appeal to the category of mystery is not to solve anything—it is merely to bring up the problem of mystery.[18] Human thought is firmly established within the subject-object dichotomy; if mystery lies outside that dichotomy, then why does it not lie outside of thought?

Obviously the solution to the dilemma, if there is one, will have to be sought in some distinction's being made within thought itself. For, "The contradiction implied in the fact of thinking of a mystery falls to the ground of itself when we cease to cling to an objectified and misleading picture of thought."[19] Marcel endeavors to bring this inner differentiation into relief in several ways. He first harks back to the Bergsonian distinction between closed and open thought: *pensée pensée* and *pensée pensante*.[20] Concrete philosophy, as a vital contact with the freshness of the real, can never congeal into the fixed forms which would imply a conquest of its object. Philosophical reflection is a *pensée pensante*, whose essence is to be a pursuit of reality, a chase which does not lose sight of but never catches up with its object. Second, he suggests a distinction between *penser* and *penser à*[21]: thinking and thinking of (or thinking upon, as the latter phrase might better be rendered if the English would stand it). Thinking only comes to bear on objectivized essences; through it we pass in review a structure of some kind. This type of thought allows depersonalization, but to think *of* someone is the act of a singular person and is brought to bear on a singular. A loving thought of a deceased friend would be an example of *thinking of*. This thought, in Marcel's view, comes to bear on the being of the beloved, not on some purported memory-image (and, of course, not on a structure, since a thou cannot be assimilated to a structure). Here then is an example of a thought which does not destroy participation: it is not an objectification, but the magical conjuration of a presence. In general we might say that if mystery is accessible to our mind at all, the thought which conceives it would have to resemble the *penser à*.

Both of these distinctions, however, are only preludes to a third which really crystallizes Marcel's thought on this matter. We have reference to the distinction between primary and secondary reflection. He agrees that reflection is integral to human existence, and his own thought should not be classified with those philosophies of life which exalt raw, uncriticized experience over wisdom. Reflection is part of life, not opposed to it, but it operates at more than one level:

> Roughly we can say that where primary reflection tends to
> dissolve the unity of experience which is first put before us, the
> function of secondary reflection is essentially recuperative; it
> reconquers that unity.[22]

It is primary reflection which severs man from the immediacy of his
situation; in the same breath that it sets up the world of objectivity it
also isolates the subject as an element over against this world. For both
subject and object, this stage represents a retreat from participation,
and therefore a retreat from existence. All kinds of cognitive gains
may thereby accrue to science, but philosophy is an explication of the
unqualifiedly actual, and philosophical thought proper only makes
its entrance with the recognition of the inadequacy of the scientific
outlook. For actuality is met in participation: the *actual* self, the *actual*
world, the *actual* God constitute my situation and are only encountered
in it. Secondary reflection, then, comes on the scene in the role of a
reflection upon a reflection. It is not so much a denial of primary reflection as a refusal of any claim to finality and exclusiveness inherent in
the latter.

Secondary reflection, says Marcel, is reflection squared, reflection
raised to the second power. Specifically, it is a recognition of the insufficiency of the categories which make primary reflection possible. An
example might serve to bring out his meaning. One of the most famous
problems raised by primary reflection is the dualism of the body and the
soul as posed by Descartes. This dualism is clearly the work of a thought
proceeding in obedience to the dictates of traditional subject-predicate
logic.

> With the categories of such a logic in mind, we shall be led either
> to consider the body and soul as two distinct things between
> which some determinate relationship must exist, some relation-
> ship capable of abstract formulation, or to think of the body
> as something of which the soul, as we improperly call it, is the

predicate, or on the other hand of the soul as something of which
the body, as we improperly call it, is the predicate... But in both
cases, body and soul, at least, are treated as *things*, and things,
for the purpose of logical discourse, become *terms*, which one
imagines as strictly defined, and as linked to each other by some
determinable relation.[23]

Now what is it which allows room for secondary reflection to
see—not the falsity—but the limitation of this viewpoint? It is, as we
have already indicated, the incommunicable experience of the body as
mine: in the sign of this originating experience, all dualism is overcome.
Secondary reflection reseizes the unity of my participated existence,
which had been dichotomized by primary reflection. One may well ask:
how can this be? How can we *think* this original participation without
reobjectifying it? Even to think of the "body-as-mine" is to stand at the
brink of conceptualizing and insulating it (since we must distinguish it
from other things). This objection gets us to the extremity of difficulty.
After all, secondary reflection proceeds by concepts, just as primary
reflection: what exempts it from the charge of objectification? Two
answers may be suggested. First, Marcel must allow some legitimate
role for the concept. Secondary reflection certainly uses concepts, and if
all conceptualizing were invalid, his whole philosophy would be under-
mined. Secondary reflection differs not in the instrument of thought
which it uses, but in the *direction* of the thought: primary reflection
tends to reify its concepts and in doing so to abstract from existence;
secondary reflection, in replunging into the oceanic immediacy from
which its concepts are scooped up, at the same time re-establishes the
primacy of the existential. To say this much, however, is only to give half
an answer. In order that secondary reflection may be moved to reroute
the impetus of thought in the direction of participation, it must be that
at some level of cognition that participation has not been lost hold of.
Otherwise, a motive to initiate the new direction would be entirely lack-
ing. This means that secondary reflection lives off an *intuition*. Marcel,

struggling to express the nature of philosophical thought, first called it
"reflexive intuition"[24] and then settled for secondary reflection as the
less incriminating phrase. But it is still right to insist on the progressively intuitive character of this reflection, and indeed it would be
inconceivable apart from the blinded intuition that underlies it. While
this intuition can never become an object of thought, without it philosophical reflection would never begin to be. As for the latter:

> It is constituted around a given which, upon reflection, not only
> does not become transparent to itself, but is converted into a
> distinct apprehension of, I do not say a contradiction, but a radi-
> cal mystery which gives way to an antinomy as soon as discursive
> thought attempts to reduce it, or, if you wish, to problematize it.[25]

Primary reflection is debarred from coping with the originating
given of participation because primary reflection represents an attempt
to translate into the language of having what is really a mode of being.
In doing so, it runs into a series of antinomies, and secondary reflection
consists precisely in the surmounting of these antinomies. Some examples of these antinomies are: I possess my body and am its master—my
body possesses me and I am its slave; sensation apprehends the world—
sensation is a subjective event shut off from the world; faith gives knowledge of reality—faith is an interesting but unverifiable subjective state.
At every turn there is the equipollent yes and no. One of Marcel's inter-
preters has aptly described the whole *Metaphysical Journal* as a dialectic
of the "suppression of problems"[26]: over and over he encounters the
inability of objectified language to express what actually occurs in an
ontological experience. Secondary reflection, confronted by the antinomies to which a thought docile to the categories of having is reduced,
is drawn to transcend these categories by a deliberate conversion to
the immediacy of being. But such a conversion can only be possible if
immediacy has never entirely forsaken the cognitive faculty. Thought
arises out of immediacy: at the point of origin a non-conceptualizable

contact is irrevocably established. It is around this point of origin that secondary reflection ceaselessly gravitates. If it could annex it altogether, knowledge would be a matter of intuition; if it lost sight of it completely, ontological knowledge would be impossible.

Something analogous to what Marcel has in mind is to be found in our recognition of the relation between a proposition and the existent it apprehends. When I express the judgment "This grass is green," in order to be said to know the state of affairs embodied in that statement, I must first take the existent and break it down into two components, a subject and a predicate. The attribute "green" then becomes a quality which the subject "grass" possesses. If I really took this literally, if I did not instinctively surmount the duality which I introduce into the unitary existent in order to possess it cognitively, I would treat the grass and its greenness as two discrete things. In other words, if I constructed the object according to the model of my thought, I would exteriorize the subject vis-à-vis its predicates. But I do not. I realize that my knowledge has severed what is in reality one: what I have distinguished exists as a unity. I surpass my own way of knowing and realize its inadequacies. How can I do this? How, except that at some level my thought has not lost intuitive contact with the existent itself? The intuition of sensation never forsakes the intellectual operation, so that at the very time that it dissects the existent it realizes the falsification in its own dissection. So with ideation in general, as a matter of fact. I realize that my mode of knowing through universal ideas misses the singularity of the existent—and to realize this, I must at some level never have lost contact with its singularity. And that means that my *thought* must never have lost contact. It will do no good to confine the intuitive contact to sense, since the intellectual faculty must have at some point an intelligible grasp of the sensible referent, or it still would have no way of correcting its own manner of knowing.

The act of judgment, then, gives us in miniature a comparison of the relation between primary and secondary reflection—a comparison only, for Marcel certainly has never used this as an example. But in a similar

way he feels that there must be an intuition underlying all secondary
reflection and making it possible. How is mystery thinkable? How do I
think love, freedom, knowledge, being? Certainly not as objects. But I
participate in them just as much as I participate in the sensible existent
to which my judgments refer. *How can I think that participation?* This
is really the epistemological problem for Marcel. To be is to participate
in being: thinking seems to loosen the bonds of participation, and to
falsify primary realities. In any effort to comprehend this participation
intellectually, the mind must be able to recognize the inadequacies of
its own objectification. But that means that participation itself functions as a blinded intuition which is not itself seen, but which enables
me to reject any thought which is not equal to expressing it—and that
includes all thought on this side of the subject-object dichotomy. In the
Thomistic system, we know existence by a *conversio ad phantasmata*; in
Marcel's thought, we know mystery by a *conversio ad participationem*.

When we do turn towards participation, what we gain is not the
apprehension of a clear and distinct something (that would be an
"object") but a perspective from which to view any statement that is
made *about* this participation. The closest possible analogy to the
role filled by the blinded intuition is probably afforded by the way the
creative idea functions in the artistic process. It is a matter of simple
knowledge—among artists, at least—that the exemplary creative idea
according to which the work is produced does not predate the work
itself: it is found in the process of creation. Now, strange as it seems,
although this conception is not precise in itself, it is to this that the
polishings and corrections of the artist are referred: if they are seen to
actuate the conception, his means pass muster; if they do not validly
express it, they must be discarded. The process of refining a painting
or poem in accordance with a conception which is itself not positively
intuited as an object of knowledge in its own right is one of the most
inexplicable processes of human experience. Yet anyone who has ever
written or painted will testify that this is what is done: our work is
judged relentlessly in the light of a conception which itself does not

exist fully until the work reveals it to us. When I sit down to write a poem, I do not know what lines shall comprise it; but as I go along, I know for certain that many lines which suggest themselves shall *not* comprise it, for they do not belong. I do not know my own conception, but I recognize what is *not* my conception.

The blinded intuition of participation functions in a way parallel to the creative idea. It hovers in the depths of my self, and restlessly forces me to regard as unfit any thought and any language which does not express its own inaccessible vision. I can never turn the blinded intuition into an object, any more than I can turn the creative idea into an object. But neither is it something negative—a mere absence: it is the root of all positivity, too positive to be expressed in language shot through with limitation. Marcel usually means by this blindfold intuition the primitive assurance of the presence of being; but we can apply it as well to the consciousness of participation as revealed in special ways. Thus, the consciousness of the body as mine functions as a non-objectifiable limit experience which forces me to regard as less than ultimate any thought which contravenes it; the awareness of the authentic participation of love performs the role of a hidden criterion which allows me to eliminate any explanation of love which does violence to this irreputable assurance; and so forth.

From all that has been said up to this point, one question that might otherwise be left obscure is practically answered: what does primary reflection reflect on? The answer is that it reflects on any participation, any immediacy. Sensation, my body, freedom, evil—are all participated realities which can be objectified by primary reflection. But something ought to be made rather clear. When Marcel talks of primary reflection, he almost always gives the impression of having a *philosophical* procedure of thought in mind; and what overcomes primary reflection is a better procedure of thought, secondary reflection. This is mentioned because it might be felt that any human thought is a primary reflection, so that the child who, faithful to the requirements of language, gradually solidifies his individuality by a steady objectification of his world, is a primary reflector. In a sense, of course, this is true: it is this kind of construction that primary reflection extends and systematizes. But this kind of primary reflection, if it is called that, is overcome through lived experience, not through thought: the child's grasp of himself as an isolated individual is left behind in love and communion, his view of the world as alien is momentarily swept away in every experience of the beauty of nature. In other words he regains participation via activity rather than thought. It is quite possible that a person's life of thought may continue to exist at the level of this primitive primary reflection while his lived experience contradicts it a hundred times a day. What Marcel is concerned with is the philosophical recuperation of participation, which is accomplished in the sign of the lived experience but constitutes an advance upon it. These remarks are inserted because ambiguity can easily arise about the interrelation of Marcel's terminology. A pressing question which certainly suggests itself here concerns the relation which exists between the various kinds of immediacy. Sensation, my body, love, faith are all immediacies but hardly all on the same level. The first two can occur—the first, certainly—infra-intellectually. But are things like love and faith possible without the mediation of ideas and language? If they are not, this means that there is an immediacy which is only made possible *through* concepts, and this in turn injects a dialectical process into the heart of participation. Marcel has never examined this question at all in his published works.

The acknowledgment of our participation is the test case for all philosophical reflection. The reason that incarnation is the central given of metaphysics is that the body is simply my nexus to the world made manifest. How can anyone help acknowledging this participation, one may well ask. But remember that it is not a lived awareness but a philosophical acknowledgment which is in question here; and remember that this would involve the recognition of the irreducible value of the founding experience of participation and consequently the grasping of myself as non-autonomous.

You will say to me: "There is no occasion to use the word temptation here. If your argument is valid, no option is left us. Can one
have a choice between what is reasonable, what makes sense—
and what is absurd?" Precisely, yes; it is of the essence of the
absurd for a being constructed as I am to be able to prefer it, on
the condition, in general, of not having recognized it as such. This
reflection of the second degree, this philosophical reflection only
exists *for* and *by* liberty; nothing exterior to me can compel me
to it; the very idea of constraint is empty of all possible content
in this register. Consequently I can choose the absurd, since it
is easy for me either to persuade myself that it is not absurd, or
even to prefer it in all its absurdity; it is sufficient that I arbitrarily
interrupt a certain chain of reflections...and thus we declare that
our liberty is implicated in the recognition of our participation in
the universe.[27]

About the last question which would naturally be raised in connection with mystery, not too much need be said now for the reason that
much of our study will be an effort to explicate it. That is, the question
of how I can be sure that mystery is not an illusion, if there is no way
of verifying it. There can be only one answer to such an inquiry: the
participation must be its own assurance. The way of asking the question
implies that we are still dealing with a subjective content of knowledge
about which we are struggling to discover whether it corresponds to
anything beyond it. But Marcel's whole point is that this is a meaningless approach in the region of mystery.[28] It continues to treat what is
essentially metaproblematic as if it were a problem posed for a secure
and completely constituted subject. But, "The metaproblematic is a
participation on which my *reality* as subject is built."[29] Therefore, he
says:

My answer is categorical: To think, or, rather, to assert the metaproblematical is to assert it as indubitably real, as a thing of which

> I cannot doubt without falling into contradiction. We are in a
> sphere where it is no longer possible to dissociate the idea itself
> from the certainty or the degree of certainty which pertains to it.
> Because this idea *is* certainty, it *is* the assurance of itself; it is, in
> this sense, something other and something more than an idea.[30]

If a question is raised about the genuineness of the metaproblematic,
there is only one way to respond: that is, by a return to the participated being. This is precisely what philosophical reflection—secondary
reflection—does. Nothing compels the doing: we could still continue
to treat a mystery as if it were a problem and perpetually attempt to
"validate" our data by means acceptable to objectifying thought. That is
why the passage back to certitude in the region of mystery is a task of
my freedom; that is why metaphysics is a "logic of liberty."[31]

CHAPTER IV

Ontological Exigence

NOWHERE DOES Marcel's constitutional disdain for systematic presentation come out more clearly than in his doctrine on being, at once so incredibly rich and bewilderingly recondite. At the same time that we revel in the vistas to which his sudden sallies of thought lead us, we feel a longing for the satisfaction which a painstaking and prosaic examination of them could have provided. Marcel now and then attempts such an exposition, but if we observe closely we watch his thought glide gently in sundry directions and issue in a series of profound insights which leave the original straightforward question swimming haplessly in their wake.

A man whose paramount concern was to convey a certain fixed understanding to his readers would do at least two things: he would set forth his own acceptation of certain words like "being" and "existence" as carefully as he could; and he would strive to deal in advance with the possible difficulties the reader might incur because of the novelty of his position in comparison with more ancient usage. Marcel does neither. The more or less abiding uncertainty of sense and scope in his connotation for the word "existence" has already been noted.[1] To this may be added the inconsistent employment of the word "being," sometimes in its ordinary universal extension, sometimes as a synonym for existence, sometimes in opposition to it—and this not merely at different stages of his thought, but in the same book and even on the same page. As if this were not enough, Troisfontaines' interpretation of the relation between *l'existence* and *l'être*[2] has now received such currency that it has largely interposed itself between the original thought and the reader—astonishingly enough, even where the reader happens to be Marcel himself. For in spite of its tacit share in the official ratification which Marcel gave to Troisfontaines' truly remarkable work (an opus which amounts to an all-but-complete concordance to the whole corpus of the philosopher, including his unpublished notes) there is reason to think that the latter's version of the distinction is more his own than it is Marcel's. Under these circumstances, how are we to proceed with our exposition of his reflections on the ontological mystery? To begin with the confusion would only compound it. Therefore, the following pages presuppose a decision as to the ultimate meaning of Marcel and seek primarily to convey that meaning, calling attention to certain discrepancies only in passing.

Let us begin by sympathizing with the plight of the willing but uninitiated reader who feels a certain haziness obtrude upon the irresistible assent which Marcel's language calls forth in him. Thus, he learns that being can only be affirmed freely,[3] and he wonders: "What being can only be affirmed freely? Can it be possible that there is anyone absurd enough to deny being? What can it mean to deny being? And yet, on the other hand, what can it mean to affirm being? If I say 'being is,' what does that mean? It certainly cannot mean that various beings are, for that is the most unhelpful of assertions. It cannot be said in reference to the 'being' which is the omnipresent checker of logic; that is a mere convenient and necessary concept, the 'widest possible category' which nobody would be concerned to make a fuss over. Then what does it refer to? What can it be which is neither a mere idea nor some individual being nor the totality of individual beings—none of which Marcel means? Does 'being' mean 'being itself,' God? Marcel nowhere says so. Then to affirm being is to affirm what?" Such a reader is brought up short by Marcel's abrupt and succinct explanation of what it means to *deny* being. To say that "nothing is" is to declare that "nothing counts."[4] It is to let oneself sink into the slough of despond where the sole conviction is that "all is vanity." How strange and how special an idea of being this introduces us to. To be is not simply to be there, or to exist, but to be of value. Being is that which resists critical dissolution, which refuses to be dissipated into the transitoriness of an empty play of appearances.[5] Being is what cannot be seen through. The pessimist turns the corrosive acid of his ill-humor upon his life and finds there emptiness of emptiness: it is a tale told by an idiot, wherein nothing signifies, nothing *matters*. To affirm being is to affirm that there is a depth in reality impervious to this nihilistic "seeing-through."

> Being is what withstands—or what would withstand—an exhaustive analysis bearing on the data of experience and aiming to reduce them step by step to elements increasingly devoid of intrinsic or significant value. (An analysis of this kind is attempted in the theoretical works of Freud.)[6]

Actually, then, for both affirmer and denier being is said in relation to a *need*.[7] "There must be being," says the one, "and I desire to participate in it." The pessimist is not one who does not feel this need, but one who, feeling it, cries out that there is nothing there to fulfill it. Pessimism is equivalent to a desperate "Oh, would that it were so..."

Marcel's reflections on being are only comprehensible in the light of this ontological exigence; the latter phrase may be rendered as the *need for being*, or better still, the *need to be*. It is with respect to this exigence that being is "defined," for "Being is that which does not frustrate our expectation."[8] Being is fullness. The experience of being is the experience of plenitude. Even more concretely, Marcel goes so far as to say that the upsurge of being is *joy*: "there is being as soon as there is enjoyment."[9] The shattering distinction between the *full* and the *empty* is infinitely more essential to a concrete metaphysics than is the distinction between the one and the many.[10] For it reminds us of what the rationalist of every variety forgets: that no objectively valid judgment bearing on being is possible, that reality is not so constituted that the mind can eliminate the possibility of despair.[11] The stark nature of despair is a witness to an absolute need, for despair is literally unintelligible except in the context of a bottomless and desperate exigence. And the possibility of despair tells us more: it tells us that we do not pass into the realm of fullness *automatically*. There is no objective counterweight to despair.[12] The world of validity provides no guarantee against emptiness; it is freedom alone which conducts us into the presence of being. Does reality contain that which can satisfy our ontological need? The answer will never come entirely from outside, since the profound "yea" of the self is the indispensable copula of existential grammar.

In scanning these semi-poetical outbursts, the first inclination of the meticulous thinker would be to remonstrate that Marcel is engaged in the most naïve of circular reasonings. For how in the world can he define "being" in terms of the "appetite for being"? An appetite is only distinguishable in terms of its object, and it looks like the sheerest mumbo-jumbo to appeal to the appetite in order to define the object. It is as if one were to define Castoria by saying that children cry for it. Look closely, however, and you see that the objection, in spite of its persuasive rationality, slurs over some important considerations. That the attempt to "define" being can be so designated only by uncommon courtesy is quite apparent. What may not be apparent is that this ineffability endows a discussion of being with further exemptions from the strictures of compartmentalized thought. Thus, there is probably no greater fallacy involved in defining being in terms of the appetite for being than there would be in defining the appetite for being in terms of being. For what the latter attempt takes for granted is that being is already thinkable by us apart from any appetitive relation to it. Just as we can conceive water as something intelligible in itself without adverting to the appetite of thirst, so it seems we ought to be able to conceive being in itself without adverting to the appetite for being. But actually this is just what is in doubt: is such a thing possible? Suppose it is the appetite which sheds intelligibility upon the object. Then would it not be true that we can only conceive the object in function of the appetite? That at least is what Marcel would hold, and we must be content to begin here with him, postponing any premature inquiries about essence, *esse*, or the relation of the one to the other until we have faithfully assimilated his point of view. Perhaps we shall find at last that his vagueness is two-sided: at the same time that it allows him to neglect many problems, it permits him to speak powerful truths whose imprecise character would scare off many a more fastidious mind.

The meaning which Marcel attributes to being can best be brought into focus by understanding what he opposes it to. The opposition he establishes is threefold: being *vs.* having; being *vs.* existence; my being *vs.* my life. Of these contrasted couples, the first receives by far the most extensive treatment, but the others serve in striking ways to reveal his true mind on this subject. We shall have to give all three careful consideration.

I. BEING AND HAVING

Marcel's analysis of the nature of having[13] is a major demonstration of his power to incorporate phenomenological analysis into a metaphysical reflection. In the last analysis, when may I speak of *having* in the strict sense? Only in those cases where I exercise a power over a thing which, up to the time of my exercising the power, has a certain independence of me. My possession is a thing which is not me, but which I attach to the circle of my self. What I have is a *thing*, an alien *quid* which I, as a *qui*, annex and over which I acquire a specific right of disposition.[14] For I only have what I can dispose of, and thus having is seen to be an activity of an autonomous self.[15] I possess my dog, or my hat, or ten acres of land. Here everything is clear-cut. But we also speak of having in other orders, where the categories begin to be fluid, as when we say "I have a headache" or "I believe I have a reputation for honesty." Only to the extent that we can isolate and define such feelings and virtues are we accurate in considering them as things possessed.[16] For I only *have* what I can show, what is transmittable,[17] or what I can regard as such. Thus, to say "I have my own ideas on that subject" is precisely to convert one's thought into a stockpile of inert bric-a-brac available for display on appropriate occasions.[18]

The limit case of all having is the possession of my body.[19] As we have seen, my situation in regard to my body is ambiguous. On the one hand, it is my prime possession, since it is in relation to my body that all other possession becomes possible: to have is to have power over, and it is my body which allows me to intervene efficaciously in real events. In this sense, it is the absolute having which is the prototype of all other possessions. Yet in a sense I cannot enclose my body within the set of categories which it alone makes possible. Since all having is exercised over another, the body as *mine* is not possessed: it is not a thing which I have at my disposal. Thus we begin to move into that ultimate area, where the categories of possession lose their meaning.

Intellectually, the only reality I "possess" is what I can characterize.[20] My ability to dissect a thing or to treat it as a sum of elements manifests that it is, mentally, at my disposal. If I regard the object as a thing possessing a certain enumerable collection of attributes, I may in turn come into possession of it by reaching out and laying hold of those attributes. I then have a "content of knowledge" in the literal sense, which I may handle with a good deal of assurance. I have, in fact, what Marcel has already described as an "object," and I am comfortably situated within the precincts of the problematic.

But a thought which proceeds in this manner is a thought which never makes contact with being. For being is the uncharacterizable.[21] Neither the being of the individual reality, nor being in the unqualified sense can be approached as a totality and "added up" in a morselized way. Surely this is unmistakably evident in the case of my own being. "*I am always and at every moment* more than the totality of predicates that an inquiry made by myself—or by someone else—about myself…would be able to bring to light."[22] A knowledge which proceeds by way of characterization must by its very nature fail to apprehend reality *qua* being, and therefore if we do have a grasp of being it must be by an untransmittable knowledge. "If the category of being is really valid it is because that which is not capable of being transmitted is to be found in reality."[23] Again and again Marcel comes back to this point: being is unshowable, not a predicate, cannot be indicated,—in a word, eludes every category in which having is involved. "For Being is, quite fundamentally, not something which we can discuss. We can discuss only that which is *not* Being."[24]

Let us not jump to the conclusion that what Marcel is speaking about here is the *esse* or act of existing of a thing, for that is not so. A reality is uncharacterizable, and therefore *is*, insofar as it is given to me as *presence*. But presence includes more than *esse*, as can be seen simply by turning to the examples which Marcel chooses. My body is apprehended as a presence; the thou is given to me as co-presence. Clearly these are not acts of being, but modes of being.

Wherever there is being there is presence. Wherever there is not presence there is not being. Now the object is an effigy which is constructed by a disengagement from the immediacy of presence, and the object may be looked upon as a mode of absence, or as a presence in the process of degradation to an absence. This means that an objectified world is a world in which being has been relegated to the background and eventually simply dispensed with. What does it mean to lose the sense of being? It means to lose the presentiment of inexhaustibility which stirs in the depths of every experience of presence.[25] Being is what quickens and refreshes—and always promises more refreshment. Once again, being is fulfillment.[26] A world which has forsworn presence in favor of the domination and autonomy which objectivity confers upon the self will of necessity be a world bereft of fulfillment.

We may not construct the world in the image of having unless we construct the self in the same image. Transposed into the order of *praxis* (activity), my tendency to see the self as the sum of a certain number of perfectly definable predicates works itself out as a tendency to reduce it to a certain number of *functions*. When that happens, there appears on the scene the "problematized man" who is the product of our rationalist-scientific-industrial civilization, in whom all sense of the ontological mystery has vanished away and over whom Marcel pronounces many a jeremiad. Everything today conspires to rob a man of his sense of being, of that living contact with the inexhaustible within himself which is the only ultimate source of fulfillment and of joy. A functionalized world produces a specialized self whose resources can be thoroughly tabulated and utilized.[27] Whatever is of having has limits. But being is beyond all inventory.[28] And man insofar as he is held fast by being is a channel of the inexhaustible. Our civilization is essentially the imposition of the rationalistic side of the human self. As a discursive reasoner, as one who indulges in primary reflection, man is above all a manipulator and a planner; but only what is possessed can be manipulated, and therefore the vision of modern civilization does not extend beyond man as a "haver."

From every side subtle influences reinforce this view. One of Marcel's favorite themes is the omnipresence of questionnaires through which a ubiquitous bureaucracy enrolls and re-enrolls the citizenry.[29] Age? Date of birth? Education? Places of employment? And so forth. What I am is supposedly then sufficiently tabulated and on this basis some higher power may then dispose of me, or rather of *my case*. For the muffled protest which arises in my being when I am judged by such a list of information is metaphysically instructive: "This is not me! Do you think you know me? But I am somewhere far beyond all this. If I could tell you…" By this, of course, a man does not mean that there are a million other details about him which the inquirer ought to know, but that there is that in him which can never be known by way of a cataloguing of details. It is not the insufficiency of the catalogue which causes it to fall short of his being, but the fact that it *is* a catalogue. Unfortunately, the more that others tend to lose sight of that "beyond," the more he himself loses sight of it. If all the world agrees in seeing him as the sum of designable functions, he is in distinct danger of becoming exactly that. The railroad conductor punching tickets, the faceless waiter carrying out orders, the elevator operator endlessly loading and discharging passengers—does not the sheer momentum of the hours serve to weld them to and identify them with their functions?[30]

Now no single factor has so contributed to this assessment of man in terms of designable needs and designable functions as the unprecedented achievements of science, especially of applied science. Technics can only utilize man insofar as he is a network of functions, and they can only minister to man insofar as he is beset with desires and fears.[31] But desire is a phenomenon of the level of having: to desire is a way of having without having.[32] To assuage the desire, a plan is devised, and the human race seems to be indefinitely proficient in the perfection of its plans. Yet this very proficiency finally proves our undoing, for we come to *put our trust* in technics in the unconditional sense. We then feel, quite simply, that they will do for us what needs to be done. But whence comes our consciousness of what needs to be done? The only need which a gaze fixed on technics can take in is a need correlative to technics, desire or fear. Therefore, "a world where techniques are paramount is a world given over to desire and fear."[33] Yet, acknowledge it or not, there is in man a different kind of need, an ontological exigence which is a demand precisely for that which no technique can confer. But how can man *need* the unpossessable? Can we say that he wants to possess it? That would not get us far. Perhaps he needs to be possessed by it. Yes, but that really means that he wants to *be* it, that is, he wants his being to unfold within it. What will happen if man tries to feed this need for the unpossessable on technics? He will be engaged in the essentially futile effort to nourish his being on the husks of having. We have said that he will experience unfulfillment, but in more concrete language that means anxiety. And thus an age which has put its trust in technics (and in the whole socio-cultural life-view which is a by-product of the technical *habitus*) will inevitably end by being an "age of anxiety."[34]

There is no attempt on Marcel's part to deny the legitimacy—even the splendor—of technics when they are pursued for proportionate goals.[35] But let the *habitus* of technics be installed as the specifying element in man's relation to reality, and the reign of *hubris* has begun.[36] To man the technician, the cosmos presents itself as matter for domination and he himself appears as an autonomous organizer. Now if he plays this role exclusively—if in fact it is the only role he can conceive—then it is no exaggeration to say that he has repudiated being. For being is not dominatable; and to experience being is to experience oneself as non-autonomous. "As soon as we are in being we are beyond autonomy... The more I *am*, the more I assert my being, the less I think of myself as autonomous."[37]

Would it not be true to say that the typical modern man, however deficient his own intellectual equipment, has a kind of imperialistic reliance on what might be called the *aseity* of science—an *aseity* which, by reflection, confers a borrowed autonomy on the individual? Science with a capital S, science-as-such, seems to be cast by the popular imagination in a role similar to that of the Absolute Self of the idealists, enjoying a like autonomy, and even positing, by an unfathomable fiat, the reality of the objective world—for we are no longer sure that something *is* until science tells us it is so. The populace, for whom the Absolute of the idealists would have remained an esoteric divinity, have no trouble in giving their allegiance to its avatar, Science, for this is a visible deity whose deeds are manifest and whose beneficence is without end. But it must not be forgotten that no matter how detached this hypostasized "Science" becomes, it is at bottom only a fictitious projection of man himself, and an unquestioning trust in Science is really a disguised but gigantic form of self-satisfaction: it is *autarkia* proclaimed without restraint and without redeeming piety. When Marcel goes so far as to connect technical progress historically with *sin*,[38] it is this that he has in mind: the final sin is *hubris*, and the man who knows reality only as matter for his having has scaled the summit of *hubris*.

II. BEING AND EXISTENCE

Although Marcel's declaration[39] that the relationship between being and existence has been a constant preoccupation of his is not borne out by the space he allots to it in his published works, it remains true that his comparatively brief discussions of that relationship help immeasurably to clarify the meaning he attributes to "being." However, we will probably point up that meaning better if we begin not with Marcel but with the very tidy (but, we suggest, inexact) distinction which Troisfontaines uses as the ground plan for his interpretation. In the latter's own words:

> Man only raises himself to it [being] by a dialectic of three stages. In the beginning, before he is even at the state of being conscious of it or of reacting personally, he finds himself engaged in a situation which he has not chosen and which nevertheless constitutes him: this is the stage of *existence*. A primary reflection analyzes this complexus, dissociates the elements which are confused in a primitive immediacy: but the *objectification* characteristic of this step, if it renders knowledge [*science*] possible, risks destroying participation. In order to remedy this, a secondary reflection, exercised on the first, permits each one to reestablish—if he wills it—communion with the real, to engage himself in *being*. Unlike existence, being, then, requires the option of the person who voluntarily maintains or recreates his union with the *world*, with *himself*, with *other persons*, and with *God*.... The guiding thread [of my work] is that *existence* here designates a participation in the real anterior even to the consciousness one takes of it...while *being* applies only to the participation in which there freely engages himself a subject who, by this very act, constitutes himself or affirms himself as a *person*.[40]

It is easy to see that there is an exact equation between this dialectic and the one of Troisfontaines' which we have earlier mentioned. Putting the two triads side by side reveals their correspondence:

community	existence
communication	objectification
communion	being

Both distinctions have this in common, that they are not as such found explicitly in Marcel. But here the comparison ends, for the first is a perfectly legitimate and illuminating explication of what is implicit in Marcel, while the second puts a strain on the original text. Reduced to bare bones, Troisfontaines' interpretation contends that for Marcel "existence" means the *imposed* situation, while "being" means the *freely accepted* situation. But if we turn to Marcel, we will find that he nowhere gives such a connotation to these words. It is not simply that the distinction is not stated by Marcel—that, Troisfontaines himself tells us—but that what is stated is often incompatible with such a schematization.[41]

The only place in which Marcel approaches a full-scale confrontation with this difficulty is in the second volume of *The Mystery of Being*, pp. 18–67. There he commences within the context of his already habitual distinction between existence and objectivity, and then proceeds to a further refinement of the notion of existence itself. This is carried on in terms of a meditation on what it can mean to *cease* to exist. It is true, he says, that a thing which has been destroyed or taken apart has ceased to exist, but "in the deepest sense of the word, has it ever existed?"[42] Was it not only a pseudo-existent to begin with? If we regard a person as a similar pseudo-existent, as a mechanism, we need not scruple to talk of his ceasing to exist. But to the extent that our human existence refuses reduction to the status of thingness, the very *meaning* of its ceasing to exist becomes obscure. There is, then, an ambiguity or indeterminacy which attaches to our predication of existence. At one level, existence is asserted of a thing which is there and yet could be elsewhere; but when, e.g., I affirm the existence of one I love, I "transcend the opposition between here and elsewhere."[43] As we ascend the scale and emerge into the region of the spirit, we catch sight of a point at which existence is no longer defective but genuine, so genuine that it seems "ultimately to be indistinguishable from authentic being."[44]

And yet though I can feel, as it were, the distant tremors of the merger of existence with being, it would be too much perhaps to claim flatly that the being of a person is patent to me. Certainly the claim would be excessive in my own case: there seems to be a forever unbridgeable gap between me and my being.[45] My being is the reality to which I withdraw in a state of recollection—a reality with which I can never fully coincide. Ever distant yet ever present, it eludes my grasp. My own existence I can confidently assert, but my being is not so much vaunted as it is accepted humbly as a perpetually bestowed gift. Actually the use of the phrase "my" being is already in danger of distorting things, since the possessive hints at an intrusion of egocentricity. That is one reason Marcel steers clear of a formula like "my existence is ordered to my being,"[46] for it is only in the proportion that my existence ceases to gravitate about my exclusive self that it takes on authenticity: so that at that dimly felt limit where authentic existence merges with being, it is not my being that is in question, but simply being. Still if we put the accent on my *being*, rather than on the first word, we do well to begin with this rather than with a concept of being-in-general. For such a concept we would inevitably tend to treat as either a universal predicate or a universal subject, according to the categories of traditional logic, and in each case we would have plunged into a blind alley. Being cannot be enclosed within the traditional logical cubbyholes, for "being, in the full sense of the word, cannot be treated as a datum."[47] And again Marcel must have recourse to the ontological exigence in order to make clear what being really signifies. The terrible emptiness which ensues in a functionalized world, a world drained dry of being, is a testimonial in reverse to the fact that being, when present, is fulfillment. Here Marcel not only adds, significantly, that this fulfillment takes on meaning only from the point of view of creation, but he appends a crucial specification in regard to the ontological exigence. The exigence for being, he says, is linked to the "exigence for perennialness" by a bond which "cannot be broken."[48] It could hardly be any more clearly stated that in Marcel's mind the need to be and the need to be eternal are one and the same need. The being which is the unexposed side of the ontological exigence, that being whose presence is felt as fulfillment, is raised on the pillars of eternity. If this is not plain enough, we need only listen to his declaration in regard to the ontological value of love. To say that one loves a person is to say: "Thou, at least, shalt not die." This means, says Marcel, "Because I love you, because I affirm you as being, there is something in you which can bridge the abyss that I vaguely call 'Death.'"[49] To affirm the beloved as being is to affirm him as eternal. Most revealing is his remark that it is undoubtedly the sight of the decay of individual beings which prompts to the nihilistic denial of being, "to announce that being does not exist, that is to say, that there is nothing of which it can be asserted that it is indestructible or eternal."[50] We could hardly want a plainer statement than that. Nor is it a late development of Marcel's thought, for he had already written in the *Journal* that "there is no being save in eternity."[51] In extending this statement we might justly render it as "to be is to participate in that which is eternal." And so it is this notion of participation which closes the circle of Marcel's reflection upon itself. For the fulfillment which signalizes the presence of being is a concomitant of participation: it *is* participation transmuted into consciousness.

A full interpretation of these remarks must wait until our third point has been covered, but enough has been said to see that Marcel does not mean by "being" precisely what Troisfontaines says he does. I do not accede to the realm of being simply by freely accepting my situation, but by recognizing that the roots of my situation go down into the eternal. Being is the eternal dimension of my existential situation. Being is that to which I aspire. The special privilege of spirit is to suffuse the presence of being—in such a way that in encountering a spirit I find his participation in the eternal so manifest that I can make no sense out of his *not* being. Spirit is the channel of being: to experience spirit is to experience the influx of the eternal. Conversely, one who has not become spirit cannot be aware of the presence of being. How does this apply to a man at Troisfontaines' "third stage"? Whether or not he has really reached the level of being depends upon the manner of his acceptance of his situation. I can transform my existential situation into a vehicle for being if I accept it in the sign of the eternal. The level at which I respond is the essential thing. Not just any free acceptance of any situation transforms it into "being." My situation is a bearer of being only insofar as it is transparent to the spirit, to the eternal. Now it would be quite correct to advance the suggestion that for Marcel a true acceptance of my situation is only possible in the sign of the eternal.[52] Father Troisfontaines surely understands his distinction in this manner.[53] Yet even so, it is still not the free attachment to my situation which ushers me into being, but my free attachment to being which enables me to accept my situation.

III. MY BEING AND MY LIFE

For the final light on Marcel's connotation for the word "being" we have only to appeal to his distinction between "my being" and "my life." Two steps are involved in this distinction. There is first the preliminary clarification in which it is brought out that my life can in no sense be likened to something which I *have*. I cannot administer it, for instance, as if it were so much capital that I can dispose of like the executor of an estate.[54] Nor can I convert my life, in particular my past, into a kind of film which has been projected onto the screen of consciousness: my life is not a succession of images at which I am a spectator.[55] One might think, then, that Marcel would automatically adopt the obvious alternative (as he did in the case of "my body") and say "I *am* my life." The fact that he also repudiates this expression[56] shows us that his formulas are always in some sense provisional: the formula "I am my life," while just as meaningful at one level as the same statement in regard to my body, would obscure rather than clarify the truth he is immediately concerned in bringing out.

For he sees it as perhaps the central characteristic of man that he is a creature who can say of himself: "My being is not identical with my life."[57] Does this sound strange? To give it meaning, we have only to advert to the power which man has of *evaluating* his own life: for approval or condemnation, in hope or despair, he can take a stand before his life considered as a whole.[58] Of course only the most obtuse would construe this as evidence for a literal cleavage within the personality: the "I" that evaluates is somehow the same as the "I" that is judged. But what this possibility does impress upon us is the fact that my self is not reducible to its objective manifestations. The reality of the self lies beyond its finite and material expression. It is precisely here that there looms up the threat of a betrayal, for there is a constant temptation facing man to reduce his being to its overt manifestation. Our world not only permits but even invites such a betrayal of our being: "the spectacle of death…can…be regarded as a perpetual provocation to denial and to absolute desertion."[59] Despair is the profound grief of the soul which proclaims that there is no being—and consequently that there is no way to locate my being beyond my life. It is probably at this point of his philosophy that the thought of Marcel sounds the most typically "existentialist" chords. He surely regards the possibility of betrayal and despair as a pivotal datum for metaphysics. No one who has not felt the vertigo of non-being[60] can be expected to be alive to the compensating presence of being. Metaphysics is not a purely impersonal science, carried on in the snug security of objective categories. It is "a means of exorcising despair."[61] For if the "essence of the world is perhaps betrayal," it is nevertheless also true that it is of the essence of betrayal "that it can be refused and denied."[62] Now, what carries us beyond the reach of despair is not some reassuringly irrefutable argument, for the very fact that despair is possible is an unmistakable indication that the last word does not belong to argumentation: a world which is so constituted as to permit of despair *must* not be capable of total objective determination.[63] Therefore the response of the self to the objectively ineffable invocation of being is a qualifying factor in the exorcising of despair.

No metaphysical thought is possible without a conversion (*con-versio*) of the whole self to a source of fullness which is accessible only to my freedom. Such a conversion is possible only in a being capable of recollection, and that is why recollection must play an indispensable part in a concrete ontology: to be recollected is to enter into the mansions of my being, through whose portals being itself makes its entry.

Now the realization that my being is somehow situated before and beyond my life brings with it a second realization: "My being is something which is in jeopardy from the moment my life begins, and must be saved."[64] My being is at stake in my life. It may be that this is the sole meaning of my life: it is an ordeal in which I must hold fast to something which has been entrusted to me, Marcel may well quote with approval the words of Keats, "the world is a vale of soul-making,"[65] since the principal meaning he himself gives to the soul is based on a similar view. The concept of the soul as "form" has no attraction for him because a form is everlastingly safe—nothing can threaten it.[66] But if the spiritual soul of man is the surrogate of being, and if being is at stake in his life, then the primary meaning of soul must be conceived with reference to this "ontological hazard."[67]

The sum and substance of Marcel's thought on this matter may be put in this way: in my life I am a carrier of more than my life. "My being" is the transcendent dimension of my life. This is reiterated in various ways: "Human living," he will say, seems "essentially the living of something other than itself."[68] The concrete witness to the transcendence of my being in relation to my life is given by the reality of sacrifice.[69] A whole metaphysics is potentially contained in the meditation to which the paradox of sacrifice gives rise. The paradox, we say, for what appears to the observer as an irrevocable loss is experienced by the one who lays down his life as absolute fulfillment. If we restricted ourselves to the perspective of his life, it would be absurd to say that a man achieved self-fulfillment by becoming a corpse; only if we shift to a different level of comprehension is it understandable how the act which cuts short his life can, as an answer to a call which comes from within his very depth, be the culminating expression of his self, or, more accurately, can be the act by which he effects a juncture with his true self. No one can characterize this as empty rhetoric, since the stark nature of the sacrificial act is beyond the depredation of mere words. And nothing can obscure the fact that the one who sacrifices himself *must* (declare it or not) feel his life to be at the service of a beyond which is more than his life. This beyond is not exactly other than himself, or at least he does not feel entitled to consider his self apart from inclusion within it. That, after all, is the meaning of invocation: I cannot feel my being to be simply *external* to a reality which I experience as invocation. Only that to which I am *bound* can call upon me; where the call is unlimited, as in sacrifice, then the nature of the bond is unlimited. This is another way of saying that I am bound to it in virtue of what I am. A man who sacrifices his life is implicitly aware that to move toward the source of the invocation is at the same time to move toward his own being. And so the final form of Marcel's distinction between my being and my life is both the profoundest and the simplest: "what is deepest in me is not of me."[70] At this point we may expect a veritable chorus of nettled professionals to exclaim: "But what a sorry excuse for philosophical analysis! This statement is mere shameless piety!" No, says Marcel: this is strict philosophy, and no one can be a metaphysician except on the *inside* of this affirmation.

CHAPTER V

Access to Being: Fidelity, Hope, Love

HIS WHOLE philosophical development, Marcel says, has been domi-
nated by a twofold preoccupation: on the one hand there has been
"what I shall call the exigence for *being*" and on the other "the obsession
with *beings* grasped in their singularity and at the same time caught up
m the mysterious relationships which bind them together."[1] The meth-
odological import of this dual concern only becomes apparent when we
realize that it does not, in Marcel's eyes, imply a conflict of interests—
or even a divergence of interests. While there may be a rough truth
in saying that the latter "obsession" has found its most direct outlet
in his dramatic activity, and that it is the preoccupation with being as
such that stamps his properly philosophical work, such a facile appor-
tionment would neglect a rather crucial question. That is: how does
our thought raise itself to being-as-such? Now, many of the classical
metaphysicians would assume that the ontological research requires
a systematic washing-away of the diversity of individual experience
in order to permit the intuition of being in its antiseptic unity. The
dilemma is easily expressed: either I immerse myself in the interplay of
singular subjects, in which case "being in itself" will come to be looked
upon as a convenient fiction or a pure abstraction in no way corresponding to what is really real (the singular); or I concentrate on being

considered in its unity and transcendence, in which case I must make abstraction from the besmirching diversity of individual beings. But it is against this dilemma above all that Marcel sets himself: on the contrary, he declares,[2] "The more we are able to recognize the individual being as such, the more we will be oriented and directed toward a seizure of being as being." Thought does not seize being via an abstraction in the direction of generality, which prescinds from the life of subjectivity (and intersubjectivity) but by a descent into incommunicable subjective experience, empathetically relived at its saturation point of singularity.

We have already seen[3] that Marcel regards the words of E. M. Forster ("It is personal life and it alone which holds up the mirror to infinity...") not as a literary extravagance but as an exact translation of a philosophical conviction which he himself fully shares. Access to being is had through intersubjectivity. For what is being? It is the source of my assurance that my existential situation is eternally grounded. But this assurance, as we have seen, is not an expressible proposition. It is, as it were, the intelligible face of participation. It is itself a participation; that is, the intellectual act by which I am assured of the presence of being represents a new level of participation in being. But this act is not the uncontaminated product of an autonomous segment of the self which I could call *pure reason*. It is the product of the entire self expressing itself to itself, and uttering being in doing so. I can only become aware of the saving presence of being insofar as I am a singular, free, creative, spiritual subject. And I am such a subject only as a member of a spiritual society, not as an isolated ego. Therefore it follows that those acts which found me as a subject-in-communion are also the acts which give me access to being.

> [T]he concrete approaches to the ontological mystery should not be sought in the scale of logical thought, the objective reference of which gives rise to a prior question. They should rather be sought in the elucidation of certain data which are spiritual in their own right, such as fidelity, hope and love.[4]

Being is plenitude. The invocation to plenitude is made through communion. If we assent unqualifiedly to the reality revealed in communion, we have assented to being, for spiritual communion is grounded in the fullness which is being. Our assent, however, is a free one, and therefore refusal always remains possible. In fact the world seems so constituted that refusal is a permanent temptation. How can we cling to the eternal ground of communion in the face of the evanescence of time and the ultimate negation of death? How are we still "selves," distended as we are across an irrecusable emptiness? Every affirmation of being is an affirmation that is made in the teeth of denial and despair. To affirm being is to hold fast to being. To hold fast to being is to turn with longing to the assurance which arises in the depths of communion.

I. FIDELITY

"Being as the place of fidelity."[5] At a certain moment of time this formula is emblazoned across Marcel's consciousness with an irresistible suggestiveness, as if its truth were the fountain out of which the multiple insights of his thought spring and to which they return. And with good reason. For his prolonged meditation on the ontological implications of fidelity will easily serve as a paradigm for Marcel's philosophical method; in the course of it we gradually come to understand how a descent into intersubjectivity is simultaneously an ascent into transcendence.

What does it mean to be faithful, and on what conditions can there exist a being capable of fidelity? Let us take a simple instance.[6] I have been to see my friend in the hospital. His life is drawing to an end; he knows it, he knows that I know it. In the presence of the terror which each day advances nearer, in the presence of his loneliness and heart-wrenching attempt at courage, my whole being was hooded with pity, with a necessity to stand with him at all costs. I promised faithfully to come back and see him again very soon. When I made that promise, my feeling was completely sincere. But several days have passed and what I felt on that occasion is just a memory. I tell myself I ought to go, that he deserves my sympathy, that I ought to feel the same way. Through conscientious self-flagellation, I can even conjure up a kind of abstract facsimile of the sympathy I felt, but its unworthy falseness inspires repugnance in me. The question is, am I bound by the promise I made, and if so, why? Why should a momentary emotional experience of the past exercise any domination over the present? It would seem to be nothing less than hypocrisy to give myself out for what, at present, I am not. What possible virtue can there be in such insincerity? Let us go back to the moment of making the promise in order to grasp the difficulty in all its force. I promise to return on the basis of my emotion, but I cannot bind myself to feel that emotion tomorrow, and it seems that I have no right to bind myself to act in accordance with an emotion I do not feel. In order not to compromise myself, my commitment ought to contain a condition: "If my feelings do not change…" Therefore the pretense to unconditionality which makes a promise to be a promise would seem in the same breath to make it a perfect act of insincerity. Quite briefly, to promise is to lie.

Here we have the straightforward expression of an "ethics of honesty" like that espoused by André Gide. For such a view purity of heart consists in an ingenuous response to the unsullied demand of the instant: only thus will I refrain from a betrayal of my true self. Now there is quite evidently a dialectical refutation which suggests itself here: we can only set up the principle of fidelity to the instant as a *summum bonum* insofar as we transcend the instant.[7]

This rebuttal is legitimate, but insufficient. The question is: *how* do we transcend the instant? If fidelity is a victory over time, it must not be thought of as an entrenchment in some kind of formal identity not involved in the temporal flow. Certainly, one requirement of fidelity is a unity of the self beyond and across the immediate states of consciousness: it is literally unthinkable that I be united with another unless I am united with myself. But it is not a pre-constituted self that is in question here. I do not give a self which I already have, but a self which I acquire in giving it. Through fidelity I transcend my becoming and reach my being. But the being I reach is not a being which was already there: *it is only there inasmuch as I reach it.* That is to say, the self which fidelity reveals is a self which fidelity *creates.*[8] When Marcel talks of "creative fidelity," he has not lost the reins on his language. He means it quite literally. Fidelity creates the self, the self as non-object. That is why the ethics of sincerity is simplistic nonsense.[9] The objector pictures my future self as somehow there, waiting for me, like the image on the next reel of a film that is being run off; it is as if I must wait and see what this self may be like, and refrain, in the meantime, from making commitments which would betray it in advance. A little thought shows up the crudity of this view. The future is not there waiting for me; it is only given with my free cooperation. The self to which the charge of insincerity might apply will not exist unless my free fidelity delivers it.

However, all kinds of misinterpretation would still be possible, if we stopped at this.[10] One might tend to think that the essence of fidelity consists in an upright and unflinching adherence to one's "word." We might regard it as an affair of self-respect; phrases like "it is a matter of principle," "my honor is involved," spring naturally to mind. Now such a way of looking at things would ultimately reduce all fidelity to fidelity to oneself: the other becomes a mere occasion for testing and manifesting how well I maintain the figure I wish to cut in my own eyes. That such an attitude occurs, everyone will recognize, but is it really correct to call it fidelity? In a passage of marvelous phenomenological acuteness, Marcel distinguishes real fidelity from this rather harrowing type of "constancy."[11] A "constant" person will conscientiously undertake to fulfill in my behalf all the expectations he perceives me to have of him; his conduct will be irreproachable, so much so that it almost seems to deserve a certificate of merit from me. But what is the trouble in all this? In relation to this man, I feel myself to be the incidental beneficiary of a course of discipline which he imposes on himself, an absent third in relation to the tête-à-tête between him and his *persona.* In other words, what is missing is *presence.* Fidelity is not an arid dedication to the preservation of one's title to self-esteem; its axis is not the self at all, but another. It is the spontaneous and unimposed presence of an I to a Thou. This sheds an indispensable light on the "self-creation" which has been spoken of. The creation of the self actually is accomplished via an emergence to a *thou* level of reality: I create myself in response to an invocation which can only come from a thou. It is a call to which I answer "present." In saying "here" I create my own self in the presence of a thou. Marcel succinctly declares that fidelity is "the active perpetuation of presence."[12]

Finally, contained in every appeal from a finite thou, there is in it and through it, an appeal to fidelity itself. There are not only the discrete invocations which scattered selves fling out to us, but along with them each and severally, there is the persistent appeal for us to exist at the level where fidelity makes unassailable sense. We are called, in short, to be persons, to be selves, to found ourselves in eternal and unqualified meaning beyond the sum of our conscious states.

How do I exist, in the concrete, beyond the moment? What is it which bridges the flow of human time? As we have seen, it is not some univocal identity borne along intact from moment to moment. Such a unity is an abstraction which exists only in the order of thought or knowledge; man in the concrete is immersed wholly in time. My eternal being is the being that is involved in time. Fidelity implies an ontological permanence,[13] but a permanence which exists in time—for only an idea does not so exist. In Thomistic language, it would be said that the unity in question can only be an analogical unity. Leaving terminology aside, the question is: how do I affirm myself as both transcendent in relation to my individual states and as non-contingently identical with them? How do I resist my dissolution into a stream of passing instants, without renouncing those instants? Only by assuming the instants into a unity which is created in, across, and through them—into an unfinished unity which continually needs moments in order to re-create itself as unity. This unity can only be a unity of direction, or will, or response. Although we have used the word "creation" of this process, we might better have said "co-creation" or "creative response," in order to avoid the insinuation of autonomy. The human self is finite. Its self-creation is only conceivable in terms of a response to an invocation.

All this comes down to a thesis which Marcel had espoused at the beginning of his philosophical life in the *Metaphysical Journal*: faith alone founds the singular person.[14] There he had averred that only faith can bridge the gap between the thinking self and the empirical self: only by accepting contingent circumstances as a gift from a transcendent can I see them as anything but absurd. I recognize them as mine insofar as I acknowledge them as participants in a vocation to which I am called. This recognition creates my self; apart from it I am split down the middle, between pure thought on the one hand, and the sheer opacity of empirical experience on the other. The substitution of "fidelity" for "faith" is a precision, since it removes the suggestion of supernatural, dogmatic belief which the earlier expression unnecessarily carried.

This doctrine naturally calls to mind the passionate assertion of Kierkegaard that to be a self is to exist in the face of God.[15] More pertinent for us, however, are the words of Royce who, here as elsewhere, is doubtless the original source of Marcel's thought. The person, Royce declares,[16] is an *ethical* category: there only is a person inasmuch as there is acceptance of a certain task assigned to us by the Absolute: "You will know that you are a Self precisely insofar as you intend to accomplish God's will by becoming one."[17] And he agrees with Marcel in the view that the self is not a datum, but an ideal[18]: the *actual* unity of the self is an achievement in the order of freedom.

The metaphysical role of fidelity now comes to the fore. This role is twofold. Fidelity reveals the uniqueness of my own mode of existence and it reveals the true face of being. On what condition can there exist a being capable of fidelity? Only on the condition that such a being transcend the status of a determined "thing." A being who is faithful is also one who can betray. The realm of fidelity is the realm of freedom. The self which exists through fidelity is a creative discovery and not an automatic fact. But this has a consequence: if the ultimate verdict on reality is a work not of an abstract epistemological subject but of an existing self, then the mode of existence of that self is a factor in that ultimate verdict. Is the world absurd or is there that which answers to the ontological exigence? *Who* answers this question? It is always *I* who answer. But who am I? Whereon do I stand when I answer? If I stand on abstract thought or on a solitary ego, I will answer in one way; if I stand on fidelity, I will answer in another. The intelligibility which is revealed in the realm of existence which fidelity makes possible is simply not there for a self which does not inhabit this realm, and which does not inhabit it in *thought*. Thus, whether like Camus, I declare that man's situation is absurd and the last word is with Sisyphus, or whether with Marcel I proclaim the fullness of being, will never depend on purely logical thought; it will depend on the existential stance of the self which affirms. Because fidelity creates *me*, it creates the meaning which is ultimately present to me.

The implicit call to fidelity to being via self-creation can and probably must become explicit. Marcel often assumes it as an explicit invocation and slips unobtrusively from a discussion of fidelity to a thou to a discussion of fidelity to being. While a bit unsettling, this is undoubtedly not fallacious, since a fully self-conscious person could not fail to detect the fundamental invocation which alone gives sense to separate fidelities. In the long run it will not be a matter of trying to rise from an understanding of the individual fidelities to an absolute fidelity, but of understanding how "by setting out from that Absolute Fidelity which we can simply call Faith, the other fidelities become possible, how it is in it and without doubt in it alone that they find what guarantees them."[19]

It is now quite evident that what we have all along been calling "fidelity to being" could just as well be called "fidelity to God." An appeal can only issue from a thou, and being as the presence that calls for fidelity can be nothing but personal, or supra-personal. And yet the alternative expression was used deliberately. There seems good reason to believe that fidelity to a transcendent may precede a well-defined conception of a deity: in fact, it is perhaps in function of our fidelity that the true notion of God can be sculpted, as we shall see. The more our un-rationalized response to being takes cognizance of itself, the more perfect becomes our conception of the being that evokes it. In no case, however, is fidelity tied to a specific dogmatized version of the Absolute: insofar as it remains adherence to a presence, it always overruns our attempts to delineate its object, for "the more effectively I participate in being, the less I am able to know or to say *in what* I participate."[20]

II. HOPE

Of all the "concrete approaches" to the ontological mystery, hope is the one which most unambiguously announces its references to transcendence. So much is this true that a phenomenological analysis of hope passes almost immediately into an elucidation of its hyper-phenomenological roots; the transcendent vector seems to be not eventual but dominant from the beginning. With fidelity and love, the transcendent implications must be carefully substantiated, but hope is actually inconceivable except as an immediate, if implicit, appeal to a transcendent. Nevertheless, we will do well to begin with hope on the mundane level, and proceed from there.

Let us take the case of a man suffering from a fatal malady—a malady that has been so certified by the doctors attending him. To the outward eye his case is closed; it is merely a matter of waiting for time to accomplish in fact what is already achieved in principle. And yet the man persists in hoping for recovery. His hope takes the form of an unwavering refusal to reckon on possibilities[21]: for anyone can tell him that his recovery is not contained among the possibilities which the cosmos has in store. But he hopes. He takes his stand within a realm where "the sum total of possibilities" is a meaningless phrase. Through his hope he exists in a realm of creative being which is beyond such inventories. Despair is bound up with what is inventoriable.[22] Hope rears itself on the active refusal to succumb to despair, to acquiesce in the tabulability of being. It is not so much a wish, or an obstinate desire, as it is a prophetic affirmation: "I shall get well."[23] In this, Marcel thinks, it is akin to will, whose fiat is also a defiance of the world of what "can be."

It goes without saying that this claim of hope, which may look so arrogant to the observer, is not drawn from the resources of the ego. There is nothing in the ego to warrant it; in fact, a man wholly consumed in the ministration to his own psyche would probably be incapable of hoping. Disponibility is the presupposition of hope—disponibility that begins in finite communion and is consummated in the total openness that turns the soul to a source beyond the visible world.[24] For hope is essentially an appeal to a creative power with which the soul feels herself to be in connivance. As such it is the opposite of self-aggrandizement. Patience and humility are the indispensable concomitants of authentic hope, of hope which is at the same time trust and love (for these are not separable). The efficacy of hope lies in its forswearing of egoistic armament. To hope is not to thrust oneself forward, but to retire absolutely in favor of an absolute. Hope has no weapons. It knows no technique; it could know none, since techniques avail only in the world of having: but that world has no room for hope, only for success or failure.

Have we said too much too fast? Have we, perhaps, skipped over those homely instances of hoping which might cast uncertainty on our interpretation? No doubt there is a certain scale of hope.[25] Often it seems to be directed towards rather trivial objects: "I hope the Dodgers win the pennant" hardly seems to bear out our lofty asseverations. But in cases like this it is clear that a vestigial reference to a transcendent has been infused with an element of egoism which all but obliterates genuine hope; for here my hope is at best regarded as an amulet which can enhance my position against "those others." Hope is not against another[26]; this is one of the things which distinguishes it from desire. The truth of this is best seen in cases where hope is exercised on behalf of another: the mother hoping for the safety of her son who has been reported missing in action; the patriot hoping for the liberation of his country now under the heel of an oppressor. Such examples of hope enforce a realization that the necessary condition for hope is communion.

Hope can in no way be directed to a weakening of communion. All we need do is contrast hope with optimism.[27] In the latter attitude a man, for sentimental or purportedly rational reasons, buoyantly maintains that "everything will turn out for the best—you'll see." He presumes to correct the vision of others in the light of what "he himself" perspicaciously observes. Hope, however, does not take place in the circle of the "I myself": its nature is distorted if it is treated as an accoutrement of a subject who is in on a secret withheld from others. Hope that plumes itself is not hope. The subject of hope is a subject in need of others; its hope is all the purer inasmuch as it hopes for all. The authentic formula of hope, according to Marcel, is: "I hope in you for us."[28] Even where the "we" element is not to the fore, there can be nothing in the experience to exclude it.

Note the double orientation of this formula. Not only is it founded on the intimacy of communion, but it is said in the face of a thou to whom the appeal is made. The true *nisus* of hope is revealed not by the individual objects to which it is directed on earth, but by the creative presence before whom it arises. "I hope that..." is only a tentative and partial formulation of an underlying absolute appeal. What distinguishes true hope is the manner in which it continually surmounts the apparent voiding of its prophetic affirmation and renews it perpetually. Thus, the invalid who proclaims "I shall be well again" may hurl this prophecy straight under the wheels of the juggernaut, death, which seems to overwhelm his hope. At the extreme point, his "I hope that..." has metamorphosed to reveal the simple and absolute "I hope..." which all along lay concealed beneath it.[29]

What was hidden then becomes manifest: that the archetypal hope is the hope of salvation.[30] The individual objects which seem to preoccupy it can all in turn be transcended and the soul embowered in an unconditional trust which excludes unfulfillment. And yet how can this be? To hope in someone is to extend credit to him, to trust that we may count on him not to let us down. This is true of all hope, but our credit is exhaustible except when it is a question of hope in all its purity.[31] To hope invincibly is to extend unlimited credit to reality. Now, acting in this way, we seem to lay ourselves open to the disappointment of not having our demand fulfilled, and it is against this imprudence that the "responsible investors" of life caution us. Hope is a risky business; we can avoid foolish risks by not expecting too much. Not only the ignoble humanisms but a doctrine as sublime as Stoicism inclines to this safe view; the distinction between what is in my power and what is not has as one of its aims the forestalling of the inquietude of vain longing. Insofar as it combats the unruly multiplicity of desires, the doctrine can be noble; but hope is a casualty along with them, and the death of hope leads not to *apathia*, but despair.

But why despair? Why not a reign of good sense? For it is a plain fact that people go on hoping when they have absolutely no grounds for hope; in such cases their behavior takes on the aspect of self-delusion and its correction would seem like a restoration of sanity. Suppose the sick man is as a matter of cold fact doomed: then he is just being dishonest with himself and probably cowardly in refusing to admit it. The best we could say for him is that his hoping might find a psychological justification through contributing to some slight prolongation of his life, but it certainly does not presage an objective truth. Or take the mother who hysterically persists in hoping that her son will return when the fact of his death is incontestable. In the second case is not hope mere wishful thinking, and in the first the more or less adequate intellectual translation of an instinctive drive for self-preservation? How can we claim ontological significance for such behavior?

Contained in this line of attack is the assumption that a man ought not to hope when he has no sufficient reason for hoping. Thus put, the objection is ambiguous. If it means that a man hopes for reasons which appear insufficient to an observer, it is undeniable but a strictly idle observation. If on the other hand the subject himself recognizes the insufficiency of his reasons, then he will not really hope at all. But in reality this *kind* of question does not arise for the "I" who hopes: it is a question that would only occur to him in the degree to which he detached himself from his hope and became an observer. It assumes that hope is a response consequent upon a weighing of probabilities, and asks it to present the arguments which warrant Its existence. Hope, however, consists precisely in a refusal to be measured by the shrewdness of the calculating reason. Is it then irrationalism—fideism? We must distinguish. If the invalid's or the mother's affirmation is judged exclusively as a proclamation in regard to an event in the objective world, then it is liable to denial: "This man will not recover," "This boy will not return." But actually the hope of each is ultimately installed in a region which transcends that of "facts": the subject's only "reason" for hoping is his dim consciousness of existing in that region. It is a *presence* which evokes hope, not a cumulation of probabilities. Borne up by a communion whose very atmosphere is eternal, unreservedly disponible to the Absolute Presence which enfolds this communion, the soul moves ceaselessly beyond the reach of critical thought; and this movement reveals the "intelligible core of hope," for "what characterizes it is *the very movement by which it challenges the evidence upon which men claim to challenge it itself.*"[32]

Then why cannot the process be a grand illusion? If hope offers no arguments and does not admit of being verified, then what guarantees its truth? If the "presence" that floods hope is known only to the one who hopes, what forbids our suspicion that it may be a hallucinatory concoction of the subject? But this way of putting questions remains imprisoned in a mode of thought which must conceive subject and object as external to each other. It is always then possible to wonder whether the object is as "really real" as the autonomous subject which questions it. Hope, however, knows nothing of such an object: it arises in the recesses of a presence which it is strictly impossible for it to regard as external to itself. Hope is an "unverifiable," if one likes, but no more so than any mode of awareness that bears on presence. Existence is never a *demonstrandum*; whether it is a question of the self, the cosmos, or the spiritual strata revealed in hope, not argument but participation has the last word. Hope guarantees itself. Through it we participate in a world of indisputable actuality. And here is the crucial point: we participate freely. The conditions which underlie hope are exactly the same as those which make despair possible. At any moment we are capable of freely slackening the ties that bind us to the fullness of being. The role of the omnipresent specters of death and time has already been discussed, but other temptations loom. The foolproof world of the problematic, for instance, can exercise a fatal attraction for a certain type of temperament which finds satisfaction in its endless stretches of sheer certitude and tends to view hope as a scandal of the intellect and an embarkation across an unknown sea. Yet let there be no mistake: the reluctance to take a chance may prevent a man from hoping—but to hope is not to take a chance. This is the outsider's view of it. When we pass beyond the pale of the problematic we are not in the province of the "as if," the "maybe," or the "what can I lose?" Nothing could be more foreign to authentic hope than sentiments like that. To hope is not to gamble—not even to make the famous wager of Pascal. Hope is metaproblematic: as an act it is no longer possible to dissociate it from that on which it bears. That means that it gives us entry into a world which is indubitably real. To hope is to be beyond doubt—but to be beyond doubt freely. The presence which reassures us exists after the manner of an invocation, and it is there only as long as our creative response permits it.

III. LOVE

Many of the things which it would be necessary to say about Marcel's doctrine on love have already been said in our discussion of communion.[33] The remarks there made of the dimension of reality revealed in the experience of the thou can be applied equally well to the nature of love. More and more Marcel approaches the position that any experience which opens us to another can be called love, until in the end we may not only say that communion is founded on love, but that communion *is* love:

> But we cannot fail to see that intersubjectivity, which it is increasingly more evident is the cornerstone of a concrete ontology, is after all nothing but charity itself.[34]

If this is so, then we are already able to enumerate the main features of love: it does not bear on a closed essence, but rather opens on to an infinity—a presence which no tabulation can exhaust[35]; the beloved is beyond characterization and judgment, since these can only be brought to bear on an object[36]; love reaches the being of the beloved, and not merely an idea of him.[37] Some points need elaboration. It must be reiterated, for example, that love is beyond the subject-object dichotomy[38]: our thought inevitably tries to objectify the I-Thou union into a relationship between discrete elements, but in so doing falsifies it. The intimacy of love is a primary mode of being, irreducible to any other. Marcel brings this out in two ways. First, he repeats here what he has said elsewhere of fidelity, that love is not the act of a previously constituted self, but an act which creates the self: loving creates the lover.[39] Second, he says that even the thou may not be as primitive as the total experience of intimacy. In speaking about the thou, "I objectivize a particular aspect of the experience of intimacy. From the core of the *us* I subtract the element that is *not-me* and call it *thou*."[40] The trouble is that in speaking of the thou I automatically tend to convert it into a him. Secondary reflection must continually remind me that both the I and the Thou exist only in the creative communion which sustains them.

More than one question crops up here. In the first place, if love really reaches the being of the other, then how can it be exposed to error? And yet it is no uncommon observation that love is often bestowed on unworthy recipients and callously betrayed by them. Does this not make it look as if the love which all along had thought itself to have made contact with the being of another person was really flitting around a fictitious idea of its own devising? "You are not what I thought you to be and I no longer love you" is the exclamation wrung from a man when the scales of illusion have dropped from his eyes.

Now one way of clearing up the confusion inherent in such an objection is to recollect that love reaches a being without characterizing it. The thou which is loved cannot truly be assigned predicates—is not reached as an essence. However, the danger is that in actual fact we do give him predicates, and it seems that our love is conditioned by those predicates: he is always partly a "he" for us. To love a person is really to *expect* from him: and yet, to expect such and such because he is such and such would be to turn the beloved into a characterizable it. When our expectations are not fulfilled, we disappointedly declare that our love was misled. The way Marcel sometimes states the situation[41] might lead us to think that he is putting the onus for deception on the one who is deceived: if he had only not allotted the other predicates, if only his love had been great enough, he could have purified it of objectivity and therefore of the liability to deception. This, however, is a foreshortened explanation. The real root of deception lies in the fact that the finite thou will not admit of such purification. The creature is for us not only a thou, a presence, but always simultaneously to some degree a *that*, an object which is in our view.[42] For that reason it may be doubted that our love for a creature can ever be unconditioned: an unconditioned love could only bear on a pure presence, and no creature is a pure presence.

Here is the point at which love reveals its transcendent orientation. Insofar as love, even of a creature, bears on a thou, it rises beyond the entire order of *things* and of the destruction which preys upon things: "Love only addresses itself to what is eternal, it immobilizes the beloved above the world of genesis and vicissitude."[43] To love a being, as we have seen, is to say to him: "Thou at least shalt not die." It will do no good to say that nevertheless he *will* die, *since* all things come to an end, for the prophetic affirmation of love is precisely a proclamation that the beloved as beloved is exempt from the penalties of thingness: the fate which lies in wait for things cannot overtake "that by which this being is truly a being."[44] The more we love him, the more we comprehend him as authentic being, the more we can be assured of his perpetuity. At the limit where total assurance becomes possible, it could only be because his thingness is swallowed up in an absolute and indefectible presence. Really to love a creature, Marcel would agree, is to love him in God. Only in the absolute does the promise of eternity with which all love is redolent attain to unconditionality. This is not a matter of inference or argumentation: it simply means that our experience of presence is truncated and our assurance sapped unless they arise within an enveloping absolute.

Not only perfect love but all love insofar as it *is* love, is haunted by this illimitable presence. That is the meaning of the prophetic "thou shalt not die": through my love I grasp you as participant in a presence which cannot fail. The more I love you, the surer I am of your eternity: the more I grow in authentic love for you, the deeper becomes my trust and faith in the Being which founds your being. There is no question of loving God or creature, since the more I really love the creature the more I am turned to the Presence which love lays bare. That is why Marcel believes that there is a "subterranean connection" between faith in its ontological plenitude and the unconditioned love of creature for creature: even where there is no explicit faith in God "this love is not thinkable, is not possible except in a being capable of such faith, but in whom it is not yet awakened; it is, as it were, the prenatal palpitation of that faith."[45]

Nor is the vaunt of love against death open to the charge of being merely a subjective *wish* for immortality: the affirmation abdicates completely in favor of that which is affirmed. Love is metaproblematic. It is "the active refusal to treat itself as subjective,"[46] and thus far forth must appear to itself as perfect knowledge: indeed "in the measure in which it is now no longer permissible to dissociate being from appearance we can say that it *is* perfect knowledge."[47] There is no dualism between love and its principle of justification: love is charged with cognitive potentialities to the precise extent that it is love. It is not that love is blind and knows nothing; it is simply that reflection only discovers its cognitive value insofar as it negates itself completely as reflection—insofar, that is, as it ceases to pose love as an appearance whose correspondence to a reality needs to be demonstrated. At this point reflection passes over into secondary reflection, whose function "will consist essentially in demonstrating that the refusal to treat itself as subjective is transcendent in relation to the criticism to which primary reflection would claim to subject it."[48]

CHAPTER VI

Creative Testimony

LET US return at this point to the expression "being is," a phrase from which our discussion long since set out, but whose meaning we are now in a much better position to appreciate. That the experience of being is allied in Marcel's mind with an intuition, however obscure, of plenitude, inexhaustibility, and eternity, should now be apparent. Being, we may say, signifies that which overflows two dichotomies: the dichotomy between the subject and the object in knowledge, and the dichotomy between the subject and the predicate of a proposition. Now, the role of language and the logical structure of thought in laying bare the presence of such a plenitude is ambiguous. There is no doubt that at some point they must be attached to being. But what is too clear is that both language and discursive thought are instruments of objectification and that in their most useful forms they achieve the perfect transmitability which is the hallmark of the problematic—of the realm where the question of being is held in abeyance.

What must be the nature of the being which is constructed according to the requirements of logic? It must be a suitable term of reference for a network of implications. But this is a mere *simulacrum* of being. There is actually nothing more in it than there is in the implications: it only serves as a peg on which to hang the latter. Being is what superabounds above the categories of logic; being is beyond all inventory. From what source is our awareness of such an ineffable drawn? Certainly not from within the logical structure, whose objective reference is suspended from a more profound intuition. Logic may sanction and enforce the assertion: "There are beings"; but here "being" only means "a term of reference which stands as a subject for the set of predicates I shall propose in regard to it"—in other words, being here means "object." No requirement of objective thought suffices to impose the other affirmation: "There is being." For here "being" means "that whose property it is not to be a term of reference for any proposition couched in the language of subject and predicate." Being is neither a subject nor a predicate; therefore a thought which must regard everything as either subject or predicate cannot as such reveal the presence of being—or even give it meaning.

Note that the contention here is not that conceptual thought contains no ontological dimension, but that the recognition of such a dimension involves more than conceptual thought. That which enables us to recognize the insufficiency of all concepts cannot itself be a concept. Similarly, if we are to be able to believe that there is still reality beyond the epistemological dichotomy of subject and object, the kind of assent (and even the kind of thought) cannot be the same as it is on this side of the subject-object dichotomy.[1] So understood, being can only be divined as an uncharacterizable plenitude. The question all along has been: is there any referent for our idea of "being" when that is taken to mean a reality which transcends these two dichotomies? For Marcel this question resolves itself into another: how do I affirm that there is a referent for my idea of being, so conceived?

We have seen that Marcel feels that the great danger in every deliberately "speculative" approach is that the thought will be torn loose from its ontic moorings and begin to measure itself by the requirements of the structures of communication. To avert this danger, he prefers to approach the ontological mystery via the evocation of concrete experiences like fidelity, hope, and love, where the infinity that permeates empirical reality will be irresistibly plain. But we cannot help being aware that although these experiences are *lived* evocations of plenitude, they do not become effective in thought until the mind tells itself that they open to transcendence. In other words, the recognition of the transcendent value of love, hope, or fidelity, is not merely love, hope, or fidelity: it is these things raised to the level of self-recognition. It therefore remains for us to inquire further into the nature of the thought which accomplishes this recognition. To do this, we need only bring to full focus an idea which looms very large in Marcel's thought, but whose definitive role he himself does not altogether seem to have recognized. This is the idea of creativity. When we have finished, perhaps we will even conclude that the conception of being as creativity is the synoptic insight binding his whole philosophy together; it will surely be our central interpretive insight.

Certainly, the notion of "creation" is a recurring theme in his thought, and it would seem that the gentlest of shoves will cause his piecemeal positions to fall into place, and allow the intuition ruling them all to strike us. Where shall we bestow the first shove? Let us begin with the following statement of his: "As soon as there is creation, in whatever degree, we are in the realm of being."[2] The reader who overcomes his logical queasiness and unblushingly converts that proposition will have uncovered the secret source of Gabriel Marcel's thought: "As soon as there is being, in whatever degree, we are in the realm of creation." Take hold of that, and you are in possession of the lever with which to move his philosophical world.

Any such claim will naturally necessitate a close meditation on the meaning of "creation," with the alternative of utilizing it simply as an emotive symbol, as is too easily done. Art is "creative," we all well know, and so is stage-acting, and someone in this era of dynamic conservatism must surely by now have talked of business enterprise as "creative" activity. At length we are dealing with not much more than an honorific catchword. And yet, in the more genuine instances of its everyday use, the emotional reaction which the simple pronunciation of the word so spontaneously evokes is really quite instructive. Why is the thought of creation so exhilarating? The constant intelligible content embedded in the word would seem to involve some variation on the theme of "*ex nihilo*." True, the strictly philosophical notion of creation may be beyond most people's grasp, and is certainly beyond their purview in using the word. But the idea of *new being*, in the unqualified sense, is the omnipresent feature in every predication. Novelty, freshness, revelation—this is what creation means. Still, this is not enough, for the newness that floods creation is not a *mere* novelty: not another element in a process of addition. It is not a "more": this kind of novelty would be likelier to have an exacerbating effect on the spirit than to recreate it. An absolute freshness which has the appearance of being eternal: is not this exactly the impression which the authentic creations of music, art, and poetry inspire in us? Not only that, but one who *beholds* them feels himself in the beholding, to be likewise made anew and beyond beginnings. An ultimate paradox, which can only be understood when we understand that the experience of creation is the experience of the source. The source is the beginning, which is also the end. One who stands in the source transcends time; but the paradox is that we need time to stand in the source.

Creation is the revelation of inexhaustibility. For the new being which wells up in creation does not diminish anything else. In *coming* to be, it does not subtract anything from eternity. And in coming *to be*, it does not subtract anything from plenitude. Rather, it is drenched in eternity, and it is not only the promise of plenitude but its expression. There is no bottom to a work of art. In its presence the conception of the "routine" passes out of view. The routine is the repetition of the already complete: for one who files cards or turns bolts, each day repeats the last. Time itself is complete for such a man: it loses its inner dimension and becomes the physical unit of measurement of which Bergson spoke. A day then is literally an extent of twenty-four hours; his work extends over eight of these hours—extends, literally extends, as only spatial simultaneities can extend. The residue of inner duration is experienced only as a kind of drag, impeding the progress from the initial to the terminal point in his spatially extended day. But creative activity does not take place in spatial time. It participates in the eternity of its product. One whose attention is creatively engaged will say that he did not notice that time had gone by. Naturally, for he has withdrawn into the creative moment which does not have any spatial extent. Here, there is only the present: and for one who dwells in that present it becomes inescapable what he meant who said that the moment is the cross-section of time and eternity.

It should now be evident that in opposing creation to routine we do not mean to equate it with sheer becoming or restlessness. Restlessness, the ceaseless search for innovation, is only superficially contrasted to dull routine. Creation is what renews; insofar as new sights and sounds revivify the spirit (and they surely may), they are creative experiences. But one who feverishly seeks them out, who accumulates them, has re-entered through a different door the quantitative prison of the office worker. For fundamentally the latter's predicament is that the reduction of his life to a collection prevents him from experiencing time as the influx of plenitude. The voracious pseudo-Romantic substitutes for the homogeneous units of the drudge an ever more heterogeneous series of experience-units, but that is all that he does; for he, too, treats his life as a collection, and only labors to make the collection *interesting*. No, the "newness" of creation does not connote an innovation, but a newness whose *essence* is to be new, and which therefore can never be old. A newness, then, which is the breath of the eternal.

We need not confine this to works of art. The notion of creation has application far beyond the boundaries of artistic activity. All contemplation is creative—precisely because it loses contact with time as measured succession and rejoins the incommensurable moment. Let us not say that contemplation consists in withdrawing from the stream of time; it consists, rather, in descending into *real* time, and forsaking its abstract *schema*. A watch is a meaningless contraption for one rapt in contemplation: it would literally make no sense to him. And by contemplation is meant any contemplation, not simply religious rapture. I am, for example, fond of walking by a certain small river. It is not far from the city, and the noises of the busy streets only slowly fade as I enter the woods through which it runs. But I am patient. For after a little while another noise, sweet and familiar, will begin to steal through the trees: first a rustle, then a murmur, then a muffled roar, the sound of the waterfall greets my ears. I sit on the bluff rocks which line its sides. It is not a large fall, but the air is filled with its voice. The crystal river rides to perfect and pellucid stillness at its cap before it takes the plunge. The sun punctures the white spray, and releases a perfume which blends with earth and green leaf to produce an odor whose first scent brings oblivion. Time—outward time—ceases to be. There I sit and watch the rushing of the water over rocks: water, moving water, which brings peace, and promise, and renewal. I could watch forever: in fact, in a sense each moment is forever, since it occurs in a realm in which measurement has no meaning. This, beyond doubt, is a creative experience. There should be no hesitation in calling it that. It would be artificial to confine our use of "creative" to the fine arts. Love is creative[3]; so is prayer; so, in fact, is every true experience of communion. Even a simple thing like cheerfulness may be creative; or the exhilaration felt on a beautiful day. All these things are creative. They are absolute beginnings which thrust me into the plenitude which is beyond beginnings. This is what Marcel is getting at when he says that wherever there is joy, there is being: for, wherever there is joy, there is creation.

There is a second feature which all creativity has in common: in it, the categories of giving and receiving are surmounted. Marcel himself makes much of this. In one of the typical phenomenological analyses which lead on to a hyperphenomenology, he brings out the fluidity of these categories even in their ordinary application.[4] What does it mean to "receive"? At a purely ideal limit, reception may take on the aspect of total passivity; it is in this way that the wax seems to receive the imprint of the stamp. But if we think of the nature of hospitality, of what it means to "receive" a person ("*chez moi*," with all the overtones of the French expression) it takes no great acumen to realize that what happens here is not intelligible in terms of a sufferance. To receive a guest is to admit another into the zone of my person, to allow him to participate in a reality which is properly mine. At this limit, "receiving" is indistinguishable from "giving": I only receive by giving, and in the end, perhaps, by giving myself. This becomes still plainer if we examine artistic activity. Is the artist a giver or receiver? We can show the impossibility of an answer to such a question in more than one way.[5] Take the creative idea. Is this an idea which the artist has and then gives to reality? Hardly. The artistic idea is not *possessed*, it is not a mechanical blueprint which precedes its embodiment and serves as a pattern to be applied readymade to things. It is *found* in the work that it *produces*. If that is a paradox, perhaps it is a pivotal one. The artist does not know what he is going to do until he does it. With the last stroke of his brush, his conception is fully revealed to him.[6] He receives it from the work to which it has given birth. As Marcel would say, we are in the region where invention and discovery coincide.[7] Has the poet made his poem or discovered it? Both and neither. For both are categories which do not apply to a creative process: they are illicit importations from a less ultimate realm of being. The poet does not first invent his creative idea, and then incarnate it in words; he discovers it by incarnating it. It comes to be in the creative process.

The same thing can be said on a grander scale. Traditionally, the artist has been thought of as "inspired." But surely inspiration does not mean reception in the sense of passivity. He is only inspired insofar as he *acts*. Yet in acting, he does not behave as an autonomous subject. He is not in control of his next move. For instance, by no effort of will can the poet bring the next word into being. When I act autonomously, the situation is otherwise. I can declare: "I shall open the window" and be assured, within the limitations of contingent being, that I shall do just what I say—the future is in my control and will occur as I decree. But if I say: "I must find the right word for line three," no assurance exists that I shall manage it. Yet even so, this action is not outside my power

in the same sense, e.g., that the movement of the planets is outside my
power, nor even in the same sense that the modification of the processes
taking place in the marrow of my bone is outside my power. For in these
cases I am passive in the face of what is imposed on me from without. In
creation my action is neither autonomous nor heteronomous. In regard
to it, the Stoic distinction between what is in my power and what is not
collapses completely. A true work of art is more than mine; it testifies to
a gift from transcendence. Yet the reception of the inspiration is itself
an act of the subject.

> What Rilke teaches us better than anyone…is that there exists
> a receptivity which is really creation itself under another name.
> The most genuinely receptive being is at the same time the most
> essentially creative.[8]

And it is impossible to break down the creative event into juxtaposed
elements, one contributed by the subject, one contributed by being. The
work is entirely mine and entirely a gift. It is a response to an invocation. And even here we must be careful: I can testify to the existence
of an invocation precisely insofar as I respond to it. My response is my
testimony: it is creative testimony, in the same way that the sacrifice of
the martyr is a creative testimony.

And in these last words we meet again the paradox which the
mind that seeks to express the spiritual dimensions of reality constantly
encounters. Is it not paradoxical that testimony be *creative*? Should not
testimony simply declare and recognize what is, and not create it? The
paradox is eased when we realize once and for all that to create is not to
make; it is not a productive activity whose principle is entirely within
the self. If anything can, the artistic process ought to tell us that the
creative self is not an autonomous subject. But further than this:

> At the root of all creation, visible or not, one discovers the same
> presence, and, I will add, the same summons of Being to the soul

which it invests, but also the act, identical in its infinite specifica-
tions, by which the soul gives testimony of this same presence.[9]

If then, Marcel declares that the theme of creative testimony has assumed
a paramount place in his thought, this is the reason. His preoccupation
is to justify the affirmation that "being is": but every such affirmation
must take the form of creative testimony. Religion, art, and metaphysics
are all creative testimonies. This is what he means when he says that no
objectively valid judgment bearing on being is possible; for an objectively valid judgment is one which prescinds from the subjectivity of the
subject, while a creative testimony is one in which the subject and reality are mutually affected—even mutually created. The martyr's witness
to his God, and the metaphysician's witness to transcendence have this
in common, that they are not the acts of an autonomous subject. Rather
they are acts through which the subject comes to be—just as the creative
activity of the artist brings his actual self into being.

It cannot fail to strike us now how many similarities this question
has with the classical dilemma in regard to grace and free will. There
it is a matter of understanding how the two components of a moral
action—grace and free will—are related to one another, of deciding
which "comes first," and of expressing their interconnection in such
a way as to misstate neither God's premotion nor man's responsibility. And it cannot satisfactorily be done. Nowadays we are reduced
to stressing the *mysterious* nature of freedom. Freedom exists, and
we testify to it in every free action, but the explanation of *how* it can
be overtaxes the tensile strength of our language. This is a key point,
for the dilemma in respect to freedom is not an isolated instance but
a *type* of the dilemma which will confront us every time we come up
against a genuine ontological datum. In language we have already used,
the "mystery" of freedom is one example of what Marcel means by a
philosophical mystery. In language we are now using, the paradox of
freedom is the paradox of creativity in general. For freedom is most
evidently a creative action. Here are all the elements we have mentioned

above. In it there is a coincidence of giving and receiving. Thus: is the free action *mine* or is it a product of God's grace? Do I give it or receive it? Whether we like it or not, such categories are transcended here just as much as they are transcended in the realm of artistic activity. The free action does not flow from me as from an autonomous subject; it is altogether mine and altogether a gift. No matter how much we struggle to get the parts properly sorted out, no matter how much we insist that there must be some small portion of the free act which is only mine and not God's (or else I cannot be held responsible for it), the effort is futile. Long experience has habituated most of us to accepting the fact that this is so, and that the how of freedom cannot be adequately conveyed in human language. All that Marcel asks us to do is to recognize that what is true of freedom is also true of every other datum in which being (considered as plenitude) is revealed to man.

As a "matter of fact being is only revealed to my liberty, and upon reflection that may actually be the *meaning* of freedom: a free action is one in which being, *qua* plenitude, is revealed. Of course, as long as we persist in confining our attention to freedom of choice, we will not see this. Liberty will appear to be a property of an autonomous self poised dramatically between various alternatives. One who is conscious of liberty in this way experiences the self as a kind of citadel impregnable to hostile forces. He experiences it as an innervating power, radically independent, belonging to itself alone, living by a glorious and indominable fiat. But there is a fatal distortion in all this:

> At bottom I can only say rightly that I *belong* to *myself* in the measure that I create, that I create myself; that is to say, let us recognize it, in the measure that metaphysically speaking, I do not belong to myself.[10]

In other words, to create oneself is not to belong to oneself, it is to belong to more than oneself. The passage to liberty is effected at the interior of belonging. Liberty is not an anarchic affirmation of self, but an acknowledgment, a welcoming of ontological belonging—or, says Marcel, of what we might as well call "creative belonging," for the two expressions have in his eyes "exactly the same value."[11]

There is no denying the paradox involved here. As we have noticed before, the greater the interiorization of an act, the greater is the degree of freedom, so that at the limit to say "I am free" is equivalent simply to saying "I am I." To be a self is to be free. But it now seems that at that limit where I am most myself, I am no longer autonomous.

> I really think that the idea of autonomy, whatever we may have thought of it, is bound up with a kind of reduction or particularization of the subject. The more I enter into the whole of an activity with the whole of myself, the less legitimate is it to say that I am autonomous. In this sense, the philosopher is less autonomous than the scientist, and the scientist less autonomous than the technician. The man who is [least] autonomous is, in a certain sense, most fully involved. Only this non-autonomy of the philosopher or the great artist is not heteronomy any more than love is heterocentricity. It is rooted in being, at a point either short of self or beyond self, and in a sphere which transcends all possible possession; the sphere, indeed, which I reach in contemplation or worship. And, in my view, this means that such non-autonomy is very freedom.... Here I will point out just one thing; the self-evident truth that in the scale of sanctity and of artistic creation, where freedom glows with its fullest light, it is never autonomy.[12]

At the point where I participate most unreservedly in being, the notion of autonomy ceases to apply to me. We are forcibly reminded of the statement of Jaspers: "There where I am myself I am no longer only myself."[13]

Freedom of choice is, after all, a surface manifestation. It is a void and uninteresting phenomenon taken in abstraction from the real freedom which underlies it. I may, for instance, accept or reject a bribe, and

appear to be acting autonomously in doing so. But the outward component of my action, and even the inward component insofar as it bears
on a specific course of action, lives off a more profound freedom, the
consent or refusal to the call which being continually issues in the depth
of the soul. At the depths, freedom is not autonomy but again a belonging. For the very conception of freedom is empty except as it has reference to value[14]: and a value is not something in relation to which I am
autonomous. A value gives me to myself founds my self: by belonging
to it, I am. This is what Gabriel Marcel has in mind by creative belonging. And it is at this point that the full *ontological* significance of his
notion of "disponibility" comes out. We affirm being freely; freedom is
a belonging; therefore the disponibility which makes belonging possible
is a constituent of metaphysical knowledge and not only a moral virtue.
Freedom is not a matter of clenching my fists against intrusion from
the outside. It is a relaxation, a letting-go, a letting-be of being (to shift
into the Heideggerian terminology). To experience being is precisely
to experience oneself as non-autonomous. To experience oneself as
non-autonomous is to experience oneself as a continuing creation.
In this light we are not surprised to hear Marcel declare: "I think that
the roots of the problem are clarified from the moment when one has
understood that disponibility and creativity are allied notions."[15] With
these last considerations, the final door swings open in our exhaustive
exploration of the Marcellian conception of "being." And that door
is labeled "value." The realm of being is the realm of value. The two
conceptions are only artificially divorced.

> One thing now seems reasonably clear: being cannot, it is certain,
> be indifferent to value: it could only be so if one were to identify it
> as a crude datum considered as existing in its own right, and that
> we are not justified in doing.[16]

In other words, it is impossible to give meaning to the experience of
being apart from the experience of value. If being is fullness, values are

the heralds of being. One who experiences the summons of truth or justice experiences a reality to which literally nothing can be opposed: it is still possible to refuse the summons, but this is not done by choosing another alternative. There is no real alternative to values like truth or justice; in refusing them I refuse myself: I refuse to be, I withdraw from the plenitude to which they invite me. Values are not something other than being: they are the glimpses we catch of being. Or they are the rays of being, as Marcel says in a metaphor which it would be impossible to improve on:

> For what we call values are perhaps only a kind of refraction of reality, like the rainbow colors that emerge from a prism when white light is passed through it.[17]

Values all have their principle in being. And there is no doubt that being can only mean transcendence. For plenitude can only be experienced in a vertical direction: whatever enters as an element into our language or our thought obviously cannot, in the nature of things, be fullness—nor can the entirety of such elements be fullness. If there is fullness, it must be experienced precisely as a beyond. Marcel says in so many words that "the exigence of being coincides with the exigence of transcendence."[18] And with this the role of values emerges: if they are the heralds of being, they are the heralds of transcendence. Sartre to the contrary notwithstanding, a value is just what will not allow itself to be chosen. As Marcel says, a value takes an incommensurable for granted.[19] On the other hand, because they are transcendent, they ought not to be spoken of as if they were objective essences which the subject encounters as "outside" him. To speak so would be to use inappropriate objective language; the spirit exists beyond the distinction between interior and exterior.[20] They are imposed on me, if one likes, but only as appeals are imposed. They are really in me, insofar as I am to create myself. Transcendence, after all, is not beyond me in the sense of being external to me; transcendence might even be defined as that which is

not myself but which can never be external to myself. To experience
transcendence is, consequently, to experience the upsurge of my own
self.

> Value…is the very substance of exaltation, or more exactly it is
> the reality that we have to evoke when we try to understand how
> exaltation can change into creative force… What we are really
> aiming at is not an emotional paroxysm, it is an upward rising
> of the very being which may be expressed, and indeed most
> frequently is expressed, in an absolute self-possession, a calm in
> some way supernatural.[21]

The link between value and being is felt again in the aura of eternity
which surrounds the experience of value. We have seen that to apprehend the beloved as being is to say to him "thou shalt not die"; but this
is only a special case of the prophecy which every value proclaims.
He who exists in the world of being, of plenitude, moves in a region
immune from death. For,

> If death is the ultimate reality, value is annihilated in mere scan-
> dal, reality is pierced to the heart.… Value can only be thought
> of as reality…if it is related to the consciousness of an immor-
> tal destiny.… In a world of scandal where absurdity had gained
> the upper hand, that is to say, where what is best and highest
> was at the mercy of blind forces…there would not perhaps be a
> single value which was not in danger of appearing ludicrous and
> suspect.[22]

How similar this is to the famous Platonic argument for the immortality of the soul which is contained in the *Phaedo*, it is not necessary to
stress. There Plato pictures the soul as most similar to what is simple,
unchanging, and divine (the Forms), and as therefore sharing in the
eternity of what it resembles. Marcel singles out value as the habitat of

the person, and appeals to its transcendence to establish the person's ultimate victory over death[23]; he holds that "value is the mirror wherein it is given to us to discern, always imperfectly and always through a distorting mist, the real face of our destiny."[24] Is this a "proof"? Not if by a proof is meant an objective demonstration which leaves our subjectivity and our freedom aside; for that kind of proof is possible only in the world of universal validity, in the world which is not being. In the realm of being, any assent that is given must be a function of our freedom. We can hold back from recognizing the ultimate significance of value, but this reluctance always has the character of a *refusal* and not simply of a speculative suspension of judgment. He who denies that the values out of which the human communion lives are "really real" betrays that communion. In this instance the spirit of truth and the spirit of fidelity join hands. The intellectual assent to the eternity which value proclaims is the cognitive counterpart of the creative fidelity through which we adhere to communion and to the presence which speaks through communion. Death cannot have dominion over a being capable of an authentic experience of transcendence.

Being, liberty, value—this is the final triumvirate of notions which gains us full entry into the Marcellian ontology.[25] And the notion which spans them all is the notion of creation. Marcel could easily agree that we create our own values—but he would hasten to add that it is therefore true to say that our values create us. For every true creation is a mutual coming-to-be of subject and object. Creative experience is the birth of the transcendent in a spiritual subject, and it is the birth of the subject in transcendence. Creation is the renewal of being: and every time we really experience truth, or justice, or a human person, we experience it for the first time. We have said before that to "be" is to participate in that which is eternal. But we can only participate creatively in the eternal. Human communion itself, insofar as it *is* communion, is a creative pursuit of the eternal. Even more, since all creation is a mutual birth, communion is the *ec-stasis* of transcendence. The transcendent comes to be in communion, just as it comes to be in any work of art, only that here both the painter and the pigments are free beings—since they are one and the same. The secret of human communion is that in being communion it is more than human. If philosophy is a quest for the *ontōs ōn*, there can be little doubt of Gabriel Marcel's verdict. Being is spirit: and spirit is creative communion. The transcendent is not a supreme "thing" but the eternal and absolute thou at the heart of all communion. Unless the transcendent is so conceived, we are in danger of falling into idolatry.

Since this is the meaning of being, the consequences for the philosophical reflection which aspires to comprehend being are inescapable: this reflection must also be creative.[26] That is, it does not simply find: the exigences which impel it are part of the meanings which it discovers.[27] In thought, too, we can only participate creatively in the eternal. The thought which weaves eternal truth is *free*. It is creative—it thrives by a continual receiving from the blinded intuition which underlies it; and that receiving is in itself a giving.

CHAPTER VII

Drama of Communion

To BE complete, a study of Gabriel Marcel's thought must surely include a consideration of his plays. He himself does not regard his drama as in any sense irrelevant to his philosophical life, but rather emphasizes their intimate connection. "It is in and through drama," he tells us, "that metaphysical thought grasps and defines itself *in concrete*."[1] We have reason to expect, then, that an acquaintance with his theatre would help to sensitize our understanding of his philosophical approach.

Nevertheless, a word of caution has to be sounded. In turning to his drama, we must not search for "illustrations" of his philosophical positions, for to do so would be to misconceive the relation between the two sides of his work. He does not devise his plays in order to convey in more vivid fashion conclusions which he has already arrived at "intellectually." This sort of "thesis-drama" didactically-minded playwrights have practiced in all ages. While it runs the evident risk of allowing non-theatrical elements to usurp the sovereignty of the stage, and the ensuing risk of gaucheness or boredom, there is no need to doubt that telling dramas might be written in this way; it is quite clear that certain plays of Sartre are of this type (*The Flies*, for one, or *No Exit*). Whatever its possibilities, however, it is a strictly derivative theatre, and Marcel does not proceed in this way. His theatre is not tributary to his philosophical thought; the bond between them is simply the bond of the similar exigence from which they spring, and to which they are independent responses. Not only is the drama's philosophical implication not thrust upon the reader, but it is likely to be hidden from the author himself. This last fact has often been remarked. Far from being illustrations of his philosophical positions, Marcel's plays often contain in dramatic form insights which are only raised to the level of philosophical recognition years later. A theme is thus present in his theatre *before* it is present in his philosophy. The most famous case of this is probably the conception of "mystery," a notion which first comes to light not in his journals, but in a scene from *L'Iconoclaste*.[2] This is not a solitary instance; if we want a specific source for the later Marcellian views on faith, we would do well to turn to *Le Palais de Sable*; on intersubjectivity, to *Le Quatuor en Fa Dièse*; on indisponibility, to *Le Coeur des Autres*; on death, to *Le Monde Cassé*. Marcel's own fondness for referring to his plays is simply a way of being true to his own dictum: he proceeds to his philosophical insights by an explication of his drama.

Marcel informs us[3] that his need for dramatic creation stretches far back into his childhood, and thus it clearly antedates any philosophical undertaking. But the easiest way to be convinced of the independent character of his theatre is simply to read the plays; what we find there is such an obvious dramatic gift, so clearly following its own logic, that the question of autonomy vanishes. It cannot be sufficiently observed that Marcel possesses a gift for dramatic construction which is, quite simply, expert. He is a master of the well-made play. We find in his drama no fumbling scenes and no mere stringing together; the touch is always sure and swift, the plot complex and firm, the momentum unfailing. Here there is none of the formless outpouring of a Beckett or Ionesco, but a play rigorously yet unobtrusively structured, in which the articulation considerably heightens the aesthetic pleasure. This is all the more remarkable in that Marcel's plays belong to the drama of reflection and hence could easily become stalled in the "talky" in the manner of some other French dramas—as Anouilh's *Antigone*, Giraudoux's *La*

Guerre de Troie n'aura pas lieu (done in English as *Tiger at the Gates*), and perhaps, too, Camus' plays. Marcel's plays avoid this because of the richness of "action" in the ordinary sense: things happen, there is no dullness or tedious waiting. What it comes down to is that he has, in the main, arresting stories to tell, and a facility in telling them. It is true that the stories and the "happening" that they entail are interior dramas and demand an audience capable of a certain degree of reflectiveness; we cannot easily envision these plays as magnets for Broadway theatre parties or garment manufacturers entertaining buyers. The kind of seriousness they call for is possibly best understood by analogy with that demanded by certain modern fiction, say that of Henry James or Joseph Conrad,[4] or even more closely, that of a novelist like E. M. Forster. This type of story will never be "popular" in one sense of the word, but that in no way prevents it from being fascinating. Marcel's plays will probably never be "popular" but they remain fascinating, and only await a theatrical public which will bring to them the same level of consciousness that many readers have learned to bring to the best modern fiction.

Mention of the interior nature of Marcel's drama turns us to the most inescapable similarity between his drama and his philosophy: the concern for communion. To characterize Marcel's theatre as a "drama of communion" is an over-facile way of evoking its central theme, and requires expansion. We have seen that for Marcel, authentic human existence *is* existence-in-communion; it is the thou who gives me to myself. Nothing could bring out more starkly the distance between the views of Marcel and Sartre than two brief lines from their plays. "Hell," says a character in Sartre's *No Exit*, "is just—other people."[5] Contrast this with the exclamation of Rose Meyrieux in *Le Coeur des Autres*, "There is only one suffering, it is to be alone."[6] Beatitude, says Marcel, is from the other—and yet what his drama does is to make us realize the tenuous and fugitive nature of this communion. It is not something achieved once and for all, but rather a standing challenge. The tragedy of human life is that that mode of existence which is its depth and fulfillment is ceaselessly threatened. Marcel's drama, then, might better be called a "drama of the checks to communion"; he limns in his more quiet way the same plight so explosively portrayed by Eugene O'Neill in *Long Day's Journey into Night*.

The great aim of life is to know and be oneself; but we can only know ourselves insofar as we are open to others. Authentic existence, then, is liable to two threats: incomprehension of my own intentions can vitiate my communion with others, or indisponibility to others can estrange me from myself. With this in mind, Marcel calls his theatre the "drama of the soul in exile"[7]; the soul which has lost its way and is uncertain of its own bearings is also alienated from others. Why are we strangers to ourselves? The predicament must surely be put down not to some psychological aberration on the part of some (which might be avoided by others) but rather to the antinomic situation in which our mode of existence places us.[8] There is a polarity between being and having at the very core of our lives. As soon as man wants to know himself—to grasp himself, as we significantly say—he is in danger of alienating himself. Self-knowledge is not really something I can have, since my self is not really something that I have. The objectified schematic forms in which we strain to express and possess our true being turn out to be so many blind alleys. Nor must this be taken merely as a quandary for cognition. My seeking to know myself in a certain manner is simply one side of my seeking to *belong* to myself, and the impossibility of this produces an inner deprivation which could lead us to think of Marcel's theatre as a "drama of indigence." The search for self is really a search for the peace of being, but this is a search in which man has always more or less lost his way; and so the soul in exile is also the soul in want.

No one escapes from this antinomic predicament and the resulting obscurity and impoverishment, but some men suffer from it more markedly than others. One man erects his "ideals" into a *simulacrum* of himself[9]; one immolates himself in favor of his official pose[10]; one contracts his being around certain attitudes with which he chooses to identify himself.[11] Immured in these prisons, each is debarred from the communion through which alone genuine self-knowledge can

issue—not as something I possess, but as something I am. The person-
ages in Marcel's plays often strike us as men hiding behind masks—
masks which we do not have to think of them as having assumed
volitionally, but which nevertheless seal them off in their own ego (and
seal the ego off from itself, if such an expression is permissible). Self-aggrandizement disguises itself as generosity,[12] morbidity as deep love,[13]
heartlessness as artistic consecration,[14] aridity of soul as devotion to
"culture."[15] "Every man is a liar" may be taken as a motto of this drama,
provided that we realize that we are dealing here not with explicit
mendacity, not even with veiled hypocrisy, but with something much
deeper and more difficult to eradicate: with the potential for self-dis-
guise which is practically synonymous with the opaque and antinomic
state of human existence itself, from which an authentic human life has
to be wrested. As we watch Marcel's characters locked in this struggle
for identity and authentic self-knowledge, we find it easy to justify still
another title which has been applied to his drama, that of a "theatre of
sincerity."[16]

To call Marcel's drama an "interior" one is simply to say that it
fulfills in a most unmistakable way the destiny of all serious theatre.
For all significant drama, no matter how "external" it may superficially
appear, is ultimately interior. Here we should recall the precision which
Francis Fergusson has made in respect to the Aristotelian dictum
that tragedy is an imitation of action[17]: the action in question is not
the succession of surface scenes, but the underlying action of human
life. It is not the "plot" which constitutes the fundamental action, but
the harrowing passage of the soul through the straits of time. Fergusson divides the tragic rhythm into three moments: purpose, passion,
perception.[18] There is first the resolute pursuit of an aim to which a man
abandons himself; second, the suffering caused by the frustration of this
aim; third, the recognition of the disparity between the private, individual purpose, and the ultimate reality which swallows it up. *Oedipus Rex*
is the evident example[19]: Oedipus purposes the discovery of the guilty
man and the lifting of the plague; suffers the agony of suspense and

eventual revelation of his parentage; perceives as doomed all human effort to set itself against *anangkē*. Or rather, we should say in this case, the audience takes the third step in his behalf; for the movement of tragedy is accomplished not only on the stage but in the souls of those who participate by beholding and who are thereby raised to a new level of consciousness at which the epiphany of meaning takes place. In the Greek tragedy, of course, what stalked the stage was not a rationally graspable meaning, but a meaning-beyond-meaning: an ultimate order of things underlay the superficial order, and the tragedy consisted in the incommensurability between man's purposiveness and the inscrutable ultimate reality; it was in the recognition of this incommensurability— this terrible and just commensurability—that the epiphany of meaning consisted.

Is there anything analogous to this tragic rhythm in Marcel's plays? The parallel would appear to be quite close, although the scale is greatly reduced. Certainly, he is preoccupied with "action" in Fergusson's sense, the inner voyage of the soul, but the likeness appears to be more minute than that. Of course, the whole mood of Marcel's drama is totally different from the ancients; in language, in technique, in psychological probing, it is modern to a degree. And yet the three phases are anal-ogously fulfilled. We may regard the need for self-knowledge and for communion as the general animating purpose behind Marcel's drama. The masks which his characters wear inevitably work to frustrate this purpose. The fundamental "action" of the drama consists in the dialec-tic of self-discovery by which the successive layers of mask are stripped off, and the passion or suffering lies precisely in this remorseless and agonizing process. What of the third stage, the epiphany of meaning? Here we must be careful. We should not expect that at the denoue-ment the audience will see the characters as they "really are," for this would seem to imply that the author has offered us a solution, that he has sorted out the tangled motives and allotted the proper portions of praise and blame all around. This would reduce the level of his drama to a relatively uncomplex psychological play such as, to take a simple instance, George Kelly's *Craig's Wife*. But only problems have solutions, and the truth about human life is not like the solution to a problem. And so we come upon the most striking feature of Marcel's drama: the sense of the ambiguous which everywhere pervades it. The meaning which breaks out at the end of his plays is simply a profound awareness of the desperate ambiguity of the human soul. To extend the analogy with the classic tragic rhythm, we might regard this ambiguity as playing a role similar to that which *anangké* played with the Greeks. It is the sign of that which is left over when man's reason has done its utmost: it is the overplus, the residue that resists judgment, and thus also the sign of the plumbless beyond to which human life opens.

All of this could be made much plainer by an appeal to the plays themselves. It will be useful, then, to insert at this point a synopsis of several of Marcel's works. Which plays should be selected? Marcel's playwrighting career has been long, productive, and signalized several times by drama awards.[20] For practical reasons, however, it seems advisable that the three plays available for the English-speaking public (fortunately, among Marcel's finest) should be included; after that, it is a matter of personal preference. *La Soif* (or *Les Coeurs Avides*) has been the fourth choice. It is an excellent play, but any brief sampling of Marcel's dramatic corpus must omit at least a half-dozen works of great merit. Among these, *Le Palais de Sable*, *Le Regard Neuf*, *Le Coeur des Autres*, and *Le Dard* might be singled out for special praise. Most to be regretted is the lack of a representative of his later period, in which his plays have tended to be occasioned by political or social currents; the best of them is probably that excellent play, *Le Dard*. As for his comic theatre, we can do little more than indicate its existence, and its real, though secondary value. His comic gift, however, is in evidence in his serious plays, running through them like a skillful counterpoint. Of the four plays that have been included, *Ariadne* suffers most from a summarizing treatment; several important characters and sub-plots have had to be omitted and the marvelous interweaving effect is thereby largely lost.

A MAN OF GOD

The life of Claude Lemoyne, a Calvinist pastor, runs a trying but established course; it is the life of an exemplary and selfless servant of his
flock. Within this devout but perhaps sunless routine, a simple message
from his doctor-brother, Francis, acts as a catalyst for tragedy. Michel
Sandier, the real father of the minister's daughter Osmonde, is dying
of tuberculosis and begs to be allowed to see his daughter before his
life ends. Shortly after their marriage, twenty years before, Claude's
wife Edmée had confessed to her adulterous involvement with Sandier,
and begged his forgiveness. Overwhelmed by the revelation, coming
in the midst of a secret and cruel trial of his Christian faith, Claude
had somehow found the strength to forgive the sin, and mysteriously
this arduous self-overcoming had restored his own faith. The wrong by
mutual agreement had been canceled out, and twenty years of married
life have borne witness to the cancelation. Yet now, what of Sandier? Do
not both Christian love and ordinary human kindness require Claude
to accede to his request? Would it not be cruel to refuse? But Edmée
is horrified. How can he even contemplate such a thing? Any man of
normal feeling would react with spontaneous revulsion. Claude's scrupulous soul-searching casts a new light on his forgiveness of her. Was it
after all just a conscientious professional gesture? Was she a pawn in a
game played between his ego and his Deity? "Yes, you forgave me," she
cries, "but if it wasn't because you loved me that you forgave me, what
was your forgiveness for? ... What good is it to me?"[21]

Ironically, though, her own motives are impugned by Sandier, who
is now allowed to visit their home without his identity being revealed
to Osmonde: was she really remorseful, or didn't she merely opt for
the security of a wifely role rather than the risks of an irregular life, no
doubt relying on Claude's dutiful absolution? In his wasted condition,
Sandier seems to Edmée like a living symbol of the mockery enacted by
their cowardice and egoism. Her accusations go right to the foundations
of Claude's life, for whatever the ultimate truth about him, he is a man
for whom it is supremely important to be counted on the side of what

is good. But his suffering is to be increased. His daughter Osmonde, suffocated by her style of life and tempted to a liaison with a married man, appeals for her father's aid against the surveillance of her mother, from whom she is increasingly estranged; in the ensuing bitter scene an admission of her true parentage is rung from him. Osmonde reacts with sympathy for him; she takes it for granted that he has just found out, instinctively feeling the duplicitous character of any forgiveness, and he numbly allows her to be confirmed in the mistake, for her words "...if I thought you'd been acting a part all these years..." have completed his destruction.[22]

In retrospect, his being seems to him to be a painstaking construction rather than a human life at all: "I am not a man," he cries, "I wasn't even capable of loving like a man, of hating like a man."[23] Even his religious vocation, he tells his mother, now seems to have been a task assumed as part of the role of devoted son to demanding and punctiliously high-minded parents. The last remnant of the real which is left him is Osmonde's love, but when, inevitably, the truth comes out about his knowledge of her mother's sin, her family's last hold over her is broken; she simply lets go, and allows herself to be swept rudderless into a new life.

To all appearances, Claude's world now lies in ruins around him: his daughter is gone, his wife envenomed against him, his faith is shaken, his manhood in question, his past a fake, his whole life a poor joke. At this precise point, a nursemaid-parishioner is ushered in, bearing flowers for the Lemoynes' wedding anniversary and prating piously about the debt which her sick employers owe to the kindness of the minister and his wife. "There's not many pastors like you, Sir, that's what I tell them at home."[24] This scene has a multiple poignancy. We feel the intrusion of the public image for which Claude has desiccated his own life; we feel the walls of the future closing in on the lives of Claude and Edmée. And yet, the sudden reversal of perspective is not without its glimmer of hope. Is there perhaps a truth in this perspective too, which could yet contain the seeds of deliverance? Perhaps, but our attention is fixed on the sadness of the moment, distilled into Claude's muffled appeal, "To be known as one is…"[25]

ARIADNE

Doctors have assured Ariadne Leprieur that the virulent tuberculosis which had necessitated her long confinement in a sanitarium has left her, but her life is still arched over by illness. Could we almost say that her malady and the remote mountain life she thinks it to necessitate are congenial to her? For Ariadne is an extraordinary woman: raised in strict Protestant piety, advanced in the habit of solitary meditation, apparently possessed of an almost reckless consideration for others, she plays the part of a distant providence in more than one life. Unable to endure the climate of Paris, she finds no difficulty in conferring liberty of action on her husband Jerome and her wealth makes it easy for her to provide him an allowance to supplement his insufficient income as a music critic. Jerome, who chafes under the incongruous arrangement, is in love with Violetta Mazargues, a young violinist. Ariadne discovers the liaison and in a strange scene actually encourages the girl to continue it, but makes her swear to keep her (Ariadne's) knowledge from Jerome, who would only suffer from it. It is as if Ariadne's illness had placed her beyond all conventions and beyond conventional ways of reacting; what would be oddity in others is simply normal for her. Baffled yet drawn by the unfamiliar depths of Ariadne's personality, Violetta allows a tenderness and conspiratorial closeness to develop between them.

But magnanimity stretched beyond certain limits begins to resemble an infiltration. Jerome becomes more and more strained by the bizarre triangle, yet does not have the vigor to make the break towards which the honest and courageous nature of Violetta urges him. Something ties him to Ariadne. In turn Violetta pleads for release from her promise of secrecy. But Ariadne reveals the precarious balance of Jerome's wellbeing: before their marriage he had suffered from homosexual temptations, and although he had won a tenuous victory over these tendencies, his condition had brought failure to the physical side of their marriage, a failure confirmed and regularized by Ariadne's state of sickness. Her love for her husband had long since reconciled Ariadne to the childless and peculiar role which had fallen to her. But as for Jerome, who knows whether a lonely existence in Paris might not have revived his tendencies? Small wonder, then, that Ariadne welcomes Violetta's love for Jerome as his salvation.

A monstrous confidence, which convulses Violetta and yet exercises a powerful spell over her, so that she feels Jerome's tortured decision to seek a divorce as somehow treasonous. The force of Ariadne's personality has become for this spirited girl a strange combination of intolerable threat, seductiveness, and standard by which other responses are to be measured. However, when Ariadne learns Jerome's intention, she is not hurt, but exalted by the prospect of a way out of their troubles, and she takes careful counsel with Violetta about how to proceed in order to preserve Jerome's happiness, even offering to end their financial worries. This is the last straw: Ariadne's drive to establish herself at the very core of a relationship from which she ought to be excluded has finished by making it contemptible in Violetta's eyes. She flees, and the later tenor of her life is indicated by the news that she is the mistress of a rich and vulgar impresario. Ariadne returns to the mountains, accompanied by her husband. There, in a final confrontation, Violetta denounces the perfidy of Ariadne, who hears herself defended by her husband, but who is herself reduced to abject despair.

THE FUNERAL PYRE

The time is 1920. Aline Fortier has lost a young son, Raymond, in the great war and her life has become organized around her deep grief. His memory is a kind of holy place which she waters and tends and preserves from the sacrilegious incursions of daily existence. Raymond's fiancée, Mireille, whose parents have died, lives with her as a daughter and loving companion, the only one who really seems able to share her sorrow. For in Aline's eyes, her husband Octave is spiritually a creature from a different planet; he had encouraged Raymond to enlist in the regiment of which he was colonel, and is even now obtusely engaged in writing a history of that regiment, a manifest proof of his deadness to grief. Mireille is a different matter. She submits to Aline's influence, apparently because she cannot help admiring the staggering proportions of her grief.

Aline, perceiving Mireille to be secretly drawn to a vigorous youth, Robert Chanteuil, who has come to live nearby, is disturbed by the thought of an alliance of such treasonous vitality, and does her covert best to cast a pall over the relationship. André Verdet, Raymond's cousin, a decent but sickly young man, is also deeply in love with Mireille. His mother discloses to Aline that his doctors are keeping the seriousness of his condition from him: his heart is so poor that he is expected to die within a short time. Surreptitiously, with elaborate respect for the girl's "freedom," Aline begins to inch her way towards a match between André and Mireille, which seems to her so much more acceptable. Octave her husband is horrified by her design and by his glimpse of the motive beneath it, and their quarrel precipitates the rupture of their airless marriage. But Aline knows her woman. In spite of the visage of suicide which the match presents to her, Mireille allows herself to be enlisted in the sacrificial drama, perhaps because it *is* a sacrificial drama and is like the culmination of the "consecrated" life she has slowly engaged herself to lead.

She marries André. A year later he has not died, but on the contrary his health seems somewhat improved. He is grateful and joyful in what he thinks is her love, but the life she leads is a pale counterfeit of happiness. On André's invitation, Aline comes to live with them. Her intentions are carefully irreproachable, but one interview is enough to shatter the unstable calm of the young people's lives. Aline is excessively overwrought at hearing of Mireille's miscarriage and she is excessively overcautious in revealing the death of Robert Chanteuil in an auto accident. André suddenly understands the circumstances of his marriage, and is grief-stricken. With every attempt to undo the damage, Aline's words leave a heavier toll of anguish, and Mireille hysterically upbraids her. Aline, apparently heartsick, leaves. But in a few moments both André and Mireille begin to fear that she will commit suicide, and the play ends with Mireille desperately seeking to call her back. Aline dead would be invincible. As Marcel himself comments, "Doubtless she will agree to come and live with them, and this, her final victory, will masquerade as a concession."[26]

LA SOIF (LES COEURS AVIDES)

In seeking to pierce through the mystery which surrounded the death of her mother, whom she scarcely knew, Stella Chartrain brings a troubled light to bear on the lives around her. Her father, Amedée Chartrain, is a man of letters of the greatest rigor of character and spirit, who never permits himself the slightest relaxation of word or gesture. An atrocious pedant and romantic, his self-pitying concern to maintain his own esteem often makes him publicly ridiculous, and the drama moves on a double plane of tragedy and burlesque, the latter remarkably reinforcing the former. Amedée has recently been remarried to a young woman, Eveline, with whom his children had become fast friends while on vacation. It is a strange match: herself a sharp-tongued, impetuous, and self-willed person, Eveline soon becomes "fed up" with her preposterous husband, and she will introduce a complicating factor into her step-daughter's search. Stella's suspicions become so wild that they give her father no choice but to reveal the truth about the long-past events: her mother had made an attempt to poison him, and he had been forced to have her committed.

Instead of allaying her fears, this intelligence seems to make matters worse, for she now begins to brood over the possibility of her mother's mental weakness being hereditary. Her family's obvious solicitude for her own fragile nervous state intensifies her obsession. When her father tries to remedy things by encouraging a marriage with Alain, the son of his cultivated friend, Mme. de Puyguerland, Eveline violently opposes the union. Marriage to this asthenic young man would be an act of despair. She decides to free Stella from her incubus by flinging out what she declares to be the "truth" of the past: Stella's mother was neither criminal nor madwoman. Her only crime? "She wished to live…that's all."[27] The atmosphere becomes unsupportable. Only Arnaud, Stella's brother, escapes the general tension. His attitude in regard to the past is simply one of reserve; somehow he feels that in this area to question is to pry, and the unconditional respect which makes him refrain from this is also what enables him to bring a ray of hope into the somber situation. When Eveline turns to him as an intelligent and friendly ally against his impossible and self-preoccupied father, he replies: "Occupied with himself…the idea has never occurred to you that there is in that the state of a being who is very feeble, very helpless… The species of indistinct thirst that devours him, he himself does not know—because it devours him."[28]

Eveline, for all her healthy humanity, cannot rise beyond her own particular way of seeing things; she can sympathize with the suffering of Stella, but not with that of her husband. What the drama does is to bring out the sadness in the soul of Amedée Chartrain through the series of perspectives in which the other characters view him. Arnaud is not far from thinking that his father's wish to justify his own self-pity actually led him to implant the murderous idea in his wife's mind. Eveline is shattered when she hears that Arnaud will soon be entering a religious order, and that her life with her husband must now pass into unrelieved vacuity. As if to confirm her mocking anticipation, Amedée returns from a journey for a final scene on the stage, his last words still cant and pretense; wearied, he drops off to sleep, and Eveline stands shaking her head. With pity, Arnaud pronounces his pathetic valedictory:

> A little while more, and all these phrases with which he bewitches himself will lose themselves in silence; this affectation by which he is duped will fall from him; he will be left alone, disarmed,

without defense, like a child whom sleep has overcome, and
who still hugs his plaything against him. Before the living man
who spouts and gesticulates, Eveline, if we could only evoke the
sleeper of tomorrow.[29]

GEORGE SANTAYANA has said that a thing is not memorable because
it is great, but the other way around.[30] If memorability is the test of
stature, it would seem that for that reason alone a high place ought to
be awarded to Marcel's dramatic creation. Some of the figures in the
plays we have just summarized simply refuse to depart from the mind.
Claude Lemoyne, for instance, is a classic of confused yearning; Ariadne
is a truly labyrinthine and unique figure; and the very grotesqueness
of Amedée Chartrain evokes our sympathy and fastens him in our
memory. To call these figures "real" is to understate the case. They are
what we can only call poetic evocations of a reality profounder than that
of the so-called "realistic" dramatists. The lack of a more poetic style in
Marcel's plays might seem to call for some reproach, or at least some
perplexity. He acknowledges his lack of lyricism but stresses that he
eschewed it voluntarily, in order to adhere as closely as possible to the
real world in which men live[31]; but in reading his disavowal of poetry,
we must qualify it in the light of his motive for clinging to the everyday:
he wants, he says, to discover the far which is in the midst of the near,
the distant at the heart of the familiar. This, one may submit, is itself a
kind of poetry, if the essence of poetry is the calling forth of the sacred
from the ordinary. The theatrical magic with which Marcel summons
the inwardness of his characters is conjuring in a high style.

To succeed in this, of course, Marcel must utilize a definite kind
of character—one who *has* an "inside." This is one of the first things a
reader becomes aware of: his people are as different as possible from
the human driftwood which the "new wave" has cast up on the shores
of our contemporary consciousness. They are not driven aimlessly by
desires and urges, but strive to act out of high human motives, to live

in the consciousness of their humanity. It is perhaps only this steadfast, though muted, note of aspiration, so rare on our stage, that permits these very modern plays to suggest a vague feeling of continuity with the classical French drama: somehow we hear distant echoes of Polyeucte, of Berenice, of Le Cid, nobly debating of honor and duty, nobly striving for moral reason against the sub-rational elements. Marcel's plays otherwise differ *toto caelo* from the rationalistic classic theatre, but there is the similar feeling that his characters are trying to get their lives under control and to put them at the service of something.

This last phrase may also serve to differentiate his drama from that of the more purely "psychological" theatre of writers like Tennessee Williams, especially the Williams of the later years. Williams' characters, where they are not simply at one with their own feelings, are mainly trying to introduce order into those feelings, to get the psychic mechanism working properly. Yet the audience is not without the nagging worry that in the end these people are nothing but psychic mechanisms, functioning well or ill. With Marcel's plays there is always the impression of something more. This "something more" is never an actor, but rather an atmosphere. His drama is a fine verification of Marcel's statement that human life is always a living of something other than itself.[32] Human life is life lived in the presence of… Of what? Of something more. The question that is addressed to the psyche drops everlastingly into the pool of concealment.

This is the meaning of the ambiguity in this drama. The appeal which Claude Lemoyne throws out cannot be answered by any human tribunal, for the reason that the human soul cannot enter into its own depths. Marcel's drama is a drama of ambiguity because it is a drama of those depths. His denouements are never solutions, because solutions are only possible at a different level. This does not mean that it is impossible to charge such people as Aline and Amedée with repulsive conduct, or that all responsibility is bathed in a sickly "understanding" and washed away. It is just that we become aware of what is left over after all judgments have been passed, a region unjudged because untouched, the ground of the ambiguous "yes, but" which is the only genuine verdict which one man can pass on another. To contrast Claude Lemoyne with Elmer Gantry is to perceive the difference between a mystery and a problem. To compare Aline with Harriet Craig or Ariadne with Regina Giddens (*The Little Foxes*) is to be aware of a different focus at work. A play without ambiguity, while it may be a fine one, is always part of the way to melodrama. Much of the power and tragedy of *Long Day's Journey* arises from the torturous ambivalence in every heart, A character without this ambivalence is probably an embodied abstraction. Marcel's characters are concrete individuals—and therefore ambiguous.

So far does this extend that he professes himself unable to give any "authoritative" interpretation of the character of Ariadne.[33] Is she wretch, fiend, saint, or what? He cannot say—for he did not produce her, he created her, and having done so, she escaped his possession and began to lead a life of her own. This life he had to respect. The drama could not serve as raw material for philosophical reflection unless it, in its turn, were a genuine process of discovery and not a mere exercise in artfully presenting what was already prosaically known. Marcel proposes an apt comparison between the freedom which God gives creatures and that which the dramatist gives his characters.[34] The role of finite guiding providence which the dramatist plays is not a mere manipulation, and so surprises await him in the course of creation. Ariadne's ambiguity in the eyes of her own creator should not be taken as a special case; there is no reason to think that Claude Lemoyne, Amedée Chartrain, and (with more reservations) Aline Fortier do not carry a secret concealed not only from audience but from author as well.

It is just this turning us towards the incommunicable center of human personality that Marcel regards as the genuine role of drama. The proper function of drama, he says, is to disquiet us,[35] to arouse secondary reflection.[36] But remember that secondary reflection turns towards participation and therefore towards the blinded intuition of being which is the cognitive counterpart of participation itself. If therefore we were to say that the drama is one means by which the blinded

intuition of being can recognize itself, this would only be a paraphrase
of Marcel's own statement. Drama places us in the presence of human
life and therefore of the element in which human life is lived; in evoking
the center, it evokes the presence which is at the center. Marcel's drama
is suffused by the light of mystery because that drama unfolds at the
center. It is not "religious" drama in a banal, confessional sense, as if it
were propaganda on behalf of the beyond. Here, as elsewhere, mystery
is not *éclairé* but *éclairant*.[37] We do not encounter the transcendent
as something which is set over against human experience, but as that
experience itself insofar as it is an *intimation*. The myth of Orpheus
and Eurydice provides a beautiful symbol of our situation[38]: we only
experience the grace of a mysterious beyond so long as we do not try to
turn and behold it full in the face. It is present precisely as that which
cannot be beheld. Out of the welter of human intentions, heightened by
the dramatist's art, there emerges an inkling of something that uncon-
ditionally *matters*.

It is for this reason that death plays such a crucial role in Marcel's
drama. Briefly put, death is the supreme test for communion. This is a
two-sided statement, for, as test, the death of the beloved being may be
either supreme threat or supreme possibility. This does not come out
quite so prominently in the plays included in this chapter as it does in
other works of Marcel, but it is not missing. The point is that the death
of the beloved being plays no objective and automatic role, but is rather
an appeal that can be responded to in different ways. Crass forgetting
of the being of the other, as if he were a thing which had ceased to
function, is naturally one reaction, but Marcel does not concern himself
with responses of that kind; he concentrates on attitudes which might
seem to be potential in communion itself. Aline, for instance, in *The
Funeral Pyre*, obviously feels herself to be faithful to her son, but
there is every reason to think that her tenacity involves a distortion of
love: from one side, it is an offshoot of a certain taste for misery, and
from another, a kind of aggressive "laying-claim" to the dead boy—a
laying-claim not without its competitive aspect and not unmarked by a

complacence in the special esteem to which her grief entitles her. There seems no doubt that the grief of her husband and Mireille is much purer, although she has managed to confuse the latter so thoroughly that the girl becomes estranged from her own sorrow. This need to cling to the physical presence of her son, the need, almost, to re-instate his physical presence, so that in his cerements he blights the lives about her, is already impure. For if death is able to polarize communion, it is only because it purifies it of this need for palpability. "To see, to hear, to touch her," says Jacques in *L'Iconoclaste*, speaking of his dead wife. "A temptation to which the purest part of you is not subject," replies his friend, Abel.[39] This is not angelism, but only the recognition that if communion is to be preserved in the face of death, it cannot be by any means satisfying to the imagination but by a release from such means, a release which is also a transcending. If death purifies love, it is mainly by enabling it to shed all accoutrements of "having"; the dead beloved is no longer one who can be "had" at all. If he may still *be* for me, it is only because I exercise a kind of absolute forbearance in the face of his physical absence. With this forbearance, however, the absolute context of human existence suddenly offers itself to view. "If there were only the living, Gisela," says Werner Schnee in *Le Dard*, "I think that the earth would be altogether uninhabitable."[40] From this standpoint, a partial answer may be given to an objection which some might raise to Marcel's drama, as well as to much other modern theatre. A play taken up with "psychological" relationships between individuals may be thought to occupy much too narrow a stage: it gains the delicious interest aroused by subtlety of perception, but loses the grand context that alone can lend lasting stature to the drama. Put in one way, of course, the objection sounds like a lament for the passing of the mythic consciousness. All modern western drama is individualistic and thus might be open to this charge. The great modern dramas of an earlier period, however, still trail clouds of cosmic significance because they deal with grand figures, like kings and heroes, in whom the importance of human life is bodied forth and whose careers are therefore not merely personal chronicles but representative histories. With the coming of democracy, such charismatic representatives no longer exist, and there are not wanting those who hold that the possibility of tragedy has correspondingly vanished. Not only such figures but the central and unified view of life which allowed them to be representative has also been lost, fragmented into numberless pieces. It is this that prompts Fergusson's appraisal of the modern possibilities for drama: "Drama can only flourish in a human-sized scene, generally accepted as the focus of the life or awareness of its time; and such a focus no longer exists."[41] It would be unwise to become embroiled in this issue, but it is necessary to point out that if Marcel's individualistic drama suffers from certain lacks, it has this in common with the modern theatre generally.

What may aggravate the objection in his case is that his concern with the obstacles to love and communion require his concentration upon the most non-public and non-objectifiable realms of the individual's experience. That his examination is amazingly acute and highly successful might intensify rather than abate the feeling of constriction. Now, certain remarks of Marcel's will be found indirectly applicable to this difficulty.[42] He has regretted what he calls the lack of a nourishing "sub-soil" in his plays, a sub-soil which he senses and admires in playwrights like Lorca, O'Casey, and Synge. The Spanish and Irish dramatists write out of the ancient, profound, unified, and living consciousness of their people, a consciousness which often lends an almost mythic density to their drama. What can replace such a nourishment for the less fortunate contemporary dramatist? What rescues him from mere psychologism?

In his own case, Marcel suggests, it is music which helps to supply the deficiency. The privileged realm to which music gives me access is a realm which is no longer private, yet is not a mere abstract universal; it places me in the presence of what is beyond myself and yet still concrete.[43] Human life, no longer borne up by myth or a unified consciousness, may nevertheless retain its attachment to an ultra-individual context in other ways. Marcel experiences music as a healing beyond, in which the exacerbations of the everyday are assumed and transcended. It can be no coincidence that his drama, too, conveys this strange impression of a harmony retrieved from individual conflict. No drama, after all—certainly not Marcel's—is simply the juxtaposition of the roles of the individual actors. It is intersubjectivity made manifest; it is the music of intersubjectivity. Even where the lives of the individual characters contain tragic and irremediable conflicts, the dramatic representation of these conflicts serves to lift them to a realm where they are transformed. Thus, through the drama, conflict itself gives rise to hope. Not hope for the characters on the stage, but hope for human life itself. Something moves here, we feel, that is more than failure, and more than success as well. Is not this what Aristotle's notion of catharsis comes down to? We reach at length a level of human existence where even happiness becomes irrelevant, and where we are left only with the assurance that comes from hope.

It is here that we meet Marcel's grand context. He feels it to be the prime sadness of our era that life is no longer loved.[44] It is a paradox that in encountering Marcel's plays, peopled though they are by confused "souls in exile," we are stirred to a sort of creative patience which reconciles us with life and with ourselves. What his plays do is to rekindle a sense of gratitude and anticipation at the chance to be a man. This anticipation is also an assurance. It is not the assertive assurance of a "healthy-minded" optimism, for optimism is an affair of the periphery, and this assurance is more like the incandescence of hope, and can only be felt where hope is possible—at the center. Marcel, by taking us to the center, puts us, with never a word said, in a milieu where the words "all is lost" have no meaning. Thus, though his dramas are "psychological" in technique, it is not only individual longings or frustrations which are at stake, but a certain view of human life. Actually, any drama about which this statement could not be made could hardly pretend to any lasting importance. Unless the spectator who beholds the action on the stage is moved to say, not "so it is with them," but "so it is with me," the play remains relatively trivial. Drama's purpose should be to raise the question of what it means to be a man. It is Henrik Ibsen's absorption with this question that goes far towards explaining Marcel's great admiration for him.[45] It is Marcel's own absorption with this question which provides his plays with their larger significance. A life in which hope plays no part is a life without a backdrop and therefore without context; it is an occurrence in a void. Simply by *being* a drama of communion, Marcel's drama restores the backdrop of the eternal and pushes the limits of the human situation indefinitely outward.

CHAPTER VIII

Concrete Philosophy

WITHOUT IN the least sacrificing accuracy to verbal facility, we could succinctly sum up much that we have so far said about the philosophical method of Gabriel Marcel under these three headings:

1. The main point he makes: the doctrine of participation.

2. The main question that engages him: how to think participation.

3. The main answer he arrives at: participation is thought through a secondary reflection that is creative, disponible, free.

Such statements, of course, might be misunderstood, but all the material to avoid a misunderstanding already is in full possession of the reader. There should be no inclination, for instance, to confuse his conception of participation with the Platonic doctrine, when this is taken in its ordinary "essentialist" sense. When Marcel speaks of participation, he means not a participation in *eidos* or form, but a participation in *act*.[1] What we have witnessed is a series of insights in which the primacy of the actual has been established at various levels of experience. Philosophy is axised upon the indubitably actual. That is what Marcel means when he says that philosophical reflection is the active negation of the "as if."[2] Philosophical thought is reflection trained on mystery, and mystery is only accessible to participation. A merely possible mystery, a hypothetical mystery, is a contradiction in terms.

This, too, is the reason for the pivotal role assigned to the body and sensation in his thought. For at first sight there would seem no reason for him to link sense and spirit in a common fate: could not the ineradicable significance of our spiritual life be justified without the necessity of taking a position in the wearisome dispute about the validity of the senses? But the point is that sense is the first level of our participation in what is unqualifiedly *actual*.

To call it into doubt or not to take it into account would represent a falling away from the actual; and it would also be the first move towards the construction of an autonomous subject. Scholastic metaphysics has traditionally chosen to rise to a transcendent reality by a penetration of concepts drawn impartially from incarnate being (material essences) in its bare, common facticity, under the methodical presupposition that there is no privileged experience of being.[3] Marcel does not do this, since his path to transcendence is via the very privileged creative self-knowledge of the subject, and yet he places no less stress on the significance of incarnation.

This provides some basis for the—at first—almost ludicrous avowal of de Corte that Marcel is an Aristotelian.[4] There is never any question for him of an experience of the spiritual structure of reality except in all the concreteness of immediate incarnate experience. "Eternal truths," "immutable essences," "pure intelligibles," are not phrases that spring easily to his lips. Even where he speaks of values, it is not something like justice-as-such that he has in mind; values are a certain way of meeting being, and are as singular as the transcendent whose voice they are. In the last analysis, if Marcel is to be classified at all, he must—there is no doubt of it—be classified with the Platonic-Augustinian tradition in philosophy.[5] And yet if his thought tends inevitably to a philosophy of essence,[6] it is to an essence reconstructed on the primacy of intersubjectivity.[7] This is Platonism remade according to the primacy of act over hypostasized concept. It is existential Platonism. Marcel's eventual aim is to discover the spirit to itself as a participant in a transcendent act, and where the words "participation" and "mystery" are used without contextual qualification, it is of this that he is thinking. The business of metaphysics is to discern the features of the transcendent act in everything that is actual. Metaphysics is not the science of being-as-such but the science of being.

That this is Marcel's conviction of the real nature of philosophy can be rather amusingly demonstrated by reviewing his various asseverations in regard to the central concern of metaphysics. Every now and then he breaks out in a more or less definitive *eureka* that purports to express his ultimate grasp of what his philosophy is really all about. The trouble is that to the naked eye no two of these declarations look alike: and far be it from Marcel to feel any need to collate them. Let us look at a representative catalogue of these bulletins announcing his "central concern":

> The notion of a foretaste is, I feel, likely to play a more and more central part in my thinking. (*BH* 14)

> …being as the place of fidelity. The center of all my recent metaphysical development is here. (*BH* 95)

> Incarnate Being. Central Datum of Metaphysical Reflection (title of first part of *RI*, p. 19)

> Love…appears to me to be what one might call the essential ontological datum. (*BH* 167)

> The problem of the metaphysical foundation of witness is obviously as central as any. (*BH* 97)

> …it is on the ground of immortality that the decisive metaphysical choice must be made. (*MB* II, 151; cf. also *BH* 11)

> The fact that despair is possible is a…central datum for metaphysics. (*BH* 104)

...the metaphysical insecurity of the creature is the central
mystery. (*BH* 218)

It is the province of the most metaphysical thought to give its true
value to this term, [reverence, or the spirit of piety in knowledge].
(*HV* 101)

These propositions have an *axial* character for a, metaphysics
which inclines to assign to a kind of ontological humility the
place which most traditional philosophers since Spinoza have
given to freedom. (*BH* 133, f. n.)

The fundamental datum of all metaphysical reflection is that I am
a being who is not transparent to himself. (*MJ* 290)

Now obviously in running through this list (and it could be
enlarged), there is no intention of implying that there is a conflict in
these statements. On the contrary, they form both a striking example
and a striking vindication of Marcel's method of philosophizing. Each
statement is a result of a re-seeing that flashes out of his absorption
with a concrete situation. The propositions are actually interrelated, and
some might even be inferred from others, but that is not the way Marcel
comes upon them. Formulas are forgotten every time he begins his
reflections anew. The fact that nevertheless the results of these concrete
approaches resemble one another is a confirmation of the value of his
procedure and an indication of a pervading orientation to his thought. It
shows us clearly what he means when he says that his "concrete philosophy" is not to be equated with a pure, directionless empiricism.[8] Underlying everything is the blinded intuition—but this does not function as
a premise from which other statements can be deduced. Rather it serves
as a light which is shed upon and reflected by every concrete situation
into which thought plunges afresh. And what this light discovers is in
each case—*presence*. Every one of Marcel's "central concern" formulas

brings out in a different way the notion that philosophy is nurtured by an experience of presence. Ultimately this presence can only be an absolute presence. It is true that other persons and even things can be felt as presences, but our experience of presence infinitely overflows them. Pietro Prini has described Marcel's philosophy, with his approval, as an "analogy of presentiality."[9] It is a good phrase, because it conveys quickly the basic character of his metaphysics. The primary analogate in an analogy of presentiality must manifestly be a person—since a presence which is only a *what* is not yet a full presence. This means that the real metaphysical question is not "What is being?" but "Who is there?" Metaphysics is the "science" of answering this question.

How is it carried on? Through a series of concrete approaches, we are given to understand. But what exactly does the word "concrete" mean here? Certainly not simply "extended," that is, concrete in the sensist's manner, since Marcel's favorite concrete approaches are the supra-sensual experiences of love, hope, and fidelity. The thought of asking ourselves what he really means by concrete occurs rather late; for a long time we are content to skim over it, and to assume that by it he simply wants to stress the situational character of his thought, its antipathy to a conceptualization in the direction of generality. This of course is quite correct as far as it goes. Concepts need continual replenishment, and to any thought in which we do not feel the "sting of the real"[10] we grow listless and inattentive.

> For me as for M. Maurice Blondel, living thought (*pensée pensante*) only constitutes itself by a kind of ceaseless replenishment which assures its perpetual communication with Being itself.[11]

He pursues his analogy of presentiality by fixing upon specific transcending experiences in which an absolute presence irresistibly emerges. Clearly this version of concreteness does not necessarily refer to what is immediately "given": in fact, since being is never precisely given—never given, that is, as a datum which can be designated—mere immediacy cannot be what he means by the concrete. Marcel will agree that "all reflection worthy of the name…must be exercised for the sake of the concrete, on behalf of the concrete" but he will go on immediately to caution us:

> These expressions, "for the sake of the concrete, on behalf of the concrete" have about them a flavor that may surprise the unreflective mind: one might in fact be tempted to suppose that the concrete is what is given at first, is what our thinking must start from. But nothing could be more false than such a supposition: and here Bergson is at one with Hegel.[12]

He feels about the concrete the same way that he feels about the subject: it is not given, it is won. What then is the *concrete*? The closest we could come to it might be this: "It is that which is apprehended by a self in which the faculties are not dissociated." Objective thought is bound up with a certain specialization of the self. Metaphysical reflection, which is a search for the concrete, issues from a source anterior to the splitting of man into separate faculties. There is a unity in the self beyond all its division into faculties: that is, at the point where it participates in being, it participates also in unity. That is why it is erroneous to criticize Marcel's preoccupation with an experience like hope by saying that he gives a virtue of the will supremacy over intellectual knowledge.[13] Hope is not a virtue of the will for him. It is a metaphysical experience which overflows into both intellect and will but proceeds from a center in which they can no longer be distinguished. This center is the concrete in the self, and what satisfies this center, this is the concrete in reality.

Now the concrete can never become simply an object of our knowledge, since it is literally inexhaustible: it is the point of our participation in the inexhaustible. We catch hold of it by recreating it in intersubjectivity, and by pursuing it beyond the limits of the world of objectivity: "It is only by going through and beyond the process of scientific abstraction that the concrete can be regrasped and reconquered."[14] Here is the reason that our pursuit of the inexhaustible concrete does not lead us away from the concrete in the more familiar sense, the temporal human situation. We possess this inexhaustible only by manifesting it. And the human situation is its manifestation. The concrete in the self seeks the concrete in reality, and in that search the faculties are subsumed into the unity of the concrete which they serve. The sharp division between the faculties is a product of the spirit of abstraction, and the spirit of abstraction is just what cannot apprehend being. Abstraction is a legitimate operation of the mind in pursuance of definite objectified goals, but when the mind turns toward transcendence it must surpass its own abstractions, for transcendence is that which gives no hold for abstraction. The blinded intuition which the self has of such a supra-abstractive concrete is the dynamic principle behind metaphysical reflection.

Certitude is achieved through a light which proceeds from the subject,[15] and he must continually assent to its radiation. It is impossible not to bring in the term "light" here. No use to protest that it is a mere image, for in this case Bergson's view is borne out: it is the image which is closest to strict truth. Besides, as Marcel says, there is really no concept in relation to which the term can be judged metaphorical. As for its meaning, it "denotes what we can only define as the identity at their upper limit of Love and Truth."[16] Knowledge which takes place below this identity cannot satisfy our thirst for the concrete. Might it not even be said that all uncertainty begins with the dissociation of the faculties? Insofar as I am spirit, I am a certainty. Scholastic philosophy has recognized this in its conception of the "agent intellect," which may be regarded as a hidden sun of actuality and certitude deeper than all the passivities of the human person. Marcel's notion is not so very different from that, except that he regards the light that breaks from the spirit as not exclusively intellectual. Inasmuch as I am actually spirit, I am actually part of a communion whose vital principle is a transcendent act which is identically love and truth. If I could coincide with my own being fully, I would attain to this transcendence. Which again means that the search for the truth of being is a search for the true self. I reach being by becoming what (at another level) I already am, spirit. Marcel does not counsel us as philosophers to retire into the soul in order to possess this actuality. Tacitly implied in his whole thought is the understanding that our particular mode of spirituality, our existence in space, time, and matter, is not a mere accidental and negligible condition, but that it is the ordinary mode in which our spirituality comes to recognize itself. Because our intuition is blinded, because it is a source of illumination and not an object of vision, we can only become conscious of it philosophically by embodying it in works which then reflect it back to us. Philosophical thought proceeds by a series of acts of recognition[17] in which the transcendent dimensions of reality are read off as the subject comes to itself in a world of objectivity (or, as Marcel would prefer, of intersubjectivity).

To have access to the light we have "to radiate this light for the benefit of each other"[18]: and in doing so we are free. The effacement of the self so as to allow the light to pass through us unimpeded is the very meaning of freedom.[19] Such thoughts doubtless sound embarrassingly like ersatz philosophy to many ears, and yet they are far from it. Marcel's notion simply is that the ultimate meaning of being is to be descried by spirit. We see in consenting to be spirit; and in consenting to be spirit, the light which is the union of knowing and loving transfixes us. At that point we are a certainty: then if I wish to become certain, I must become a certainty. "But how can I *be* a certainty, if not inasmuch as I am a living testimony?"[20] Philosophy then is a total act. In reading Marcel we really do have the continual impression that the "frontiers are blurred between ethical reflection, metaphysics, spirituality."[21] He makes no apology for this; on the contrary, he takes it as the hallmark of the Platonic tradition:

> Between love and intelligence, there can be no real divorce. Such
> a divorce is apparently consummated only when intelligence is
> degraded or, if I may be allowed the expression, becomes merely
> cerebral; and, of course, when love reduces itself to mere carnal

appetite. But this we must assert, and as forcibly as possible: where love on one side, where intelligence on the other, reach their highest expression, they cannot fail to meet.[22]

If it is the whole man who affirms ultimate truth, Marcel need not scruple to declare: "I think we ought to aim at a restoration of that unity of poetic vision and philosophical creativity of which the great pre-Socratic philosophers offer us one of the first known examples."[23] It is remarkable to note how modern philosophy, especially as represented by the existentialists, has moved in the direction of granting philosophic value to the poetic vision. (See for instance Heidegger on Hölderlin, and Marcel himself on Rilke.) Nor does Marcel hesitate to claim that the road "which leads to holiness and the road which leads the metaphysician to the affirmation of being...is one and the same road."[24] Finally, he replies to the possible allegation that his philosophy is really mysticism with the rather startling statement: "But it is a question precisely of knowing whether in the last analysis there exists a specifiable frontier between metaphysics and mysticism."[25] Philosophy is "a certain way for experience to recognize itself"[26]; or it is "experience transmuted into thought."[27] If there are elements in experience that cannot be sorted out neatly among the separate faculties, then so much the worse for the doctrine of the separate faculties.

The concept represents the means which the spirit forges in order to accomplish this transmutation. But it needs to be continually replenished by the concrete situation. Take the famous formula to the effect that "man is a rational animal." That certainly represents one stage by which experience is transmuted into thought and the subject takes consciousness of himself. But unsustained by the rich aliment of experience it is a supremely abstract formula, and can certainly not lay claim to have taken captive the fixed essence of man. It is accurate as it stands only in relation to a question which is asked with a view to a determinate purpose, the purpose of classifying man so as not to confuse him with other specimens that are being examined. In answer to a question which goes beyond this restricted purpose, it becomes insufficient and even laughable. To the Psalmist's question, "What is man that Thou art mindful of him?" the answer, "Man is a rational animal," would ring rather hollow.[28] Perhaps the only authentic formula for man, the only formula that is not abstract, is that he is "*imago Dei*."[29] This is a thoroughly concrete formula, but because it is, the meaning has to be continually recovered from experience. It is infinitely open to completion.

In filling in the meaning of its concepts, concrete philosophy employs what has been called a probing for the unexpected profundities of the familiar.[30] Both to Marcel and to his readers this method often exhibits a great deal in common with the method of phenomenology. There are, however, important differences. Husserl's phenomenology aims to set philosophy up as a strict, presuppositionless science. Marcel begs to differ: philosophy cannot be presuppositionless and it cannot be a strict objective science. The exigences of the subject necessarily qualify the experience he probes. While Marcel certainly admits the intentional character of knowledge (all consciousness is consciousness *of*), the intentionality is a function of the level at which the subject makes his demand on the real. Besides, a metaphysical statement cannot be said to bear on a given, since being is not a given, not even in the way that values might be said to be "given"; and obviously being cannot be reached via any kind of *epoché* since it is altogether intractable to being inscribed in parentheses. Therefore Marcel is forced to refer to his method not as phenomenology, but as hyperphenomenology.[31]

How is a hyperphenomenology possible? How can a world commingled with objectivity reveal its transcendent depth to me? It can only do so if the demand I make upon it is itself transcendent. This is surely the opportune moment to bring into full focus the common origin of three phrases which flow out of the absolute center of Marcel's thought: primitive assurance, blinded intuition, and ontological exigence. We have seen in the first chapter that primitive assurance and blinded intuition are really alternate ways of expressing the same thing. Slowly the realization dawns on us that by the use of "ontological exigence"

Marcel is getting at his fundamental insight in yet a third way. Man's
assurance of the presence of being is not separable from his *need* for
being; the spirit is a light in being an exigence. This need, which verbally
would seem to denote a mere absence or lack, is actually at the bottom
of my deepest assurance of positivity. "Man is an infinite lack": but in
so apprehending himself he utters the magic word which gives him an
absolute meaning and dispels the opacity of the world. We have spoken
of the blinded intuition as shedding a light across experience, but we
might just as well have spoken of the ontological exigence doing so. I
am a source of light insofar as I *participate* in a transcendent: but the
ontological exigence is the mode in which my participation is revealed
to me. Therefore only cognition which is the product of the ontological
exigence has transcendent value. No one can be a metaphysician who
does not experience this exigence.

That is why Marcel declares that an "objective" demonstration of the
existence of God is impossible. An objective demonstration pretends
to prescind from the absolute exigence. But if a would-be theologian
really did this, no demonstration would ever be forthcoming. If he
approached the question of God's existence "impartially" or "with
detachment," as one might a theorem in geometry, he would guarantee his own failure: reality treated as pure "object" could not serve as a
premise to establish a conclusion with transcendent value. The natural
theologian must desire that God exist: he must think out of his ontological exigence. But here is the paradox: if he does think out of that
exigence, then he is already attached to the God he is undertaking to
prove. For the ontological exigence is itself a mode of participation and
it turns us to a metaproblematic reality. The proof of God's existence is
an elevation to the level of thought of the participation within which
thought arises. Usually Marcel talks as if no proof of God were possible
except on the basis of an actual faith in God; it seems to him to be
the recovery through secondary reflection of the metaproblematic reality which critical reflection upon faith has called into doubt. Actually
his philosophy does not require that the participation upon which the

proof of God's existence rests be supernatural faith: it would seem to be enough to say that the intelligible evidence of the proof is a function of a real participation, and for that the ontological exigence itself should suffice. As Marcel says:

> It is clear that the apprehension of the ontological mystery as metaproblematic is the motive force of this recovery through reflection. But we must not fail to notice that it is a reflexive motion of the mind that is here in question, and not a heuristic process. The proof can only confirm for us what has really been given to us in another way.[32]

Marcel's own manner of "proving" the existence of God, one of the high points of his thought, leans directly upon the ontological exigence. Prini has perfectly epitomized this "proof" as an "exigential inference."[33] It occurs many times in his work, forming a kind of "great dialectic" in which his entire philosophy is encapsuled.[34] Upon first reading it, one has the impression that he has reached one of the last outposts of human thought. Nor does familiarity dim one whit the wonder aroused by the initial impact of this dialectic, stunning combination that it is of rational subtlety and intuitive existential depth. Only the full presentation of the original could convey its power:

> Reflection on the question "What am I?" and upon its implications. When I reflect upon the implications of the question "What am I?" taken as a single issue, I see that it means: "What is there in me that can answer this question?" Consequently, every answer to this question *coming from me* must be mistrusted.
>
> But could not someone else supply me with the answer? An objection immediately arises: the qualifications which the other may have which enable him to answer me, the eventual validity of what he says, are observed by me; but what qualifications have I for making this observation? I can, therefore, only refer myself

without contradiction to a judgment which is absolute, but which is at the same time more within me than my own judgment. In fact if I treat this judgment as in the least *exterior* to me, the question of what it is worth and how it is to be appreciated must inevitably be asked afresh. The question is then eliminated *qua* question and turns into an appeal. But perhaps in proportion as I take cognizance *of this appeal* qua *appeal*, I am led to recognize that the appeal is possible only because deep down in me there is something other than me, something further within me than I am myself—and at once the appeal changes its index.[35]

What Marcel has given us is a new "ontological argument," which involves an implication of presences rather than an implication of concepts.[36] One who is habituated to the categories of objective thought will insist on asking *to whom* this appeal is made and how we can know that there is anyone there to answer. But to ask myself if I can check and see whether there is anyone to answer my appeal is to place myself outside of that appeal, on a purely hypothetical plane. A "someone" whose credentials I could verify out of my own resources would not be the Absolute Recourse to whom I utter this appeal. In other words the transcendent is given as metaproblematic in and through the appeal in which I invoke him. In that appeal God is given to me as Absolute Thou; aside from that appeal, God is an absent third. Therefore Marcel will reiterate that the attempt to demonstrate God "objectively" is self-defeating. "Theodicy is atheism"[37] because it transforms God into an object, a someone "about whom" I can talk as if he were not present. When we speak about God, it is not about God that we speak.[38] The attitude of characterization bears upon an absent third: God is Presence. The "attributes" of God are simply the ways in which we must conceive Him if we are to maintain Him as Absolute Presence and prevent Him from falling back into the region of the problematic.[39]

The philosopher is a man "fully awake"[40] and in being thus awake he feels the disparity between the exigence which arises in the self and the world as it is first offered to his knowledge. From this point of view, *inquietude* is a basic metaphysical mood[41] and metaphysics becomes an attempt at a *"redressement"* of a fundamentally unacceptable position.[42] The task of philosophy is to allow experience to recognize itself as harboring the promise of fulfillment for the ontological exigence. It is a way for me to assure myself that I do participate in being—or rather that *we* participate in being, since I can only feel the presence of being in communion: as Chenu says, "to participate in being and to participate in other beings are only two aspects of the same fundamental operation."[43] Concrete philosophy naturally turns towards intersubjective experiences because it is in intersubjectivity that the ontological exigence finds its deepest intimation of fulfillment. Marcel's favorite concrete approaches are, as we have seen, fidelity, hope, and love. It seems worthwhile to suggest that many other concrete approaches are possible, not all of which are as patently connected with immediately intersubjective experiences as these.[44] He himself has intimated that the time is ripe for a metaphysical explanation of the image-experience of man.[45] Since all the faculties are subtended under and permeated by the same unifying exigence, there should be no hesitation in believing that the imagination is shot through with metaphysical meaning. Man's transcendence is announced to him on all sides and by his whole being. The Freudians have only scratched the surface of symbol life. The great symbols are like shadowy guides that beckon us on to the eternal; they are the secrets whispered into the ears of the subject by the world of objectivity. Does someone say that perhaps we ought not to believe what they tell us? There is only one answer: "He who has ears to hear, let him hear!" Our "ear" is the ontological exigence. The bridge, the cave, the door, the gateway, the light in the window, the river, the ocean, the infinite spaces themselves, and the whole thronging host of immemorial images exist in a dimension totally other than the world of universal validity. They are meaningful only to the singular subject who is joined in love and longing to his fellows—but to him their meaning is inescapable. Certainly, their exploration would provide an authentic approach to the ontological mystery. Something not unlike this was attempted by Ernst Cassirer in his philosophy of myth, but he worked under two handicaps: the limitation imposed by his Kantian viewpoint and the troublesome fact that he did not really believe in the myths in the way that would have been necessary to turn them into ontological knowledge. In any case the myths present very special difficulties, which do not attach to the authentic symbol-life of man of which they are only a part. Still other concrete approaches are possible; upon some a start has already been made, Haecker has given us a "metaphysics of feeling." Further, the term "poetic knowledge" no longer sounds like dissonance to modern ears; Marcel and Heidegger have seen to that. Perhaps even the voluminous work of Maurice Blondel might be looked upon as a new concrete approach to the ontological mystery, inasmuch as it is an exhaustive analysis of the ultimate implications of human *action*, certainly a new departure. The possible approaches might be multiplied—how far, we will only know as the thinkers arise to multiply them. In the very nature of things, it would seem likely that we have just begun to tap the deep wells of being. Philosophy ought to feel free to range over the whole field of human experience and to metaphysicize whatever answers its need.

A final note of caution ought to be sounded about the scope of concrete philosophy. Marcel uses words like "engagement" now and then, but he certainly does not mean by them what we might assume if we were to draw our notions from the patter of the Sartrean existentialists. He is not campaigning for philosophers to throw themselves into political activity, to sign manifestoes, or to join committees. The philosopher is not a man of congresses: his wisdom begins with a true sense of his own vocation and a realization that there are "realms in which his lack of competence to make judgments is complete."[46] Not that he should withdraw hermit-like from the life of his nation (Marcel specifically warns against that),[47] for his philosophy is always expressed in the present and he finds his eternal truths not in some timeless heaven of abstraction, but *hic et nunc* in the human situation. But his specific task as philosopher is to save what is human in that situation, and his "engagement" is a commitment to ontological communion with other persons and with the Absolute Thou. He is a defender and creator of the universal. What is the universal? "The universal is spirit."[48] The philosopher fights for the authentic image of man against all the forces that threaten to deface it. Often today that comes down to a resistance to the enervating influences which issue from mass civilization. Here Marcel joins forces with his fellow existentialists, right down to the common phraseology. The person is one who confronts and assumes his situation; the mass man, "*l'on*," exists below the level of such confrontation and his very existence constitutes both a moral (and sometimes a physical) threat to thought and at the same time an impetration for the saving ministry of thought. Since we philosophize in the situation, no one can be a philosopher today without taking a stand within himself and, when necessary, before all men against the forces which man has let loose upon himself. We need not think only of the systematic horrors perpetrated by the Nazis and Communists on the souls and bodies of men with the aid of techniques of degradation developed to diabolical perfection, nor of the threat of a nuclear war which a torpid and thingified humanity fatalistically awaits, but of seemingly lesser yet omnipresent and insidious influences like the tides of propaganda by which all countries relentlessly subvert the minds of their subjects, or of the incredible sensationalistic trivializing and cheapening of life which is progressively produced by the mass media of every variety. When life is reduced to a dirty joke for masses of men, a concrete philosophy must testify for the universal which each man carries beneath the scoria of his outer existence. We might extend Marcel's ideas. The misery of human life in general, the filth, the pain, the poverty must (irrespective of our etiological diagnoses of it) form the object of philosophical testimony, on the alternative of philosophy deteriorating into mere pretense and philosophers into parasites on the human body politic. The exigence for being must include an exigence that all men live under such conditions that they may feel the exigence for being. Conversely, we might mention what Marcel, because of his rather saturnine view of modern times in general, tends to pass over: it is also the province of the concrete philosopher to celebrate in the temporal situation the genuine glories which perhaps only he is fitted to appreciate to their utmost. In the ventures of both condemning and praising, the philosopher runs an extra risk of error since he is engaged in "applied philosophy" and his vision may often fail; but the only way he may fight for the universal is by awakening other men to the search for it.

With these remarks our inquiry into the method of Gabriel Marcel may be declared finished and our avowed purpose of discovering what he conceives philosophizing to be, fulfilled. The reader who has followed the exposition up to this point will, it is hoped, have felt the appreciation of Marcel's method seep into his consciousness with and through the reception of the Marcellian doctrine. What is perhaps desirable now is a review of the features and presuppositions of that method as we have met them.

Marcel's philosophy, we have seen, is based on a metaphysics of participation. This participation has more than one level to it, but at each level it shares the common note of non-objectifiability. It is impossible to isolate ourselves as participants from that in which we participate, since at every level it is the participation which *founds* us as subject. Actuality is participation. My actual being is a co-existent of a world in which it is incarnate and a spiritual communion outside of which it is a mere abstraction or a possibility. I cannot divorce my actual self from this participated existence, and this consideration is what gives rise to the epistemological distinction between a problem and a mystery: a mystery is a question in which my being participates, and in which it is therefore also called into question. The central Marcellian issue is: how is knowledge in the sphere of mystery possible? Or, how are we to think participation? The answer, we saw, was that it is secondary reflection by which we reaffirm in thought our essentially participated existence. But this secondary reflection must be tributary to an intuition, or there would be no incentive for it to recognize the insufficiency of the primary reflection which has obscured our participation and set us up as an autonomous subject over against an object.

Underneath all of Marcel's thought is the conviction of a blindfold intuition or a primitive assurance of the presence of being, and it is only because the mind is haunted by this non-objectifiable intuition that secondary reflection is possible. This intuition is not an object of vision, but a principle of vision: it is that which sheds trans-phenomenal significance upon our experience, by being reflected in it. But the spirit is only a light in being an exigence, and so the phrase "ontological exigence" is an alternative expression for Marcel's basic conviction. Metaphysical knowledge is only possible insofar as man makes an absolute demand upon experience. Philosophy is the means by which thought awakens to the presence of this ontological exigence and to that which intimates its fulfillment. The risk in all purely impersonal, systematic speculation is that it will convert being into an object and lose the sense of presence upon which the very possibility of metaphysics rests. For this reason, Marcel prefers to philosophize in the area of interpersonal relationships, for here the presence of being—of that which will not disappoint the ontological exigence—is most clearly announced. Just as one might say that the very act of thought reveals the spirit to itself as a participant in an order of intelligibility (of a plenitude which negates the nothingness of absurdity), so love, hope, and fidelity reveal it to itself as a participant in a plenitude which negates the nothingness of despair.

Our intuition of being may be compared to a creative idea. It is not precisely an object of knowledge, but a presence which functions as an inaccessible standard by which any thought unequal to its embodiment—and this means all thought couched in the language of subject and predicate—is seen to be less than ultimate. It thus becomes the dynamic principle behind the whole process of philosophical reflection. But that reflection is only freely indulged in: at any moment I may surrender to phenomenality and refuse to respond to the appeal of being. In regard to a transcendental exigence, the question of illusion cannot be raised: the metaproblematic is affirmed as indubitable, says Marcel, but it is affirmed freely. Metaphysical reflection is thus a creative testimony in response to an invocation, an act which creates me in the order of thought as an authentic subject by establishing me in the dimension of transcendence. Since I am totally involved in the metaphysical question, this reflection is not the work of an impersonal mind, but of a concrete self in whom the faculties are not dissociated.[49] The meaning of being is not to be explicated by an abstraction in the direction of generality, but by a descent into the singularity which burgeons in intersubjectivity, whence by an analogy of presentiality, there is an ascent to an Absolute Presence. Thus, self-knowledge and knowledge of being are mutual achievements.

It now remains for us to consider the possible objections and exceptions to Marcel's method of philosophizing, especially as they are embodied in some representative critics. This will be done at considerable length in the last chapter, which may be regarded as an apologia, an attempted *rapprochement* with other types of thought, or a concession of shortcomings, as the particular case may be.

CHAPTER IX

Concrete Philosophy Evaluated

THERE IS, of course, criticism and criticism, and the length of reply called for varies accordingly. The first requirement of critics is that they criticize what someone has actually said. This entails, at a minimum, that they really read him—that is, that they do not regard his works as an occasion for reviewing certain pre-established theses of their own. The ideal critic ought to think of himself as a collaborator. He is actually engaged in helping the thought of an author to disencumber itself of the unnecessary appurtenances with which his private whims and crotchets have burdened it. Genuine criticism—creative criticism— exists in order to fan the fires of original genius. Nothing prevents a genuine critic, in the end, from throwing up his hands in holy horror at the obtuseness and vacuity of his subject, but even when he finishes in indignation his criticism ought to give evidence of a persistent concern to understand the meaning which he feels compelled to denounce.

In two of Marcel's commentators it is difficult to escape the impression that a persistency in such concern has met with some redoubtable obstacles, and we may offer them as instances of the kind of criticism which it is relatively easy to dispose of. The first of these is Marjorie Grene, whose *Dreadful Freedom* is an off-the-cuff treatment of existentialism in general, but whose remarks on Marcel are especially instructive in that they provide us with an example of how meaningless so-called critical reflection may become. Through her whole discussion there peers a facile contempt for Marcel stemming from comfortable prejudices and habitual categories of thought which serve as permanent and unchanged spectacles by means of which all his works are read. It is as if she had glanced hurriedly through his writings and said, "But this is the same old bosh dressed up in new clothes!" The result of this reading (or non-reading) via predetermined molds is an almost sneering dismissal, and a flagrantly superficial rendering of what he has said. Thus, his interpretation of evil as "mystery" is immediately inserted into a theological framework which he does not use and which would in no way help to understand what he means: "The world as God made it was perfect, yet it had a devil in it."[1] The best she can make out of the problem-mystery distinction is that there are "mysteries deeper than mere problems at the heart of personal existence."[2] Again, her preconceptions as to what Marcel must be meaning (since he is a *religious philosopher*) lead her to pick out just those passages which are most unoriginal and irrelevant—and then to misconstrue even these. In regard to his doctrine on the body all she says is that he stresses the notion of *flesh* over the body, that the flesh is the sign of self-centeredness and our fallen state, and that we can shift our center towards communion; the whole *philosophical* analysis of incarnation is just omitted. She speaks of his theory of love and the thou as "relief from the ills of the flesh," again obviously a one-tenth reading and a subsumption under the categories she assumes proper for a religious philosopher. As for his doctrine on communion, "all he does as far as I can see, is to present with unctuous sentimentality, a number of generalizing phrases as unconvincing as a very bad sermon on the text 'God is love.'"[3] His method "hardly deserves the name of method"[4] for "I cannot agree that there is in either of these volumes (*BH* and *MJ*) a philosophic method worthy of serious consideration—the mad dialectic of Kierkegaard makes a good deal more sense than this...."[5] She sees him as somebody who is trying to revive religious faith, detects a "thoroughly false ring"[6] to his thought, and concludes that "this is not philosophizing but a two-faced, ambiguous, and not even very clever imitation of it."[7] All in all this chapter is an astonishing performance, since it succeeds in omitting or distorting anything that is of any real importance in Marcel.

A mishap also occurs when Robert Ostermann, a Thomist, undertakes to examine Marcel. Actually, the first two of his three articles are a quite unobjectionable and even appreciative presentation of the Marcellian doctrine, and yet when the time comes for the critical evaluation in the third article, most of the lights suddenly seem to turn off. Ostermann has nothing of Grene's waspish manner, but what does nullify much of his critical worth is the determined corrective attitude to which an overly verbalized adhesion to Thomistic positions urges him. (Needless to say, many another Thomist would find Marcel's thought much more congenial; in European circles the influence of both his themes and his terminology is evident—see, e.g., de Finance's article, mentioned below, p. 161.) Ostermann's discussion, certainly animated by no bad will, is an example of what it means to situate oneself within the *simulacrum* of language and to fail to make connection with one's interlocutor. The premise upon which he bases most of his remarks is that the idea of being for Marcel is existence and only existence. "Existence is real, nothing else."[8] To his own satisfaction this conclusion is supported by two texts,[9] and his criticism is a deduction of the conclusions which would flow from these texts provided they are taken in his sense. Now, several points must be made: (1) The texts which Ostermann uses to attribute this assertion to Marcel do not justify such an ascription, since they are open to a different interpretation. (2) Marcel does not utilize the Thomistic distinction between essence and existence, so that even if he were to say "existence is everything" (and he does not) he could not mean what Ostermann takes him to mean. Without remarking on the possible ambiguity of the term, the latter forthwith goes on to refute the position attributed to Marcel on the grounds that if existence (in the Thomistic sense of "*esse*") is all there is to being, then intelligibility is

wiped out. This interpretation is clearly based on his meaning of existence: if essence is missing, then so is meaning. But surely Marcel does
not pose the problem in these terms. What is his alternative to existence? An essence which is hypostasized in isolation from the thing. It is
the *existent* which Marcel emphasizes; his basic conviction, as we have
seen, is of the indissoluble unity of *existence and the existent.* (3) Failing
all else, we have Marcel's own testimony. In the preface to Prini's work
on him, Marcel congratulates the author thus:

> I am also very grateful to you for having considered my thought
> in itself without bracketing the dangerous existentialist label to it.
> You have, besides, very well showed how it is irresistibly drawn
> towards a philosophy of essence.[10]

Nor is this an isolated remark. Marcel has more than once noted the
Platonic affinities of his thought. For instance, we have the following
explicit statement:

> But it is clear that reflection on the meaning of words must be
> directed, just as Plato wanted it to be, towards a grasp of what
> traditional philosophers used to call *essences.* One cannot protest
> too strongly against a kind of existentialism, or a kind of caricature
> of existentialism, which claims to deprive the notion of essence of
> its old value and to allow it only a subordinate position.[11]

Such statements ought to warn a critic away from predicaments of
his own devising; but having convinced himself that Marcel has really
said that being means "*esse*," he must ask "If existence is all, what is left
to diversify it?"[12] Apparently nothing, since in the Thomistic scheme
of things, existence is limited by essence. This being so, all meaning
must depart from reality and the mind must find itself "confronted by
complete undetermined meaningless existence."[13] Without stopping to
ask himself where he finds such a conception in Marcel, he explains that

because it is so, then "The logical term of Marcel's teaching is pessimism, intellectual despair."[14] This would naturally follow, since "If essence is jettisoned, the intellect is deprived of its grip on the real," and "being within the confines of this philosophy, is unintelligible."[15] By now of course all similarity between the critic's remarks and the actual philosophy of Marcel has vanished. He is telling us what Gabriel Marcel's philosophy ought to have been if Marcel had meant by a certain couple of sentences what the critic would have meant by them.

Against these merely possible conclusions, however, must be weighed the reality of Marcel's philosophy, which regards being as supremely intelligible, and which issues not in despair but in joy. The writer himself feels this discrepancy and can only account for it by opining that Marcel's religious experience must have preserved him from the pernicious consequences of his thought—an opinion which would seem the reverse of the truth, since there is every indication that it was his type of thought which led him to his religious experience. As a final example of the degree to which a man's tenacious adherence to one notion can obscure his vision, we may offer this:

> The following syllogism might be used to sum up the situation: If the intelligibility (rational determinations) of reality is due only to the essence; if reality is warped when we consider it essentially; then existence is unintelligible and reality has in it something more than intelligibility. For Gabriel Marcel, this is mystery.[16]

Not only does this passage repeat the basically erroneous theme, but thrown in is the clear implication of an equation of mystery with non-intelligibility. This is unworthy of Ostermann's own appreciation of the true meaning of "mystery" which is better explained elsewhere in his paper (although never in such a way as to break through the misunderstanding set up by his preconceived categories). We would be justified in considering this as an example of the imperialism of abstraction; for the fallacy of abstractionism consists basically in an *inattention* which,

instead of taking something on its own terms, insists upon stuffing it
into a pigeonhole labeled in advance.

There is no point in multiplying the instances of such abstractionism which mar an otherwise skillful exposition. One point, however,
may be made in retrospect. Ostermann may have been prompted to his
views by an assumption erroneously shared by many others, the assumption of an identity in meaning between "essence" and "object." Marcel,
of course, does not intend these two words to be taken as synonyms.[17]
By an "object" he means the conceptually articulated structure which
the mind projects into reality. An object *is* only the sum (or at best the
interrelationship) of a certain number of notes or functions. That is why
it does not participate in *being*. Being is plenitude, inexhaustible depth;
the object, by definition, has no depth: it is the counter of the rationalist. What is experienced is presence, not object. The object is what is
brought into being by viewing reality as if it were literally constructed
according to the pattern of human thought. If a man refuses to recognize any more in being than is required by his abstractions, then he
has reduced being to a sum, either already accomplished or ideally
achievable. The notion of an "object" is perfectly valid in the case of
an artifact, for as a matter of fact here the reality is simply what our
reason, proceeding with definite circumscribed ends in view, requires
that it be. A watch *is* the sum of a perfectly designable set of functions; a
chair *is* exactly what our way of conceiving it decrees. The "essence" of a
watch or a chair is identical with the watch or chair as "object." But that
only holds good in the case of an artifact; an artifact as such does not
participate in being (in uncharacterizable plenitude) but is a product of
conceptual thought pursuing goals perfectly proportionate to itself. If,
however, we were to proceed in the same way in regard to things which
are *not* artifacts, if we were to equate their "essence" with their "objectivity," how can we fail to see that we would be wildly wrong? An essence
is certainly not the sum of a number of concepts; an essence may be
what we aim at through our concepts, but it is perpetually transcendent
in respect to conceptualization. Marcel would not agree that it is only

qua "esse" that the thing escapes our conceptual grasp. The whole being participates in being—in inexhaustibility. If this is kept in mind, there will be no proneness to think that in surpassing objective thought we bypass intelligibility. Perhaps the supremely intelligible character of the thing is that aspect under which it is finally refractive to conceptualization. Our concepts are pregnant with ontological significance precisely insofar as they turn us continually towards the supraconceptual. The final meaning of thought must reside not in the transmittable notions which it forges, but in the perpetually renewed act which overflows all its notions. This act tirelessly seeks its term, does not find it, but maintains itself in being by this very recognition that it has not found it.

Without lingering any longer on the manifold possible misunderstandings of Marcel's thought, let us now make a start on an assessment of that thought as we have seen it, and let us do it by putting the issue in the most elementary manner possible by asking these two questions: (1) Is Marcel on proper grounds in his view of what philosophy *is*? (2) Is Marcel on proper grounds in his view of what philosophy *is not*?

1. It is now clear that Gabriel Marcel envisions philosophy (certainly his philosophy) as a matter of concrete approaches to the ultimate, involving the illumination of reality by the exigences of spirit. This necessarily means that he must give to what many have been in the habit of calling "subjective" experiences (e.g., hope, joy, and perhaps something like image-experience) an important place in his thought. Consideration of this has led some to relegate Marcel's thought to the domain of the pre-philosophical. Maritain denominates his kind of thought "not genuine metaphysics but a substitute which may possess a considerable philosophic interest, but is nothing but a substitute all the same."[18] Gilson, while lavish in his praise of Marcel, thinks of him as one who "seems to tend spontaneously towards a metaphysic of the act of existing without, however, quite attaining it,"[19] and his admiration at Marcel's philosophical authenticity is mixed with the possibly diluting belief that he is a continuator in modern times of the tradition of "speculative mysticism."[20] For Collins, too, Marcel is one who discloses

the pre-philosophical drama in which the individual either opens or closes himself to the hold of being.[21] With these sentiments, Marcel de Corte's original interpretation expressed close agreement.[22] Now the difficulty here is a fairly simple one. On the one hand, according to these Thomists, we have a metaphysics which is the science of being-as-such, and on the other hand, we have a collection of interesting "pre-philosophical" discussions. This amounts to saying that genuine philosophy must center on being *qua* being and that all else is to be regarded as a merely contingent approach to that kind of study. The justification for this, naturally, is that more than one subjective experience can serve as a propaedeutic to the intuition of being, and that therefore philosophy cannot be reduced to the elaboration of these propaedeutics. Granting the plausibility of this objection, however, what warrants the additional inference that philosophy may not be considered to *include* these experiences? Why call the philosophical analysis of fidelity "pre-philosophical"? In one sense this would seem to be a quarrel over words. The protagonist has simply chosen to confine his meaning of philosophy to the science of ontology (and its blood relatives) and to call everything else pre-philosophical. He may do so if he likes, but nothing prevents us from taking "philosophy" in a wider sense than that. We may take it to mean: "the conceptual expression of the ultimate implications of experience." We will then have as many facets to philosophy as there are kinds of experience.

Included among these will be the "subjective" experiences which Maritain would like to lay under an interdict. "Philosophy," he says, "is registered whole and entire in the relation of intelligence to object."[23] But what, after all, does this mean in Maritain's terminology? For him the object is "the intelligible density of an existent subject rendered transparent in act to the mind."[24] All knowledge, then, is objective. So, philosophy must also be objective. Someone will surely interpose here that in some way subject *qua* subject must be known to the intellect or else the very distinction between subject and object would never be made. Maritain acknowledges this when he speaks of the concomitant intuition which the self has of its own existence, an intuition, however, which "surrenders no essence to us."[25] Even though he will also admit an obscure knowledge of subjectivity afforded by the mode of connaturality (in moral, poetic, and mystic experience) still this is not knowledge by *mode* of knowledge, "which is to say, by mode of conceptual objectisation"[26]; therefore, "It would be a contradiction in terms to seek to make a philosophy of that sort of knowledge, since every philosophy—like it or not—proceeds by concepts."[27] And there we have it. But on review, what do we have? All Maritain has actually said is that by philosophy he means conceptually expressed knowledge. By no means ought that to allow him to rule "subjective" experience out of philosophy. Upon inspection his remarks are seen to conceal an ambiguity in the usage of the term "subjectivity." He means by it *either* the non-conceptualizable depth beneath all experience, *or* any experience in which this depth is a determinative constituent. By definition, subjectivity in the first sense eludes conceptual capture. But subjectivity in the second sense is not inaccessible. Why should there not be an experience which for its very intelligibility requires a reference to the subject? Subjectivity may not be intelligible as a datum given separately to the mind, but it may be the unique source of intelligibility for a whole range of experience. The meaning of subjectivity may then be seized in these experiences. There is nothing particularly startling in this opinion. Thomism generally holds that the subject only knows himself in knowing other things: the nature of the self is revealed in its manner of being related to the non-self. All that Marcel and those like him propose to do is to enlarge this approach a bit. The subject not only comes to the world as a sensory knower and a discursive reasoner, but as a singular related to other singulars, and, through the ontological exigence, to an absolute singular. He only knows himself as a singular in knowing others as singular. When he tries to transmute this concomitant knowledge into reflexive philosophical thought, he does it by a perpetual evoking and re-creating of the experience itself, an evocation which thereby serves as a blinded intuition to guide his conceptual formulation. Who is authorized to tell him that this procedure is valueless? What, for instance, gives Maritain the right to declare (in reference to Kierkegaard): "As a philosophical category, anguish is worthless… Anguish is the lot of subjectivity. It is in the philosopher, not in his philosophy."[28] Nothing justifies the inference that because philosophy must be objective (conceptually expressed) it cannot without forfeiting its status take account of subjectivity. Such a prohibition would also indicate a corresponding shift in the meaning of "objectivity." Above, it meant the conceptual grasp of a subject; now it seems to mean the conceptual displacement of the subject.

We ought to distinguish between experience and the conceptual elaboration of experience. Connatural knowledge is not in itself philosophical knowledge. But what prevents us from plumbing the depths of this experience and transmuting it into thought? Why should not all experience be capable of being metaphysicized? If there is a philosophical transmutation of the experience of change, why can there not be a philosophical transmutation of fidelity? And once conceptualized, does it not fulfill the canon of "objectivity" as Maritain has expressed it? The only fear would be that in proceeding in this way the subject might be imprisoning himself in private moods not shared by other subjects, thus lessening the value of his results. In other words, we might fear a further type of "subjectivity": the word now would mean not merely "existing in and deriving intelligibility from its reference to a singular subject" but "peculiar to one or several subjects and not shared by the generality of men." This meaning of subjectivity in turn passes over into another: "peculiar to one or several subjects and not really existing in reality." By imperceptible stages we have passed out of "subjectivity" into "subjectivism." But the entire fear is grounded on the misconception that as we descend into subjectivity we find a more and more isolated particularity, whereas the truth appears to be just the opposite. The concrete universal is the pearl hidden in the heart of authentic subjectivity. The universal is spirit, as Marcel has said. And in regard to the universal, I do not have to fear subjectivism: once and for all, a spiritual experience exists beyond the dichotomy between subject and object. It simply *is*: it neither corresponds nor fails to correspond to something else. If we look a little more closely, we will probably see that it is not really conceptualizability which Maritain uses for the touch-stone of philosophy, but a rather narrower notion—demonstrability. This develops much more clearly in the latter part of his work where he distinguishes sharply between two different attitudes to reality: (1) Cause-seeking: which is marked by a certain theoretical universality or detachment from self; (2) Salvation-seeking: which is carried on in an attitude of dramatic singularity.

The first attitude is essentially philosophical, the second essentially religious.[29] Here we have an apparently unequivocal claim that a man ought to pursue a philosophical inquiry by deliberately "universalizing" himself.[30] With this assertion Marcel would take point-blank issue. I can never discover the ultimate meaning of being by prescinding from my singular self. Philosophy could only proceed by detachment if it had delegated to religion the task of maintaining surreptitiously the parti-cipation it had ostensibly prescinded from. As long as religion fulfills this task behind the scenes, philosophy appears to itself to be the work of a purely "scientific" mind.[31] Apart from the support of such religious participation, the aberrations of this science are notorious. These aber-rations may not force us to deny that philosophy is a science, but they do enforce a realization of the non-univocal character of the notion of science. Scientific knowledge is knowledge *per causas*, we are in the habit of saying. It is demonstrable knowledge. Yes, but demonstration may not mean the same in the region of mystery as in that of prob-lem. All scholastic hassling to one side, there are, as Kant clearly saw in his initial existential seizure, three crucial philosophical questions: God, freedom, and immortality. And these three come down to one: the possibility of transcendence. Is any of these susceptible of an "objective" proof in Marcel's meaning of that term? One thousand (or one million) philosophers disagree on these basic stakes, yet each goes on straight-facedly claiming that philosophy is a science. If philosophy really is a "demonstrable body of knowledge" in exactly the same sense as the

other sciences, why has it not nailed down these issues long ago?[32] The
usual answer is that the arguments are valid in themselves but that various subjective obstacles prevent their being universally accepted. Just as
it happens in a political debate or a family wrangle or in an automobile
collision, the persons' own involvment overwhelms their judgment and
distorts their perception: and yet there is thought to be no call to deny
on that account that there really is an "objective" datum to be perceived.
This last consideration is fulcral, for it allows us to pinpoint the difference
between the philosophical situation and the ones it mentions. In settling
a dispute between the two irate motorists, how would the authorities
proceed? Would they not solicit the testimony of a bystander who could
report on what really happened? This done, the objective state of affairs
would stand revealed, liberated from the mendacious self-interest of the
individuals involved; and perhaps in a cooler moment they themselves
would ruefully admit that this was how it was, after all. But can such a
procedure be followed in the philosophical dispute? Suppose we decide
to allow an "impartial bystander" to arbitrate the controversy on God,
freedom, and immortality. To whom would we appeal? There is no such
bystander. Every subject has a stake in this dispute—a stake infinitely
higher than the ruffled pride of the motorists.[33] Can we not appeal to an
ideal bystander? This would be done simply by asking ourselves what
would be the verdict of one who could free himself from all the singular
attitudes which I and all the others suffer from. Would one with absolute knowledge decide in my favor or theirs? This is the process we go
through every time we convert ourselves into pure thought. There is an
objective datum, we feel, but in order to perceive that objective datum, I
must palliate the coloring of my singular self and put myself in the position of the impartial bystander. Then the objective elements of the situation will be laid bare, and I can construct an argument which should
convince anybody who is also willing to convert himself into an impartial bystander. My argument will be convincing in itself, and if those
others will only allow themselves a cooler moment they cannot help but
feel its cogency. Nothing to it! The only trouble is that the data I need to

construct my "scientific" argument are simply *not there* for a bystander. The only data available for a universalized mind are universalized data; as such they will be empty forms of thought, logical checkers which fit neatly into patterns of argumentation, but whose real content can be revealed only to the experience of a singular subject. The point of departure upon which an argument could be based is not available for a bystander, but only for a participator. This statement is most directly understandable with reference to freedom. One who withdrew from the stream of free activity in order to observe it and verify it from without would be acting like the child who tries to catch his own finger. The "proof" of free will is really the process by which the subject translates into conceptual language his own profound experience of his singular selfhood.[34] If he were to prescind from that experience, no possible argument could convince him of freedom.

Now, often the proof for the existence of God is thought to be absolved from this difficulty, so that it is knowledge *per causas* of the most "objective" variety. All we need, it is felt, is the common experience of sense, plus the ability of the mind to reach the third degree of abstraction, a feat that theoretically could be accomplished from any point of departure, since there is no privileged experience of being. This done, the mind makes the distinction between the contingent and the necessary, and rises to a transcendent *per modum necessarium*. But observe. The idea of "being" which I conceive is *either* a mere checker of logic, *or* it is the genuine notion of being—in which case it includes my self. If I treat it as entirely objective, it is no longer the idea of being; if I recognize its non-objectifiability, its conception includes my singular subjectivity. Being is only *there* as a datum for a singular self. Father de Finance here lends clear support to Marcel: set off from the ego, he says, my idea of being would be an empty, Kantian form. If we tried to confine ourselves to the intentional objectivity of the affirmation of being, without adverting to the order of value and interiority which the ego reveals, we would have an existence without depth, and probably at last "a non-existing existent."[35]

None of this ought to sound strange in the ears of a Thomist, since his own doctrine on the analogy of being is based on a very similar consideration. Marcel says that being is non-objectifiable; the Thomist says it cannot be arrived at by a true abstraction. Being includes its differences, for there is no way to prescind from them. In either view, in conceiving being I must conceive my self within being.[36] And this means my self in its *singularity*. If I were really to follow Maritain's precept and universalize myself, I literally would not be able to conceive being. I would not be able to pursue metaphysics for the simple reason that I would not be able to ask the metaphysical question. Here again de Finance declares himself explicitly in agreement with Marcel: my idea of being must include the very act which conceives it, so that "being" thus apprehended is neither subject nor object "for both subject and object are included within being."[37] This of necessity must change the character of the knowledge which is achieved in the sphere of being. In this case we have a "science" which cannot prescind from the singular; obviously it can only be analogically similar to those sciences which are constituted as sciences by prescinding from the singular.

These last thoughts allow us to give one last precision to the effort to clarify Marcel's approach to being and to effect a partial *rapprochement* with traditional metaphysics adequately considered. All along, the submerged premonition has been that true subjectivity is not *mere* subjectivity. Upon reflection we may now see why this is so. Since the conception of being includes both subject and object, then the philosophy of being can be *neither* a purely objective *nor* a purely subjective inquiry. This is so for the good reason that the matter of such an inquiry could not coincide with the true notion of being—since being transcends the division between subject and object. An investigation of being as pure object would give us only an illusion of knowledge; without the contribution of the subject, metaphysics would truly deteriorate into a pseudoscience for it would be dealing with a pseudo-reality, "being *qua* object." On the other hand an investigation of being as pure subject is also impossible. The exigence of the subject *qua* exigence is

turned towards the other. This amounts to saying that the transcendental exigences are not really "subjective." Exigence for being, for truth, for
goodness, are not purely subjective characteristics: they are modes of
participation in what is trans-subjective and absolutely real.

How much difference will this make in the science of metaphysics
itself? This is the question to which the continuators of the philosophical approach of Gabriel Marcel will increasingly have to turn their
attention. At the outset it is impossible to miss the great *epistemological* importance of the distinction between a problem and a mystery.
That is, the manner of assent and the manner of achieving certitude are
inescapably different in philosophical knowledge from what they are in
purely "objective" knowledge. This does not need laboring. One might
only suggest individual epistemological researches which ought to be
pursued: the thorough exploitation of the meaning of "proof" in the area
of mystery; as part of this last, an examination of the questions raised by
the use of a transcendental notion like "being" in logical propositions
and inferences which are directly adapted to carrying universal ideas;
an exhaustive analysis of the meaning of "abstraction," a word whose
surprisingly nebulous character has usually escaped notice. But once
we recognize that the exigences of the subject have a voice in deciding
the limits of intelligibility in the knowledge which is directed towards
transcendence, all kinds of problems are raised. We are provided with
an occasion to review, for example, the entire role of the subject in the
discovery of meaning in general. Once the active, constitutive role of
the subject is recognized in one case, we may be reminded of the essentially *active* nature of knowledge in all its modes. Classical metaphysics
has always acknowledged the necessity of saying that the mind *makes
intelligibility*[38]: material reality is opaque as it is presented to the senses
and must be illuminated by the agent intellect. The thought occurs to us,
however, that the conception of an agent intellect may be only a partial
description of the manner in which the spirit discovers the intelligibility
in things by sweeping them into the whole continuing process of its
quest for selfhood and being. Sometimes the agent intellect is treated

simply as a machine for the manufacture of concepts; but just as we ought to know (and such approaches as modern logic and pragmatism remind us) that the concept has no life independently of the judgment, nor of the whole teleological movement of the subject, so we ought to suspect that what we have called the "agent intellect" cannot function independently of the total dynamism of the subject. If the mind makes meaning, perhaps the principle of intelligibility is not a specialized agent intellect, but spirit in its entirety.

Reality is to be explained not *as* object nor *as* subject, but from the side of the object or from the side of the subject. Scholastic philosophy generally has confined itself to an objective approach. Nevertheless, the kind of reflection which Marcel pursues is far from unknown within scholastic circles. Thus, the proof for the immortality of the soul based upon the desire for happiness, or the moral argument for immortality, or the argument for God's existence from universal consent, all really are grounded in the conviction of the ultimate relevance of the exigences of the subject. What often gives them a rather specious appearance is that authors do not acknowledge this and labor valiantly to treat them as "objective" proofs, holding good for a neutral observer. As we bring our discussion to a close, the remark of Rousselot seems quite germane: "It follows that from the Thomist point of view a philosophy founded on the analysis of appetite or volition is legitimate, though of an inferior kind."[39] Marcel does not precisely analyze the transcendental aspiration of the will, but he does explore the concrete situations where that aspiration may clearly recognize itself.[40] There does not appear to be any real reason to deny that such an exploration is part and parcel of philosophy.

2. We may now consider the second question: is Marcel on proper grounds in what he thinks philosophy is not? It is an easy matter to discover the attributes he denies of philosophy, since he does not tire of reminding us of them. It is not systematic; it is not a universally valid science. Now the second point has already been implicitly disposed of, but let us briefly reconsider it. The obvious criticism is that all thought that is true must be universally valid: it cannot be false for one and true

for another. Even Marcel claims universal validity for his assertions; when he probes the nature of fidelity, he feels we ought to accept the truth of his conclusions; he does not look upon them as fancies of his own. Unless philosophy is to be "every man for himself" there must be a claim to universal validity. In answering this objection, we must give a very definite meaning to the phrase "universally valid": it means either "what cannot be rejected by thought except at the price of renouncing its own logical structure," or in an empirical sense "what is imposed with necessity on anyone who wants to subsume sense experience under a consistent logical order." At bottom it seems to be an essentially Kantian category. The limits of the universally valid are defined by what must be necessarily admitted in order to put coherence into experience and to establish the subject as a member of a community of minds whose thought is orientated towards that in itself which allows the community to *indicate* itself as community.[41] The "real" in this sense is the order which is correlative to an impersonal subject; reciprocally, this subject is defined by the conception of this necessary order. Not every truth need be a "universally valid" truth: that is, in order to recognize this truth it may be necessary to go beyond what is required by logical thought considered in this minimal role. Thus, such propositions as "I exist," "God exists," "People exist who love me," "The idea of being has absolute value," "History has a meaning," are true propositions, but they are not universally valid propositions. This means that I could fail to perceive their value, and yet fulfill all my duties as an object in an orderly phenomenal universe. Conversely, when I do assert their truth I must do so as more than an epistemological subject.

In the case of Marcel's bias against system, any verdict we reached would have to be based on some distinction being made with regard to the meaning of the word. Marcel's animus against system arises from two sources, one theoretical, the other apparently psychological. The second is more easily disposed of, since it is more a private difficulty of Marcel himself than a necessary requirement of his philosophy. Temperamentally, synthesis is not his strong point: he seems incapable

of constructing even a systematic exposition, much less a delineation of
reality in terms of a system. This shortcoming more than once causes
chagrin to the reader who painfully searches for non-existent transi-
tions and interconnections; as often as not the last part of his chapters
has only a nodding acquaintance, with the first. A lot of this is due to
his fear that solicitude for orderly presentation will turn his attention
from the concrete to its abstract facsimile. The danger is certainly real,
though not unavoidable. For Marcel himself the rewards of his own
method far outweigh the disadvantages, since it is to this systematic
horror of the systematic that his thought owes much of its non-deriv-
ative character.

Speculatively, he feels that any system which really rested on a total
objectification of being would be altogether impossible, since being is not
a spectacle.[42] If he is right anywhere, he is right here—but does that rule
out all attempt at systematization? To believe so would be to slight one
of the profound exigences of the subject, the exigence for unity. Unless
the mind sees things whole, it does not feel that it truly sees. And this is
no error, if we understand the nature of conceptual knowledge. Because
it is a substitute for intuition, the concept needs continual replenishment from the concrete—and *also* from other concepts. Thought is a
commerce between mind and being, but a commerce often facilitated
by the exchange within thought itself. If a "system" means the equation
of reality with the blueprint of abstractions which the mind forms of
it, obviously it could lead quickly to the death of authentic thought.
But the mind's exigence for unity is already a participation in the unity
which binds being together. To see conceptually is to see partially, but
to think is to orientate oneself towards the no-longer-partial. Therefore
the process of human thought includes an attempt to introduce into the
series of partial acts of cognition the unity whose presentiment is its
own profound mainspring. The justification for the system is not that
it is adequate to reality, but that it is *not* adequate to reality. This naturally means that an authentic system must be open of its very essence.
With regard to the spurious closed system that would interpose itself

between thought and reality, we may deliver Gilson's verdict: "Every system depends upon will more than upon understanding."[43] And yet to forswear systematization altogether is also to run the risk of forsaking the concrete: even Marcel's own concrete approaches could not be fully appreciated unless there were a framework of knowledge into which to insert them. The oscillating movement in which the human mind is embroiled (between world-view and concrete approach, conceptual framework and phenomenology) seems to be a necessary condition of the human manner of knowing. Marcel's kind of philosophy is really philosophy, but it is not all there is to philosophy; nor in order to grant it its full value do we have to hold that it is.

Under the general heading of what Marcel declares philosophy *not* to be, we may now consider at some length the negative relation he declares to hold between it and objective knowledge in general. In particular, the consignment of scientific knowledge to the realm of having tends to exteriorize completely the relationship between science and philosophy, and on this score Marcel has come under heavy fire in some quarters. A lot of the criticism undoubtedly arises because he not only fails to enthuse over or even appreciate science and technics, but because he gives indications of viewing them with profound mistrust as enemies of the spirit.

But this opposition between the spirit and technics must in no sense be regarded as irreducible. Ultimately technics are one instrument of the spirit. There is not the slightest doubt that there is, in Marcel's eyes, a place proper to technics. Then why does he spend so much of his time rehearsing the evils of technocracy? Is it a species of Romanticism which impels his protests? Is this just the thesis of William Morris or Eric Gill decked out with philosophical trappings? Ultimately, no. While there is no denying that some Romantic elements tinge his thought, it is only fair to recognize that the source from which his reflections spring is not a nostalgia for some idealized past but a nostalgia for being. A strictly functionalized consciousness is not just a social phenomenon but a metaphysical phenomenon, This is what must be kept in mind by

those who might be inclined to fall into professional disparagement of
Marcel's analyses as the sentimental outpourings of an amateur sociolo-
gist; in actuality they represent a striking application of his own dictum
that a philosophy worthy of the name must attach itself to a given situation and reach the transphenomenal by plumbing its depths. The fact
that the contemporary world rings hollow is, if correctly interpreted,
an ultimate revelation. Marcel does not deny that technics "in themselves" are—not neutral—but simply good. But "technics in themselves"
is an abstraction which cannot dictate their value in a given existential
situation.[44]

However, granted that Marcel has not fallen into the absurd error
of condemning technics *in toto* and has, as we have seen, explicitly
recognized their value, is it not peculiar that he devotes so little effort
to drawing out their positive contributions? Does he not remind us of
those newspaper columnists who will go on record as favoring labor
unions in principle but devote endless columns to denouncing their
abuses? Of all the charges levelled against Marcel, this comes closest
to having real weight—and yet it ought not to be accepted as proof of
bad faith on his part, as it almost certainly is in the case of the newspaper columnists. A preliminary classification must be made on what
it means to evaluate technics. How might a "final judgment" in this
dispute sound? There is no question of a decision such as: "Technics
are sixty-seven percent good and only thirty-three percent bad," for
that is an infantile effort to translate their ontological dignity into terms
of having (and of quantity, at that). The error is easy to detect when
put into such an explicit formulation, but often escapes notice in prac-
tice. Thus, most approaches to the problem of technology conceal an
unformulated question: "Have technics done more harm or good to
the human race?" Not only is the question unanswerable in fact, it is
probably meaningless. We can skirt such terminology and put the case
with more accuracy once we perceive that the genuine and omnipresent
property of technics is to be an *opportunity*. This does not mean to be of
neutral value, but to be offered as a *chance* to the incarnate spirit of man.

It is the spirit which confers their consequent meaning, and therefore man's verdict on technics is really his verdict on himself.

Now if Marcel realizes this, why does he not enter more enthusiastically into the manifold possibilities of technics? Two reasons must probably be assigned. The first is the incompatibility of his own temperament with the universe of science. As a literary man and a musician the probability is great that he shares the distaste of the rest of his breed for the mechanical viewpoint. While it is possible for such men to develop a theoretical recognition of the contribution of technics, they cannot be expected to go much further. Yet one might think that a philosopher like Marcel, who insists that thought must begin within our situation, could rise beyond any lacuna of temperament and extend a more cordial hand to the contemporary world. Does he not proclaim the "non-contingency of the empirically given" and refuse to retreat to the sanctuary of the non-engaged self? Then he ought to recognize the engagement at the global and historical level as well: our world situation is not fortuitous in respect to some timeless portion of the self—it makes the self, the only self we have. Therefore one might urge, as has been done,[45] that Marcel's own philosophy ought to force him to take a more optimistic view of modern technology. And, with reservations still to be made, it must be admitted that this is true. This is one of the shortcomings of his thought. But even here we must be careful. One should not fall into the shallow fallacy of equating an engagement in the situation with a passive acceptance of the situation. To "accept" our situation is to assume if, to take it on ourselves—and this is far from being incompatible with a struggle to alter its present state. When a man struggles with a vice in his character, he does not deny the non-contingency of the basic psychic structure which underlies it. The whole point in combating the evils of technics is to remember that they are part of the basic psychic structure of historical humanity. This does not mean that the present state of technology must receive that veneration which debased intellects are moved to offer to an automaton called history, but that even it must be understood as the partially genuine creation of an imminent teleology which man cannot deny without denying himself.

This question, of course, involves the more general one of the degree to which we can establish philosophically the meaning of history at all. Apparently the question does not interest Marcel; at any rate he never confronts it. What remarks he does make in passing serve only to accentuate his impatience with the euphoria of mechanical historicisms. We must realize that in the background of the French spiritual writers there looms the shadow of an unvanquished Comtean positivism, which makes it more than ordinarily difficult for them to welcome the notion of any supra-individual entelechy operative in history.[46] Yet strangely enough a rather exact statement of the issue is possible on the basis of Marcel's own philosophical insights. Not only may we enlarge his idea of the "situation" to include the empirical given of history, but his own distinction between a problem and a mystery helps to make it clear in what sense a meaning may be attributed to history and in what sense it may not. If history has any meaning at all, it can only be affirmed at the level of mystery. Marcel does not say so himself, but nothing could be clearer. No man can declare that history has a meaning as if this were a matter of objective knowledge: we are involved in history and therefore we cannot pronounce on it as something external to us. It is not something we "have" but something we are. Therefore if we can affirm a meaning at all, that meaning is affirmed as metaproblematical. Only at the level of spirit is it possible to express the fact that history has a meaning—and that affirmation is both indubitable and freely made. It is similar to my individual situation with regard to my life. How can I declare to myself that my life has a meaning? Certainly not as an objectively demonstrable bit of knowledge, but in function of my free decision to be spirit: this does not imply that the meaning is doubtful, since once I open myself to mystery it is indubitable—but freely recognized. Time radiates intelligibility only when it is illuminated by spirit. In the same way, a meaning to history is posited as beyond dispute at that moment when it is recognized as one dimension in the self-recognition of spirit. Since the self-recognition is free, the recognition of meaning is free. In that recognition there is no room for the skeptical doubt that the judgment might be erroneous, for such doubt is only possible when a within and a without can still be distinguished. But in this limit-case no such dissociation can be made: to recognize meaning and to create meaning are here one and the same thing.[47]

All this does not permit us to pass from the affirmation of the meaningfulness of history to the marking-off of perfectly defined goals and stages within history, for to do so would be to run the imminent risk of degrading a mystery to a problem. This, of course, is exactly what various philosophies tend to do: Hegelianism, Comtean positivism, Marxism, Nazism, scientism, all in their way seek to schematize and possess the inner nature of history. But history is non-objectifiable. It is not, perhaps, philosophically permissible to talk about *the* goal of history, as if it were some clear and distinct, though still undiscovered, objective. Those who talk this way invariably feel the temptation to deliver up the human person to present injustice wherever this is necessary to bring about the future ideal end. Conversely it would be erroneous to speak as if the human person were an absolute, fixed mark set against the streams of historical time. Here, too, we would be betrayed into the thought-forms of having, which must isolate in order to grasp. If the person is only a reality through participation, then these thought-forms will not enclose it. The only fully adequate formula for *the* meaning of history is theological: the world was created for the glory of God. Transposed into the philosophical language of our human side this means that the world was created in order that spirit become spirit. History is the efflorescence of spirit: this is the only truth which can be pronounced about history taken as a whole. As to which objective elements and appearances within the historical process advance this pneumaphany and which do not, that can certainly never be decided by their position in the temporal succession. Marcel rightly says that it is only to the world of technics that the concept of perfectibility can be automatically applied, since on the level of being nothing assures us that what comes after in time will not be emptier than what comes before.[48] The reverse view would amount to an intolerably superficial sort of philosophical Couéism—something like that which Spenser adopted. The best that the spirit can do is to affirm the authenticity or non-authenticity of the energies which are released through history.

The question is: Has Marcel risen to the proper affirmation in the case of technics? Our reply must be at least partially in the negative. It really seems that the mutually exclusive relationship which he establishes between objective knowledge and metaphysical knowledge smacks too much of the spirit of abstraction which he himself abhors. It dissociates what can be appreciated only in unity. Is it an accident that our age which has seen such unprecedented advance in the objectification of nature has simultaneously witnessed a parallel rediscovery of subjectivity? Ought we to look upon this rediscovery as a reaction against a process which is quite exterior to itself, set over against itself? Or is not rather the objectification the very condition of the new subjectivity? The latter view would seem to be more in keeping with Marcel's principle of the noncontingency of the human situation: here it is a matter of realizing that the mode by which we obtain self-knowledge is non-contingent. A man living in a primitive condition of society does not have the same opportunity for self-knowledge as a man living in an advanced civilization: he is potential and amorphous as a subject because his world has not been sufficiently objectified. It is not to be expected that a people sunk in perpetual slumber, like the pygmies of Africa or the Australian aborigines will develop a metaphysics. Metaphysical knowledge is not precisely *outside* of objectified knowledge; rather they are dual aspects of a coming to consciousness which is one integral process. Man's knowledge arises as a concomitant of the manner in which he builds himself into the universe. One who believes that the sun is a fiery chariot is a less apt candidate for the philosophical intuition of being than one who treats it as a gaseous sphere, and has carefully ascertained its mean distance from the earth. The advance in self-knowledge which had to intervene between the first and the second man is tremendous. (On the other hand, a man who could not be moved by the image of the sun as a fiery chariot would be a completely hopeless case metaphysically.) The subject is too vast and complex to be doctrinaire about it, but what we do have the right to say is that metaphysics should not look upon "problematic" knowledge as a threat to its own soul. Not only ought it to recognize that problematic knowledge is perfectly useful within its own sphere, but that it is useful for the deepening of metaphysical insight. Not that it *is* metaphysical knowledge but that man's way of coming to metaphysical knowledge cannot be isolated from the rest of his cognitive life. Every great advance in objectification bears within it the possibility of a corresponding advance in the appreciation of mystery.

We would be foolish indeed to think that this must happen to every individual man who is caught up in the movement of strictly objectified knowledge. It is undeniable that objectification can seduce the mind away from the ontological mystery altogether. The great mechanists of the eighteenth and nineteenth centuries are the classic examples of this kind of defection from being, and the danger is always great that the practitioner of the problematic sciences will reify his abstractions and develop a block against mystery. But the question should be raised as to whether there is not a basic ambivalence in objectified knowledge. Granted that historically it has often militated against the sense of mystery, is there any real reason why it should? That is, in a self genuinely orientated to the mystery of being, could not problematic knowledge actually contribute to his awareness of transcendence?[49] Where it does not, the fault would seem to be that *both* his problematic knowledge *and* his metaphysical comprehension are insufficiently conscious of their own inner nature. Briefly, we might ask, must all characterizing tend to obliterate the experience of presence? Take a simple case. As a child I am aware of a tree which grows near my house; that tree is a constant presence, day by day, year by year, filling many idle hours with gazing, and touching, and climbing. In fact it falls little short of being a "thou." As time goes by, I learn many things about the tree: it is called an oak tree, its roots go very deep, it draws water from the ground, internally it would show concentric circles, its leaves prosper by photosynthesis, etc. The first knowledge is in the realm of mystery, the second is on the verge of the problematic. Does the second destroy the sense of *presence* which I derive from the tree? If I identify myself altogether with the *posture* in which I characterize the tree, then the sense of presence would asymptotically approach zero. This is what Marcel really intends by problematic knowledge. One who approaches being as a *mere* observer or a *mere* characterizer does not apprehend it as being. *Anybody* could come around and characterize my tree as I learned to do. But is it not at least quite possible that I can transcend my own mood of characterizing and gather it too into the intimacy which exists between me and my tree? My father is "thou" to me but just as the sight of my father in his old characteristic mackinaw and galoshes on a snowy night could stir loving thoughts in me, so the characteristics of the tree will not destroy the experience of presence if they are thought of as characteristics of *my* tree: my tree has deep roots, inside my good old tree wonderful secret forces are working, etc. In other words an experience of a singular presence need not be obliterated by the qualities under which we know it. Certainly this is clear in the case of poetry, where the characteristics evoke the mystery of the singular.

The special problem that comes up in the case of scientific objective knowledge, of course, is that the characteristics given are universals and not properties of one singular being. Here the tendency to be turned away from presence is much greater. It must be remembered, however, that a worker who is engaged with a machine is not confined to such universals. The man fixing an auto may be applying general rules, but if he is fixing *his* auto, then the material beneath his hands is a presence, just as the flowers in the hands of the gardener are presences—even though he may know their Latin names. Even if we pass on to include mechanics who work with "anybody's" car, or to scientific theorizers who live in a land of universals—even here there is no need that their postures destroy presence. The theorizer is in worse danger, since he may give himself completely to the isolated teleology of just that part of his activity which is perfectly proportionate to success and transform the whole world into an image which would totally correspond to that teleology (into an "object"). But something else saves (or can save) him: the living presence which he approaches via his techniques may be looked upon as not this tree nor this machine, but nature itself as a total presence. Essence is a principle of creativity; science traces the extent of this creativity, but once it becomes aware of what it is actually engaged in doing, it could never believe that it has problematized the universe.

None of these remarks ought to be taken to mean that Marcel's problem-mystery distinction is invalid. On the contrary, there is every reason to believe that it will become a classic distinction in metaphysics. The important point of this distinction is not that objectified knowledge does not have its element of mystery,[50] but that metaphysical knowledge *must* be treated as mystery. Scientific knowledge is ambivalent, as we have said: it could prescind altogether from presence. In either case, the scientific datum as such is still before the mind: the scientific object as such is detachable from my self. It is a clear and distinct datum which may be absorbed by mystery but is not already mysterious. It is not of such a nature that it must be *given* as mysterious. The engine *qua* artifact is simply an "object"; the engine *qua* presence is mystery. Being can *only* be presence, mystery. The gardener who expressed and extended the mental state in which he classifies the parts of flowers would become a problematic knower, a botanist; the gardener who expressed and extended the mental state in which he smells the flower would become a philosopher—or a poet.

Yet we must remember that it is the same man who does both. And could not the very attempt to classify and to measure awaken us further to the depth in being which escapes such classification? Could, for instance, Marcel set up his distinction between the "he" or "it" and the "thou" unless the progressive objectification in thought had more and more served to reveal the non-objectifiability of the person? Or could his fruitful meditation on the "body as mine" have hit home as powerfully if the critical doubt of Descartes had not been raised?

Let us put this last question in no uncertain terms: the philosophical cognition which we may have today of the meaning and significance of incarnation is greater and richer than St. Thomas could have had, and it is greater because the Cartesian doubt intervened between St. Thomas and Marcel. In transcending the Cartesian objectification, we return not to the same notion of body which we already had but to a fuller notion, which is fuller because of the need to transcend that objectification. Without pressing matters any further, let this stand as an example of what is meant by saying that an increase in objectification may be the prelude to a heightened awareness of subjectivity. A realization of this will help concrete philosophy to become still more concrete.

In offering our criticism, let us hope that we have observed the dictum which we laid down at the beginning of this chapter. Criticism is collaboration. This has been intended in no other way. We have not meant to contravene the thought of a philosopher who is one of the most original forces of our century, but to defend the vital center of that thought and to assist it in however small a way to take the fullest cognizance of itself.

NOTES

INTRODUCTION

1. Paul Claudel, *The City*, trans. John Strong Newberry (New Haven, CT: Yale University Press, 1920), p. 20.

CHAPTER I

1. *BH* 166.
2. *BH* 135.
3. *MJ* XIII.
4. Ibid.
5. *BH* 119. Also cf. *MB* (I) 212, (II) 186; *RI* 35, 91ff.; *PE* 8; *PI* 135.
6. *BH* 171. Also cf. *BH* 28, 140; *PI* 93, 136–137; *PE* 8.
7. *MJ* VIII. Cf. *PI* 136–137.
8. *BH* 98, 114.
9. *RI* 91.
10. *MJ* VIII.
11. *BH* 28. In the context of the paragraph, "being" here means reality as ultra-subjective, but the statement will stand also as his verdict on our relation to "being" considered as fullness, as transcendence. In this opinion, Marcel finds himself in good metaphysical company. The

abundant remarks of Louis Lavelle, *La présence totale* (Paris: Aubier, 1934), probably provide the most extensive agreement. Cf. p. 12, where he speaks of "la présence actuelle et inévitable de la totalité de l'être en chaque point." The whole of this book is an assiduous working out of the co-articulation of self and being: "Il y a une expérience initiale qui est impliquée dans toutes les autres et qui donne à chacun d'elles sa gravité et sa profondeur: c'est l'expérience de la présence de l'être. Reconnaître cette présence, c'est reconnaître du même coup la participation du moi à l'être" (p. 25). Cf. also Maurice Blondel (whose *L'action*, 1893, Marcel regards as one of the greatest speculative works in the French language). In *L'être et les êtres* (Paris: Alcan, 1935), he denies that there is any problem of "going to being," for we are already in it (p. 9). Francis Callahan, S.J., *Philosophical Method in Maurice Blondel* (Fordham University, Ph.D. dissertation, 1955), declares, p. 42: "That the transcendent is implied in any and every state of consciousness is a basic point in the philosophy of Blondel" and "we are more certain of this transcendent reality than we are of anything else." Blondel insists, in *L'être*, that "nous ne chercherions pas l'être…si nous ne l'avions ou ne l'étions en quelque façon" (p. 12), and he even uses words that ring familiar, speaking of "la certitude primitive que nous possédons inaliénablement" (p. 14). Louis de Raeymaeker adds a Thomist's assent when he says, *The Philosophy of Being*, trans. Edmund H. Ziegelmeyer, S.J. (St. Louis: B. Herder, 1954), p. 57: "It is impossible to deny the absolute, which is always present to consciousness."

12. Here one might wonder whether all these levels of reality could have some claim to legitimacy. Could there not be various genuine levels of reality—a Cartesian level, an Aristotelian level, etc.? Briefly, we might suggest that for Marcel it would be a question of knowing to what these hierarchical planes of intelligibility are ordered (*MJ* 2). More generally, this question is one facet of the larger one that arises later in reference to Marcel's position on objective knowledge: how far ought he to deny ontological value to such knowledge?

13. *MB* (II) 87–97; *RI* 217; *BH* 133.

14. *RI* 235–236; *BH* 114.

15. *HV* 26.

16. *BH* 219; *MJ* 290.

17. *BH* 117; *RI* 35, 76–78, 130, 187; *MJ* 41.

18. *BH* 137, 237; *RI* 50–52.

19. *RI* 191.

20. *BH* 119.

21. *RI* 124.

22. *BH* 118, 122; *MJ* X; *MB* (I) 13.

23. *MB* (II) 188.

24. *BH* 118.

25. *MB* (II) 119ff.; *RI* 79.

26. *MB* (I) 3. The passages which Marcel is thinking of are undoubtedly those contained in English in the collection of Bergson's entitled *The Creative Mind*, trans. Mabelle L. Andison (New York: Philosophical Library, 1946). There he speaks of a "mediating image" (p. 39) which "if it is not the intuition itself, approaches it more closely than the conceptual expression…to which the intuition must have recourse in order to furnish 'explanation'" (pp. 128–129). He warns: "Let us not be duped by appearances: there are cases in which it is imagery in language which knowingly expresses the literal meaning, and abstract language which unconsciously expresses itself figuratively. The moment we reach the spiritual world, the image, if it merely seeks to suggest, may give us the direct vision" (p. 49). The intuition is like a "center of force" from which image and concept spring, but the image is closer to the depths (p. 142; cf. also p. 195). Not only does he speak of a mediating image, but he actually seeks to discover it in the thought of Berkeley (pp. 139–141). If more evidence is required for Marcel's acceptance of the fundamental metaphysical worth of imagery, we need cite only one further sentence: "These analogies which have been exploited in every age by rhetoric and poetry—hasn't the moment finally come to let their philosophical meaning break forth…?" he asks in *Existentialisme chrétien* (Paris: Librairie Plon, 1947), p. 293.

27. Michel Bernard, *La philosophie religieuse de Gabriel Marcel* (Paris: Le Cahier du Nouvel Humanisme, 1952), uses these exact words (p. 127)

and further calls Marcel's dialectic "rigorous but sinuous" (p. 92). Roger Troisfontaines, S.J., in *Existentialisme chrétien*, p. 215, speaks of his "sinuous researches." Marcel de Corte in his introduction to *Positions et approches concrètes du mystère ontologique* uses the verbally different but uncannily parallel metaphor of an "ascending spiral" to convey his own impression of Marcel's thought (p. 37): this metaphor clearly contains the same elements as that of a "winding path." Paul Ricoeur, *Gabriel Marcel et Karl Jaspers* (Paris: Éditions du Temps Présent, 1947), refers to Marcel's reflections as "fort sinueuses" (p. 50). Marcel himself informs us (*RI* 82) that a friend of his described *Être et avoir* as a "cheminement de la pensée," and he agrees that nothing could be more appropriate. The number of times that he himself accentuates the *winding* nature of this journey (besides the places explicitly cited here, see *MMS* 167; *HV* 98; *MB* (I) 136; *RI* 193) removes any doubt as to the aptness of our symbol.

28. *RI* 53.
29. *HV* 60.
30. *MJ* 316.
31. *MB* (I) 3.
32. *MB* (I) 4.
33. *MJ* X.
34. *MB* (I) 139.

CHAPTER II
1. *RI* 22.
2. *MJ* VIII.
3. *RI* 8; *MJ* 305.
4. *RI* 23.
5. *MJ* XII; *MMS* 91–92.
6. *BH* 19.
7. *BH* 219.
8. *BH* 120; *MJ* 236.
9. *RI* 24.

10. *BH* 120; *MJ* 298

11. *RI* 24; *MMS* 90.

12. *RI* 91.

13. *BH* 170–171; *MJ* 40ff., 325.

14. *BH* 27.

15. *MJ* 40. So acutely is this dichotomy felt by Marcel that some closely thought pages in his early *Metaphysical Journal* are devoted to conceiving the manner in which the gap between the reasoning self and the empirical self is closed. His solution is rather remarkable: it is only faith which accomplishes this union. It is only by conceiving myself as willed by God that I became a *mind*, a living and active reality as distinct from a thinking subject: "The act of faith…posits the non-contingence of the empirical ego.… Through faith I affirm a transcendent foundation for the union of the world and my thought, I refuse to think myself as purely abstract, as an intelligible form hovering over a world" (*MJ* 45). The exact meaning of faith here shares some of the obscurity of the first part of the *Metaphysical Journal*, but Marcel explicitly repeats: "The mind…is only created as mind by faith in God" (*MJ* 46).

16. *MJ* 32, 322ff.; *BH* 27, 105.

17. *BH* 19; *MB* (I) 133; *PI* 136–138.

18. *MJ* 17–22, 269, 274, 314–317; *BH* 10–12; *MB* (I) 88–89. Somewhere along the line it ought to be made clear that Marcel's view of the relationship between existence and objectivity underwent a change that amounted to a reversal. In the beginning of the *Metaphysical Journal* the reader will have a hard time distinguishing any difference in meaning at all. An existent is that which is given to an immediate consciousness, quite evidently an object of some kind. Truth, at this juncture, is identified with verifiability and is only applicable to the realm of existents (spatially presentable objects of consciousness). Thus one will feel that since God is not an object presented to consciousness, Marcel is perfectly consistent in denying that He "exists." Then there is a gradual change in outlook, culminating in the essay *Existence and Objectivity*. (The early *Journal* pages date from 1914, in which year Marcel wrote the whole of

Part I; Part II was written between 1915 and 1923. The essay appeared in the year 1925.) In this essay the two conceptions are disengaged and opposed. The object is the "rationally articulated spectacle" which thought sets over against itself, as it deliberately sets aside "the mode in which the object, is *present to* the person who considers it…the mysterious power of self-affirmation by which it confronts a spectator" (*MJ* 320). Idealism conjures away this sense-presence of the thing, a sense-presence which Marcel says is either identical with existence or is its immediate manifestation (ibid.). His uncertainty in regard to the latter is never explicitly resolved; having distinguished existence from objectivity, he prefers to introduce a new distinction between existence and being rather than sifting and refining his notion of existence. The result is that although existence ceases to be equated with an object that is set over against a subject, it never sheds its sensory, spatial connotations.

19. *MB* (I) 134.

20. *MJ* 25.

21. *BH* 9.

22. On incarnation, see *MB* (I) 103–124; *MJ* 124–127, 244–248, 314–317; *BH* 10–12; *RI* 26ff.

23. Jean-Paul Sartre, in *Being and Nothingness*, trans. Hazel E. Barnes (New York: Philosophical Library, 1956), uses language that frequently coincides with Marcel's in his phenomenology of the body (p. 103ff.), but with a quite disparate intent.

24. *MJ* 127.

25. *RI* 30.

26. *RI* 19.

27. *MJ* 320–327 (in the essay *Existence and Objectivity*).

28. *MJ* 21.

29. *MJ* 322.

30. Ibid.

31. *MJ* 323.

32. *BH* 11.

33. *MJ* 187, 231, 257, 277ff.; *MB* (I) 104–108; *RI* 36–39.

34. *MJ* 316.

35. For this analysis, see *MB* (I) 111–114.

36. *MB* (I) 109

37. *RI* 116–119.

38. *MB* (II) 14.

39. *MB* (II) 9.

40. *MB* (II) 8.

41. *BH* 104.

42. Roger Troisfontaines, S.J., *Existentialisme et pensé chrétien* (Paris: J. Vrin, 1948), p. 106ff.

43. For the distinction between "thou" and "he," see: *MB* (I) 176ff.; *MJ* 158, 165, 219ff.; *RI* 46ff.; *BH* 106–107.

44. *RI* 152

45. *RI* 50–52.

46. The ultimate unifier of the human personality is, of course, its presence to the Absolute Thou (see Chapter V). Nicolas Berdyaev, in *The Divine and the Human*, trans. R. M. French (London: Geoffrey Bles, 1949), also sees the unity of the personality as more an achievement than a postulate: "Man must all the while perform a creative act in relation to himself" (p. 134); "The synthetizing creative act creates the image of man and without it there would be merely a collection and medley of bits and pieces" (p. 114). Marcel never thinks of this act as anything but a response, thus ridding it of any suggestion of autonomy.

47. On this, cf. *BH* 69ff., 73ff., 127,148; *RI* 55ff., 76–77.

48. The egoistic Amedée Chartrain in *La Soif* (Paris: Desclée de Brouwer, 1938) may be taken as embodying this characteristic. About him, his wife Eveline says: "You know perfectly well that a person is worth something to your father only through the image of himself which he contemplates in the depth of his eyes" (p. 266).

49. *RI* 67–70.

50. *MB* (I) 177ff.; *MJ* 170.

51. *RI* 50–52; *MJ* 99, 145. This exact way of expressing it is Troisfontaines', *Existentialisme chrétien*, p. 227.

52. In spite of the aura of egotism which Sartre throws over the whole move-
    ment, it must be said that an appreciation of the communal nature of
    personality is present in many existentialists. Karl Jaspers, *Philosophie*
    (Berlin: Springer Verlag, 1932), declares, Vol. II, p. 58, that being is mu-
    tual being, "Miteinandersein." Paul Tillich, *The Courage to Be* (New Hav-
    en, CT: Yale University Press, 1952), agrees that "only in the continuous
    encounter with other persons does the person become and remain a per-
    son" (p. 91).

53. Jeanne Delhomme's phrase, *Existentialisme chrétien*, p. 174.

54. *Le quatuor en fa dièse* (Paris: Librairie Plon, 1925), p. 190:

    Roger: No… Ah! It is frightful to think that I have not been loved for
    myself.

    Clair: Yourself? Himself? Where does a personality commence? It was
    indeed you all the time; do you not believe that each one of us is
    prolonged in everything that he gives rise to?

55. *MB* (II) 15.

56. *MJ* VIII.

CHAPTER III

1. Josiah Royce, *The World and the Individual*, Second Series (New York:
   Macmillan, 1901), p. 166.

2. Ibid., p. 197ff.

3. For the most fully developed discussions of this distinction, see: *BH*
   100ff., 117ff., 126ff.; *MB* (I) 204ff.; *HV* 68–69; *MMS* 67ff.; and the entire
   text of *PAC*. ("On the Ontological Mystery," *PE*.)

4. *MMS* 66.

5. Here cf. Martin Heidegger, *Existence and Being*, trans. Werner Brock (Chicago: Regnery Co., 1949), p. 355: "Every metaphysical question can only
   be put in such a way that the questioner as such is by his very questioning
   involved in the question." Maurice Blondel agrees, "The Inconsistency of
   J. P. Sartre's Logic," *Thomist*, Vol. 11 (1947), p. 396: "From existentialism
   in the best sense of the word, the idea to be retained is that a practical and

militant philosophy is necessary, since in the question: 'What is Being?' I am included and compromised to the point where I can no longer answer objectively without taking a stand for or against my own existence."

6. *PE* 8.

7. *MMS* 73.

8. *BH* 144, 171–172; *MMS* 68, 94.

9. *MMS* 68; *BH* 219.

10. Henri Bergson, *Time and Free Will*, trans. F. L. Pogson (London: Allen & Unwin, 1928), pp. 220–221.

11. *MB* (I) 4–5.

12. *BH* 114, 135.

13. *MJ* 208, 298.

14. *MJ* 314.

15. *BH* 120–121.

16. *MJ* 98.

17. On this see *HV* 101; *BH* 217, 219, 221, 222, 224, 232.

18. A remark quoted with approval by Bernard, *La philosophie religieuse de Gabriel Marcel*, p. 103.

19. *BH* 126.

20. *RI* 21.

21. *BH* 31–32.

22. *MB* (I) 83.

23. *MB* (I) 93–94.

24. *BH* 98.

25. *RI* 35.

26. Jean Wahl, *Vers le concret: Études d'histoire de la philosophie contemporaine* (Paris: J. Vrin, 1932). Pages 223–269 are on Marcel. Quotation is from p. 261.

27. *RI* 35. It may occur to some that Sartre has managed to assent to participation and absurdity at the same time. But we must go behind the words. The verdict that reality is absurd is itself a kind of refusal of participation, and consequently Sartre's view of our being-in-the-world is not an acknowledgment of participation in Marcel's sense. Sartre never

does close the gap between the thinking self and the empirical self, thus indirectly bearing out Marcel's view in the *Journal* that our presence to the world can only be conceived as intelligible through faith.

28. For a similar opinion, cf. Nicolas Berdyaev, *Spirit and Reality* (London: Geoffrey Bles, 1939), pp. 11–12: "An objective interpretation of spiritual reality raises the question: Do my spiritual states and experiences correspond to any authentic reality or are they mere subjective states? But this is a fundamentally false presentation of the problem, one based on the supposition that the subject should reflect some sort of object. Actually, spiritual states do not correspond to anything, they simply are; they are the prime reality, they are more existential than anything reflected in the objective world." What is said here of higher "spiritual" states can be said, *mutatis mutandis*, about "mystery" or ontological experience in general. It is interesting to note that in agreeing that his central theme is the non-objectifiability of being, Marcel mentions that this criticism of objectivization" is made also by Berdyaev in a parallel way in his principal writings" (*MJ* VIII). Berdyaev has also noted the considerable extent of his philosophical agreement with Marcel, on pp. 275–276 of his autobiography *Dream and Reality*, trans. Katherine Lampert (London: Geoffrey Bles, 1950).

29. *BH* 114.

30. *PE* 11–12.

31. *RI* 40.

CHAPTER IV

1. See above, Chapter II, n. 18.

2. Roger Troisfontaines, S.J., *De l'existence à l'être*, 2 vols. (Paris: J. Vrin, 1953), Vol. I, pp. 42–48.

3. See *BH* 117, 120, 121, 142–143; *RI* 77–78, 187. The whole doctrine that secondary reflection is a work of our liberty implies that being is affirmed freely.

4. *MJ* 129; *PE* 5; *MB* (II) 58–59; *RI* 224.

5. A famous passage from Bertrand Russell (which Marcel quotes, *BH* 180) epitomizes one way of saying that *nothing is*: "That Man is the product of causes which had no prevision of the end they were achieving; that his origin, his growth, his hopes and fears, his loves and his beliefs, are but the outcome of accidental collections of atoms; that no fire, no heroism, no intensity of thought and feeling can preserve an individual life beyond the grave; that all the labors of the ages, all the devotion, all the inspiration, all the noonday brightness of human genius, are destined to extinction in the vast death of the solar system, and that the whole temple of Man's achievement must inevitably be buried beneath the debris of a universe in ruins—all these things, if not quite beyond dispute, are yet so nearly certain, that no philosophy which rejects them can hope to stand." Let none say that what Russell negates here is truth and value rather than being, for Marcel's contention surely stands here: being is not to be considered as a datum apart from the true and good; *ens, verum, bonum,* are not only convertible but inseparable.

6. *PE* 5.

7. On the ontological exigence, cf. *MJ* 183, 288, 290; *MB* (II) 33–51.

8. *MJ* 179. Compare this to a similar remark of Royce, *The World and the Individual*, I, p. 154: "Primarily in seeking Being, we seek what is to end our disquietude."

9. *MJ* 206. Also cf. *MJ* 236.

10. *MJ* 181, 198, 206; *PE* 3. Karl Jaspers, in *The Perennial Scope of Philosophy*, trans. Ralph Manheim (New York: Philosophical Library, 1949), turns the same insight in a different direction: "Only man cannot fulfill himself in his finiteness. It is only man whose finiteness involves him in history, in which he strives to realize his potentialities" (p. 66).

11. *MJ* 96–98.

12. *RI* 187.

13. For a general discussion, see *BH* 154–175.

14. *BH* 134, 158–159.

15. *BH* 155, 173.

16. *MJ* 309–310.

17. *BH* 134, 146, 155, 161; *MJ* 312.

18. *BH* 166.

19. *BH* 82, 84, 163.

20. *BH* 149, 158, 169. Heidegger, too, *Existence and Being*, pp. 387–388, remarks on the inadequacies of the "logical" thinking whose only concern is to make things come out even: "Nothing counts for calculation save what can be calculated. Any particular thing is only what it 'adds up to'… it is of the prime essence of calculation and not merely in its results, to assert what-is [*das Seiende*] only in the form of something that can be arranged and used up."

21. *BH* 151, 168–169; *MJ* 147–148,155, 177, 199.

22. *MJ* 199.

23. *MJ* 311.

24. *MMS* 130.

25. *BH* 102.

26. *MJ* 179, 206; *MB* (II) 45.

27. *MB* (I) ch. 2; *MB* (II) 37–38; *PE* 1–3; and the entire text of *Man Against Mass Society*.

28. *BH* 102; *RI* 97.

29. *MB* (I) 29ff.

30. *PE* 2–3.

31. *BH* 76; *MMS* 66.

32. *BH* 152.

33. *BH* 76.

34. *BH* 74.

35. For Marcel's praise of technics, see *BH* 74, 175, 234; *MMS* 41, 45, 46, 52, 61, 62, 64, 98, 154, 195.

36. *MMS* 40, 74–75; *HV* 115; *MB* (II) 87.

37. *BH* 132.

38. *MMS* 57ff. It might be appropriate here to indicate briefly the marked divergence on this point that exists between Marcel and Jaspers, who is otherwise such a kindred spirit. The latter is much more disposed to grant the ontological relevance of objective social structures and of science in

particular. What he calls "Reason" is the essence of philosophy, and science is "an indispensable constituent of Reason" (*Reason and Anti-Reason in Our Time* [New Haven, CT: Yale University Press, 1952], p. 8). The same thought is reiterated straightway in *The Perennial Scope of Philosophy*, p. 7: far from being set over against philosophy, "science is the basic element of philosophy." This is an issue to which we must return later.

39. *BH* 137.
40. Troisfontaines, *De l'existence à l'être*, Vol. I, pp. 44–45.
41. Jean Wahl, *Vers le concret: Études d'histoire de la philosophie contemporaine*, seems to approximate the truth more closely when he contrasts being to existence as a different *realm*: participation in love is the type experience for being, while incarnation in my body is the type experience for existence (pp. 244–249; cf. also pp. 257–258, 266). While this is based on an examination of the *Metaphysical Journal* alone, it is not superseded by anything in the later works. Paul Ricoeur, *Gabriel Marcel et Karl Jaspers*, takes practically the same view: existence and being refer to different *levels* of participation. He works out an ingenious device to match some important Marcellian themes off against the ways in which the subject can retreat from participation, at each level: existence, evacuated, leaves abstraction; being, evacuated, leaves nothingness and despair (pp. 56–58).
42. *MB* (II) 25.
43. *MB* (II) 27.
44. *MB* (II) 27.
45. *MB* (II) 31.
46. *MB* (II) 33–34.
47. *MB* (II) 37.
48. *MB* (II) 61.
49. *MB* (II) 62.
50. *MB* (II) 59.
51. *MJ* 184.
52. In his mind, only faith can attach us irrefrangibly to the concrete. Cf. *MJ* 41–45, 86, 234.

53. Not only is this clear from the context, but he has said as much in private conversation with the writer. It must be quite evident that the exceptions here taken to Troisfontaines' schema center on his terminology. That Marcel's philosophy envisions a threefold movement such as he describes, there is not the slightest doubt. But Marcel already has a habitual usage for "being" and "existence" and it would have been better if Troisfontaines had retained his earlier nomenclature and called his book *De la communauté au communion*. When this was suggested to him, his unexpected reply was that this had been the title originally intended.

54. *BH* 130.

55. *MB* (I) 189–190.

56. *BH* 87.

57. *BH* 199. Also cf. *BH* 71, 118; *RI* 106; *PE* 12–13.

58. *BH* 95, 110.

59. *BH* 119.

60. *RI* 100.

61. *BH* 87.

62. *BH* 119.

63. *MJ* 96.

64. *BH* 199.

65. Ibid.

66. *BH* 25.

67. *BH* 89

68. *MB* (I) 171.

69. See *MB* (I) 165ff.; *BH* 84; *RI* 106.

70. *BH* 227. For similar views on the significance of sacrifice, cf. Heidegger, *Existence and Being*, p. 390: "Sacrifice is a valediction to everything that 'is' on the road to the preservation of the favor of Being.... Sacrifice is rooted in the nature of the event through which Being claims man for the truth of Being." (Here "that-is" translates *das Seiende*, "Being" translates *Sein*.)

CHAPTER V

1. *RI* 192.
2. *RI* 193.
3. See above, p. 9.
4. *BH* 119.
5. *BH* 41.
6. *BH* 41ff., 47ff.; *RI* 205ff.
7. *BH* 110.
8. *RI* 223–224. And of course it is also creative in the sense that it liberates me from egocentrism and constitutes me as a source for the similar liberation and renewal of others; it is part of the disponibility which allows me to be a power of radiation.
9. *BH* 50ff., 110, 198–199, 231.
10. *BH* 53ff.; *HV* 129–132; *RI* 214–216.
11. *RI* 199–204.
12. *PE* 22.
13. *BH* 96, 120.
14. *MJ* 41–45.
15. See the whole of the essay *Sickness unto Death* in Søren Kierkegaard, *Fear and Trembling* and *The Sickness unto Death*, trans. Walter Lowrie (New York: Doubleday Anchor Books, 1954), especially p. 173.
16. Royce, *The World and the Individual*, II, p. 275.
17. Ibid., p. 277.
18. Ibid., pp. 287–288.
19. *RI* 218.
20. *RI* 80. Cf. *BH* 122.
21. *BH* 79; *HV* 46–49.
22. *BH* 102.
23. *BH* 79; *HV* 10, 53, 66; *PE* 19–20; *MB* (II) 153ff.
24. See *BH* 73–80; *HV* 2.
25. *BH* 91, 94; *HV* 29ff.; 41.
26. *HV* 10, 33, 39, 49, 58.
27. *HV* 33–36.

28. *HV* 60.

29. *HV* 32; *MB* (II) 162, 172, 180.

30. *BH* 80; *HV* 46–47.

31. *HV* 55ff. Cf. similar thoughts on fidelity, *MB* (II) 76–84.

32. *HV* 67. See also pp. 63–66.

33. See above, pp. 25–32.

34. *MB* (II) 170.

35. *MJ* 64, 158; *RI* 152.

36. *MJ* 220ff., 232.

37. *MJ* 223.

38. *MJ* 304; *MB* (II) 154.

39. *RI* 50–52. See Bernard's explanation, *La philosophie religieuse de Gabriel Marcel*, p. 65.

40. *MJ* 303.

41. *MJ* 231ff.

42. *MJ* 157.

43. *MJ* 63.

44. *MB* (II) 154. Nicolas Berdyaev, in *The Divine and the Human*, attributes a similar ontological significance to love. "Love is connected with personality and it demands that personality shall be immortal" (p. 137). Cf. also pp. 125 and 164, and the almost identical parallel to Marcel in *Spirit and Reality*, p. 100: "Love is an eternal affirmation of the being of the human personality."

45. *RI* 179.

46. *MB* (II) 62.

47. *MJ* 63.

48. *MB* (II) 62.

CHAPTER VI

1. Such a conception does not sound initially unlike what Jaspers means by "the Comprehensive" (*das Umgreifende*), whatever is the eventual use he makes of it. How closely it resembles Heidegger's "*Sein*" it must be left for

others to determine. On the other hand, Marcel's "being" emphatically does not resemble Sartre's "*etre-en-soi*" (which if closely examined might prove to be simply a blank universal noumenon correlative to an epistemological subject): the notion of presence is inapplicable to the "*en-soi*," while it is central to the meaning of "being" in Marcel. Tillich's "power of being," like Jasper's "comprehensive" bears an initial compatibility with Marcel's notion.

2. *BH* 150.

3. For Marcel on this, cf. *HV* 220.

4. *RI* 40–43, 120ff.

5. *RI* 123ff.; *HV* 146, 264.

6. *MB* (II) 117. For Marcel's assimilation of philosophical reflection to artistic creation, see *PI* 133–134.

7. *RI* 87–88.8.

8. *HV* 264. Again we find echoes in Heidegger (*Existence and Being*, p. 311), this time in the essay "Hölderlin and the Essence of Poetry," where he speaks of the poet as one who intercepts divine signs: "This intercepting is an act of receiving and yet at the same time a fresh act of giving."

9. *RI* 16. Cf. *PI* 107–108 and Berdyaev, *Spirit and Reality*, p. 154: "The problem of creativeness is the fundamental problem of the new spirituality. But in essence spirituality is always creativeness, since freedom and activity are the attributes of spirit. In creativeness there are two elements: that of grace, of inspiration coming to man from on high, of genius and talent possessed by man, and that of freedom, having no external cause and determination, but forming the new elements in the creative act."

10. *RI* 130.

11. Ibid.

12. *BH* 173–174.

13. Paul Ricoeur, *Gabriel Marcel et Karl Jaspers*, quotes this statement on p. 259. It is from Jaspers' *Philosophie*, II, 199.

14. *MMS* 26.

15. *RI* 75.

16. *MB* (II) 44.

17. *MMS* 122.

18. *MB* (II) 128.

19. *HV* 143.

20. Marcel, it seems, ought to agree with the words of Berdyaev, *The Divine and the Human*, p. 141: "When the question is asked in books on aesthetics whether beauty is objective or subjective, it is an entirely wrong way of putting the matter"; p. 143: "Beauty even when it is simply contemplated requires the creative activity of the subject. Beauty is not objectivity, it is always transfiguration."

21. *HV* 142–143.

22. *HV* 152–153.

23. There is no question, of course, of Marcel's regarding values in anything like a Platonic manner; they only exist as incarnated in a situation, not as abstract entities. See *HV* 155.

24. *HV* 153. An interesting comparison of Marcel's thought with the value-philosophy of Dietrich von Hildebrand has been made by Alice Jourdain in her contribution to *The Human Person and the World of Values: A Tribute to Dietrich von Hildebrand* (New York: Fordham University Press, 1960). Her paper, "Von Hildebrand and Marcel: A Parallel," may underestimate the very real divergences between the two thinkers, however.

25. Fittingly enough, this is also the title which Marcel gave to one of his unpublished lectures. It is mentioned by Delhomme, *Existentialisme chrétien*, p. 170.

26. This being so, the objection of de Corte, in *La philosophie de Gabriel Marcel*, is wide of the mark. He declares that Marcel's method of philosophizing is "une contamination patente de la métaphysique par l'activité poétique" (p. 70). Marcel ought to consider this a perceptive appreciation rather than an indictment.

27. *PI* 18.

CHAPTER VII

1. Quoted by Fessard in his essay in *La Soif*, p. 7.

2. *L'Iconoclaste* (Paris: Librairie Stock, 1923), p. 47.

3. In "The Drama of the Soul in Exile," included in *Three Plays* (New York: Hill and Wang, 1958), p. 14.

4. It should be stressed that the basis of this comparison is the level of reflectiveness in these writers, not its manner. As far as technique is concerned, Marcel has none of the sometimes laborious and slow-moving style of the nineteenth-century writers; he is much more nimble and more "interesting." The comparison with Forster is probably clearer and not subject to this reservation.

5. Jean-Paul Sartre, *No Exit*, adapted from French by Paul Bowles (New York: Samuel French Inc., 1945), p. 52.

6. *Le Coeur des Autres* (Paris: Librairie Grasset, 1921), p. 111.

7. *Three Plays*, p. 16.

8. On this, see Fessard, essay in *La Soif*, pp. 14–19; and Joseph Chenu, *Le Théâtre de Gabriel Marcel et sa signification métaphysique* (Paris: Aubier, 1948), pp. 50, 118–120.

9. The minister Claude Lemoyne in *Un Homme de Dieu*.

10. The politician Moirans in *Le Palais de Sable*.

11. The leftist-professor Eustache Soreau in *Le Dard*.

12. Ariadne in the play by that name.

13. Jeanne in *Le Mort de Demain*.

14. Daniel Meyrieux in *Le Coeur des Autres*.

15. Amedée Chartrain in *La Soif* (*Les Coeurs Avides*).

16. See R. Jouve, "Un Théâtre de la Sincerité," *Études*, 5 et 20 Avril, 1932.

17. In *The Idea of a Theater* (New York: Doubleday Anchor Books, 1954), pp. 48, 161.

18. Ibid., p. 31.

19. Ibid., pp. 38–47.

20. Marcel has been awarded Le Grand Prix de Littérature de l'Academie Française and Le Grand Prix Nationale des Lettres. *Le Dard* won Le Prix Brieux and *Le Chemin de Crête* (*Ariadne*) Le Prix Hervieux.

21. *Three Plays*, p. 59.

22. Ibid., p. 93.

23. Ibid., p. 97.

24. Ibid., p. 113.

25. Ibid., p. 114.

26. Ibid., p. 21.

27. *La Soif*, p. 240.

28. Ibid., p. 275.

29. Ibid., p. 288.

30. George Santayana, *The Life of Reason* (New York: Scribner's, 1953), p. 68.

31. *Three Plays*, p. 15.

32. *MB* (I) 171.

33. *Three Plays*, pp. 26–27.

34. The comparison was made at a conference given at Hunter College, New York City, November 13, 1961.

35. See M.-M. Davy, *Un Philosophe Itinérante: Gabriel Marcel* (Paris: Flammarion, 1959), p. 208.

36. *MB* (II) 66.

37. See Charles Moeller, *Littérature du XXe Siècle et Christianisme* (Tournai: Casterman, 1953–1960), Vol. IV (1960), p. 219.

38. Ibid., p. 129. For Marcel's fondness for this myth, see *PI* 7, 35.

39. *L'Iconoclaste*, p. 47.

40. *Le Dard* (Paris: Librairie Plon, 1936), p. 87.

41. Ibid., p. 237.

42. The remarks were made at the Hunter College conference cited above.

43. *BH* 136.

44. On this, see Moeller, *Littérature du XXe Siècle et Christianisme*, pp. 158ff., 244. It is the central theme in *Le Monde Cassé*.

45. On Marcel's fondness for and admiration of Ibsen, see Davy, *Un Philosophe Itinérante: Gabriel Marcel*, pp. 80–83.

CHAPTER VIII

1. *RI* 33. As he there says, in many respects his views on this subject are quite close to those of Louis Lavelle.

2. *RI* 107.

3. See for instance Fernand van Steenberghen, *Ontology*, trans. Martin J. Flynn (New York: Wagner, 1952), p. 20.

4. Introduction to *PAC*, p. 39.

5. He himself senses this, and most commentators add their agreement. Cf. the following pages in these authors already cited: de Corte, p. 63; Prini, pp. 80–81, 120, 129; Colin (in *Existentialisme chrétien*), p. 30; Bernard, p. 84, 91, 138–139.

6. Marcel's statement. Introduction to Prini, p. 7.

7. *MMS* 85.

8. *MJ* VIII.

9. Prini, p. 117.

10. *RI* 89.

11. *RI* 22.

12. *MMS* 119.

13. The charge of Robert Ostermann, "Gabriel Marcel: Existence and the Idea of Being," *The Modern Schoolman*, Vol. 32 (November 1954), pp. 19–38, on p. 29.

14. *MMS* 119.

15. *MMS* 196. Not that he is the source of this light, says Marcel; he is more like a screen that reflects it. The notion of mystery as light, as the supreme source of intelligibility, is a recurring one. Cf. *MB* (II) 119–124; *RI* 79.

16. *MMS* 197.

17. *MB* (I) 139.

18. *MMS* 197.

19. Ibid.

20. *MB* (II) 129.

21. D. M. MacKinnon, in the introduction to *BH*, p. 2.

22. *MMS* 7.

23. *MMS* 29.

24. *BH* 85. In the English translation, "being" is spelled with a capital, which is not correct.

25. *RI* 190.

26. *RI* 25.

27. *RI* 39.

28. Cf. *HP* 22.

29. Cf. *HV* 23–24.

30. MacKinnon, in the introduction to *BH*, p. 2.

31. *RI* 106.

32. *BH* 121.

33. Prini, p. 119.

34. For this dialectic, see *BH* 124–125; *RI* 92ff., 188ff.; partially, *PE* 6–8; *MB* (I) ch. VIII.

35. *BH* 124–125. The Augustinian character of this approach does not have to be emphasized. Karl Jaspers' notion of the limit-situation as a springboard to transcendence or as our mode of coming to awareness of transcendence has the same resemblance to an "ontological argument." He agrees that a proved God is no God at all; accordingly, "only he who starts out from God, can seek him. A certainty of the existence of God, however rudimentary and intangible it may be, is a premise not a result of philosophical activity" (*The Perennial Scope of Philosophy*, p. 32).

36. Colin, in *Existentialisme chrétien*, p. 104.

37. *MJ* 64. Also cf. *MJ* 32, 98, 228; *MB* (II) 176; *RI* 226ff.; *BH* 81.

38. *RI* 53. Also cf. *MJ* 137, 156, 160, 261, *passim*.

39. *BH* 121, 147.

40. *RI* 105.

41. This is the theme of *L'homme problématique*.

42. *MJ* 288, 293; *MB* (I) 8.

43. Joseph Chenu, *Le Théâtre de Gabriel Marcel et sa signification métaphysique*, p. 71.

44. Although all, perhaps, are only ultimately meaningful relative to it.

45. In *Existentialisme chrétien*, p. 293. Cf. also the beautiful remark in *HV* 256: "Are we perhaps in the world in order to utter the primitive words which clothe earthly experience with a body; house, bridge, water-spring, orchard, window, and again pillar or tower, but also to translate that intimate inward being of which things in themselves are unconscious?"

46. *MMS* 81.

47. *MMS* 86, 91.

48. *MMS* 7.

49. Because of this, we have suggested that the metaphysicizing of experi-
     ence can be pursued beyond the areas that Marcel explores, for instance
     in the image-life of man. In this connection it is relevant to call attention
     to the very instructive observation of Robert C. Pollock, "A Reappraisal
     of Emerson," *Thought*, Vol. 32 (Spring 1957), pp. 86–132, in respect to
     Emerson's effort to reconstitute and validate the symbolic consciousness
     of man. "The images," Pollock quotes Emerson as saying (p. 119), "the
     sweet immortal images are within us—born there, our native right." This
     article contains other examples of a partial affinity between Emerson's
     thought and existentialism in general and Marcel in particular. To cite of
     the latter only one: All thinking is at bottom a "pious reception" Pollock
     quotes Emerson, for "when we discern justice, when we discern truth, we
     do nothing of ourselves, but allow a passage to its beams" (p. 96). Cf. the
     very similar remark of Marcel's, above, p. 136.

CHAPTER IX

1. Marjorie Grene, *Dreadful Freedom* (Chicago: University of Chicago Press,
    1948), p. 124.

2. Ibid., p. 127.

3. Ibid., p. 129.

4. Ibid., p. 127.

5. Ibid., p. 128,

6. Ibid., p. 130.

7. Ibid., p. 132.

8. Robert Ostermann, "Gabriel Marcel: Existence and the Idea of Being," p.
    20.

9. The two texts are: "c'est *d'être* qu'il s'agit, non de *l'être*," in *Journal metaphy-
    sique* (Paris: Gallimard, 1927), p. 202, and "En faisant de l'être un sub-
    stantive." We learn, says Ostermann, "nous semblons en effet nous de-

mander implicitement quels sont les prédicats qui lui conviennent. Or ceci est inintelligible" (ibid., p. 181).

10. In Prini, p. 7. (This preface was written in 1950.)

11. *MMS* 85.

12. Ostermann, "Gabriel Marcel: Existence and the Idea of Being," p. 22.

13. Ibid., pp. 24–25.

14. Ibid., p. 27.

15. Ibid.

16. Ibid., p. 30.

17. It cannot be gainsaid that some of Marcel's remarks would give the impression that he does make such an equation, but even so it is usually clear from the context that he is using "essence" in a consciously pejorative sense for definite purposes, and not as a Thomist would use it. Thus when he says that love does not bear on a "closed essence" the word is clearly a symbol of a fallacious epistemology and is taken as such: it means the essence considered as the sum of a number of notes. Again, his tendency to disparage "characterization" might lead us to think that he must wind up in some kind of pure indeterminacy. But his point simply is that a being is not the sum of the characteristics we attribute to it: to apprehend it as *presence* is to apprehend it as non-characterizable fullness. This might be looked upon more as a defense of essence than a denial of it. He wants to regard essences not as "objets éclairés" but as "présences éclairantes" (Prini, p. 8, Marcel's preface).

18. Jacques Maritain, *A Preface to Metaphysics* (New York: Sheed & Ward, 1948), p. 52.

19. Étienne Gilson, *Existentialisme chrétien*, p. 7.

20. Ibid., p. 8.

21. James Collins, *The Existentialist* (Chicago: Regnery, 1952), p. 148.

22. Marcel de Corte, *La philosophie de Gabriel Marcel*, p. 72.

23. Jacques Maritain, *Existence and the Existent*, trans. Lewis Galantiere and Gerald Phelan (New York: Pantheon, 1948), p. 72.

24. Ibid., p. 13.

25. Ibid., p. 69.

26. Ibid., p. 71.

27. Ibid., pp. 71–72.

28. Ibid., p. 145.

29. Ibid., pp. 124–125.

30. We do not overlook the fact that Maritain would hedge his own statement around with qualifications, but the qualifications would all be made for the sake of maintaining the essential rightness of the statement.

31. We remind the reader of Marcel's connotation for "science": by it he means a knowledge which bears on an "object" in his strict sense of that word. Since metaphysical knowledge proper does not deal with an item within the ken of a detached observer, but with the "being" which spans the subject-object dichotomy, and ultimately with *transcendence*, then the meaning of science cannot be univocal with respect to metaphysics and the other sciences.

32. While we may recognize that non-philosophical sciences differ in important respects (as to methods, norms, etc.) they are at least identical in the sense that they are all concerned with "objects." Not so with metaphysics: being is not an object.

33. Note that all that is said here is that participation is the necessary soil of philosophical truth. Nothing that is said should be construed to imply that all error or disagreement in philosophy would be ended if the response to the invocation to participation were always given.

34. This even holds good of the famous "metaphysical" argument, which is based on the premise that the object of the will is the good-as-such: anything but a purely verbal assent to the truth of this premise would involve an existential grasp of the self as an élan towards the absolute.

35. Joseph de Finance, "Being and Subjectivity," trans. W. Norris Clarke, *Cross Currents*, Vol. 6, No. 2 (Spring 1956), pp. 163–178; quotation is from p. 168.

36. Someone might object that if in order to conceive being I must explicitly conceive what is implicit in it, then I could not conceive it without conceiving a chipmunk, a razorblade, and a slime mold, since these are not

extrinsic to being either. But this would be somewhat captious. These all exist for me under the aspect of object and it is only my self which introduces the totally other dimension of subjectivity.

37. Ibid., p. 166.
38. Cf. Pierre Rousselot, S.J., *The Intellectualism of St. Thomas*, trans. Fr. James E. O'Mahony (New York: Sheed & Ward, 1935), p. 99.
39. Ibid., footnote to p. 55.
40. Of course he does not regard it as an aspiration of the will, but simply of the subject, since he does not advert to the division of faculties.
41. A fine description of this way of conceiving "reality" is given by Royce, *The World and the Individual*, I, pp. 225–264; and not only given but approved of in large measure by Ernst Cassirer, *Substance and Function*, trans. W. C. Swabey (New York: Dover Publications, 1953), c. 1923, pp. 271–308.
42. This illusion of a successful total objectification is exactly what vitiates idealism in his opinion, as we saw in Chapter II.
43. Gilson, *Existentialisme chrétien*, p. 3.
44. *MMS* 41–42.
45. Ricoeur, *Gabriel Marcel et Karl Jaspers*, p. 175ff.
46. Ibid., pp. 171–172.
47. Cf. *RI* 104.
48. *BH* 187.
49. This, as we have already seen, is Jaspers' opinion, and here he provides a corrective to Marcel.
50. That is, science simply neglects the ultimate mystery within and upon which it builds its structure of secure problematic knowledge.

BIBLIOGRAPHY

WORKS BY MARCEL

Philosophical Works

Being and Having. Trans. Katherine Farrer. Boston: Beacon Press, 1951.

Le déclin de la sagesse. Paris: Librairie Plon, 1954.

The Decline of Wisdom. Trans. Manya Harari. London: Harvill Press, 1954.

Être et avoir. Paris: Fernand Aubier, Éditions Montaigne, 1935.

L'homme problématique. Paris: Aubier, 1955.

Les hommes contre l'humain. Paris: La Colombe, 1951.

Homo viator. Paris: Aubier, Editions Montaigne, 1945.

Homo Viator. Trans. Emma Crauford. Chicago: Regnery, 1951.

Journal métaphysique. Paris: Gallimard, 1927.

Man Against Mass Society. Trans. G. S. Fraser. Chicago: Regnery, 1952.

La métaphysique de Royce. Paris: Aubier, 1945.

Metaphysical Journal, containing the essay *Existence and Objectivity.* Trans. Bernard Wall. Chicago: Regnery, 1952.

Le mystère de l'être, 2 vols. Paris: Aubier, 1951.

The Mystery of Being, 2 vols. Chicago: Regnery, 1951.
  Vol. I: *Reflection and Mystery.* Trans. G. S. Fraser.
  Vol. II: *Faith and Reality.* Trans. René Hague.
  Both volumes have been published by Regnery in paperback form.

The Philosophy of Existence. Trans. Manya Harari. New York: Philosophical Library, 1949.

The Philosophy of Existentialism. New York: Citadel Press, 1961. (This is a paperback reprint of *The Philosophy of Existence.*)

Position et approches concrètes du mystère ontologique. Introduction par Marcel de Corte. Paris: J. Vrin, 1949. This essay is contained in translation in *The Philosophy of Existence.*

Présence et Immortalité. Paris: Flammarion, 1959.

Du refus à l'invocation. Paris: Librairie Gallimard, 1940.

Royce's Metaphysics. Trans. Virginia and Gordon Ringer. Chicago: Regnery, 1956.

Plays

Titles are arranged in the order of their composition, except for the comic theatre.

Le Seuil Invisible. Paris: Grasset, 1914. This contains *La Grâce* and *Le Palais de Sable.*

Le Quatuor en Fa Dièse. Paris: Plon, 1925; piece finished in 1919.

Trois Pièces. Paris: Plon, 1931. The plays were composed between 1919 and 1921. They are: *Le Regard Neuf, Le Mort de Demain, La Chapelle Ardente.*

L'Insondable. Paris: Stock, 1959. The play was composed in 1919.

L'Iconoclaste. Paris: Stock, 1923. Composed 1920.

Le Coeur des Autres. Paris: Cahiers Verts, Grasset, 1921. Composed 1920.

Un Homme de Dieu. Paris: Cahiers Verts, Grasset, 1925. Composed 1921.

L'Horizon. Paris: Aux Étudiants de France, 1945. Composed 1928.

Le Monde Cassé. Paris: Desclée de Brouwer, 1933.

Le Fanal. Paris: La Vie Intellectuelle, supplément, 1936.

Le Chemin de Crête. Paris: Grasset, 1936.

Le Dard. Paris: Plon, 1936.

La Soif. Paris: Desclée de Brouwer, 1938. This play was republished under the title *Les Coeurs Avides.* Paris: La Table Ronde, 1952.

Vers un Autre Royaume. Paris: Plon, 1949. This contains *L'Emissaire* and *Le Signe de la Croix.*

La Fin des Temps. Paris: Realites, 1950.

Rome n'est plus dans Rome. Paris: La Table Ronde, 1951.

Mon Temps n'est pas le Vôtre. Paris: Plon, 1955.

Croissiez et Multipliez. Paris: Plon, 1955.

La Dimension Florestan. Paris: Plon, 1958.

Théâtre Comique. Paris: Albin Michel, 1947. This contains four plays: *Colombyre*, or *Le Brasier de la Paix*, composed in 1937; *La Double Expertise* (1936); *Les Points sur les I* (1936); *Le Divertissement Posthume* (1923).

The only plays of Marcel translated into English are those contained in the volume *Three Plays* (New York: Hill and Wang, 1958.) This contains *A Man of God* (*Un Homme de Dieu*), *Ariadne* (*Le Chemin de Crête*), and *The Funeral Pyre* (*La Chapelle Ardente*).

For a complete bibliography of Marcel's works, including all his drama and music criticism, and all his articles, see the second volume of Troisfontaines' work listed below.

The William James Lectures which Marcel delivered at Harvard in the fall of 1961 will be published early in 1963 by Harvard University Press (no title yet assigned); these are especially interesting for the extended review of his dramatic work that Marcel gave in the course of the lectures.

WORKS ON MARCEL

Bagot, Jean Pierre. *Connaissance et Amour: Essai sur la Philosophie de Gabriel Marcel.* Paris, Beauchesne, 1958.

Bernard, Michel. *La philosophie religieuse de Gabriel Marcel* (appendix by Marcel). Paris: Les Cahiers du Nouvel Humanisme, 1952.

Chaigne, Louis. *Vies et Oeuvres d'Écrivains.* Paris, Lanore, 1954. Tome 4.

Chenu, Joseph. *Le théâtre de Gabriel Marcel et sa signification métaphysique.* Paris: Aubier, 1948.

Colin, Pierre. "Existentialisme chrétien." In *Existentialisme chrétien* (*q. v.* under Gilson).

Collins, James. "Gabriel Marcel and the Mystery of Being," *Thought*, Vol. 18 (December 1943), pp. 665–693.

Davy, M.-M. *Un Philosophe Itinérant: Gabriel Marcel.* Paris: Flammarion, 1959.

De Corte, Marcel. *La philosophie de Gabriel Marcel.* Paris: Chez Pierre Tequi, n. d.
_____. *Introduction* to Marcel's *Positions et Approches Concrètes du Mystère Ontologique* (*q. v.*). In this introduction de Corte considerably altered his original assessment of Marcel.

Delhomme, Jeanne. "Témoignage et dialectique." In *Existentialisme chrétien* (*q. v.* under Gilson).

Dubois-Dumée, J. P. "Solitude et communion dans le théâtre de Gabriel Marcel." In *Existentialisme chrétien* (*q. v.* under Gilson).

Fessard, Gaston. *Théâtre et mystère*. Essay published as an introduction to *La Soif*, pp. 7–116. Paris: Desclée de Brouwer, 1938.

Gilson, Étienne. "Un exemple." In *Existentialisme chrétien: Gabriel Marcel.* Présentation de Étienne Gilson. Paris: Librairie Plon, 1947. Textes de Jeanne Delhomme, Roger Troisfontaines, Pierre Colin, J. P. Dubois-Dumée, Gabriel Marcel.

Hocking, William Ernest. "Marcel and the Ground Issues of Metaphysics," *Philosophy and Phenomenological Research*, Vol. 14, pp. 439–469.

Jourdain, Alice. "Von Hildebrand and Marcel: A Parallel." In *The Human Person and the World of Values: a Tribute to Dietrich von Hildebrand.* Ed. Balduin Schwarz. New York: Fordham University Press, 1960.

Miceli, S.J., Vincent P. *The Life of Communion and Community in the Philosophy of Gabriel Marcel.* Unpublished doctoral dissertation, 1961. Fordham University Library, Bronx, New York.

Moeller, Charles. *Littérature du XXe Siècle et Christianisme*, 4 vols. Tournai: Casterman, 1953–1960. Vol. IV includes a lengthy discussion of Marcel.

Murchland, C.S.C., Bernard G. "The Philosophy of Gabriel Marcel," *The Review of Politics*, Vol. 21 (April 1959), pp. 339–356.

Ostermann, Robert. "Gabriel Marcel: The Discovery of Being," *Modern Schoolman*, Vol. 31 (January 1954), pp. 99–116.
____. "Gabriel Marcel: The Recovery of Being," *Modern Schoolman*, Vol. 31 (May 1954,), pp. 289–305.
____. "Gabriel Marcel: Existence and the Idea of Being," *Modern Schoolman*, Vol. 32 (November 1954), pp. 19–38.

Prini, Pietro. *Gabriel Marcel et la méthodologie de l'invérifiable* (lettre-préface de Marcel). Paris: Desclée de Brouwer, 1953.

Ricoeur, Paul. *Gabriel Marcel et Karl Jaspers: Philosophie du mystère et philosophie du paradoxe*. Paris: Éditions du Temps Présent, 1947.

Sottiaux, Edgard. *Gabriel Marcel, Philosophe et Dramaturge*. Louvain: E. Nauwelaerts, 1956.

Troisfontaines, S.J., Roger. *De l'existence à l'être*, 2 vols. (lettre-préface de Marcel). Paris: J. Vrin, 1953.

_____. "La notion de *présence* chez Gabriel Marcel." In *Existentialisme chrétien* (*q. v.* under Gilson).

Wahl, Jean. *Vers le concret: Études d'histoire de la philosophie contemporane*. Paris: J. Vrin, 1932. Pages 223–260 are devoted to Marcel.

Among studies of existentialism which devote chapters to Marcel's thought are: H. J. Blackham, *Six Existentialist Thinkers* (London: Routledge and Kegan Paul, 1951); James Collins, *The Existentialist* (Chicago: Regnery, 1952); Kurt F. Reinhardt, *The Existentialist Revolt* (Milwaukee: Bruce, 1952); David E. Roberts, *Existentialism and Religious Belief* (New York: Oxford University Press, 1957).

While they are not actually "on" Marcel's thought in the sense of being expositions, the following two books are especially interesting in being highly original works which are strongly under the influence and inspiration of Marcel's thought: Henry G. Bugbee, Jr., *The Inward Morning*, preface by Marcel (New York: Collier Books, 1961); Ralph Harper, *The Sleeping Beauty* (New York: Harper, 1955).

CLUNY MEDIA

Designed by Fiona Cecile Clarke, the CLUNY MEDIA *logo depicts a monk at work in the scriptorium, with a cat sitting at his feet.*

The monk represents our mission to emulate the invaluable contributions of the monks of Cluny in preserving the libraries of the West, our strivings to know and love the truth.

The cat at the monk's feet is Pangur Bán, from the eponymous Irish poem of the 9th century. The anonymous poet compares his scholarly pursuit of truth with the cat's happy hunting of mice. The depiction of Pangur Bán is an homage to the work of the monks of Irish monasteries and a sign of the joy we at Cluny take in our trade.

"Messe ocus Pangur Bán,
cechtar nathar fria saindan:
bíth a menmasam fri seilgg,
mu memna céin im saincheirdd."

Made in the USA
Middletown, DE
07 February 2025

70431140R00133